Other SIGNET Books
You Will Want to Read

THE
ROCK STORY

by

JERRY HOPKINS

A SIGNET BOOK from
NEW AMERICAN LIBRARY
TIMES MIRROR

Acknowledgments

Excerpts from "Rolling Stone Interview: Eric Clapton," Copyright May 11, 1968; "A Rotting Corpse, Stinking Up the Airways" by Tom Donohue, Copyright Nov. 23, 1967; "The Groupies and Other Girls," Copyright Feb. 15, 1969, courtesy Rolling Stone, Straight Arrow Publishers, Inc.

Excerpts from "Balls of Fire" by Andy Wickham, Copyright July 19, 1968; "Rock's Fifth Column" by Ian Whitcomb, Copyright Sept. 13, 1968; "Column by John Carpenter," Copyright May 10, 1968; "Jefferson Airplane" by John Carpenter, Copyright May 10, 1968, courtesy the *Los Angeles Free Press*.

Excerpt from "It's Happening" by J. L. Simmons and Barry Winograd, Copyright 1966 by J. L. Simmons and Barry Winograd, Marc-Laird Publication, courtesy the authors.

Excerpts from "I Call on Dick Clark" by Pete Martin, Copyright Oct. 10, 1959; "When Four Nice Boys Go Ape!" by Richard Warren Lewis, Copyright Jan. 28, 1967; "Meet Gloria Stavers" by William Kloman, Copyright Nov. 4, 1967, reprinted with permission of *The Saturday Evening Post*.

SIGNET TRADEMARK REG. U.S. PAT. OFF. AND FOREIGN COUNTRIES
REGISTERED TRADEMARK—MARCA REGISTRADA
HECHO EN CHICAGO, U.S.A.

SIGNET BOOKS are published by
The New American Library, Inc.,
1301 Avenue of the Americas, New York, New York 10019

FIRST PRINTING, MARCH, 1970

PRINTED IN THE UNITED STATES OF AMERICA

My Sweet Lady Jane,
When I see you again,
Your servant am I
And will humbly remain.

PREFACE

I conducted a little poll the other day. I went out on the Sunset Strip and into Van Nuys (which is in the San Fernando Valley, a suburb of the Sunset Strip) and then into two or three other Los Angeles neighborhoods. I started asking kids why they liked rock music. Kids starting about eight years old and running into the middle twenties.

Nine out of ten said, "It makes me feel good."

Jerry Hopkins
Laurel Canyon, 1969

Contents

PART-1:

The History

1

We're Gonna Shake,
Rattle & Roll

The roots are in blues and country.

Blues came from the black—from the field hollers and work songs of slaves and the gospel chant and spirituals of small Negro churches in the South. The blues. A term which broadly covers the mass of forms and styles of music created by the American Negro. The blues. Now being sung by everyone.

Country music developed in the Ozarks and Appalachians during a time when generations were detached from the accelerating urbanization of America, and later, in another form and style, in the dust bowls and plains of the Southwest. Bluegrass. Cowboy songs. Country and western. C&W. Also being sung by everyone now.

Fifty years ago the forms were as segregated as their makers were. Whites heard Negro music and Negroes heard the white man's music, but there was very little of the rhythmic and vocal cross-pollination that is common today. True enough, popular jazz and minstrelsy had generally reflected the white man's use of black rhythms. But this was not a merging of the individual musical efforts or styles that was to come later as rock developed—when again the white man took from the black, but this time he gave something in return. When blues and country music merged, rock 'n' roll was born. That oversimplifies matters, but with this as a base . . .

Go to Nashville.

In 1925 (when "hot jazz" was all the rage), a new radio program, *Grand Ole Opry*, debuted on radio station WSM in Nashville. The performers on that show mirrored precisely the strain of country music that came from the mountains of West Virginia, Kentucky and Tennessee: Uncle Jimmy Thompson, aged 88, fiddled jigs, reels and country songs for an hour, while his niece, Eva Thompson Jones, played piano and sang. They set the pattern for the weekly broadcast that has issued from Nashville since. And Nashville became the capital of country and western music.

Many of the artists who appeared on *Grand Ole Opry* were also making records then. In fact, the first country hit came two years earlier, in 1923, when Wendell Hall sang "It Ain't Gonna Rain No Mo' " for RCA Victor. Another RCA artist at the time was Jimmie Rodgers, "the singing brakeman," who sold more than twenty million records between 1927 and 1935. Rodgers probably was the most important figure of the time, abandoning much of the nasal twang that had turned so many away from country music and creating a flock of disciples—Lefty Frizzel, Ernest Tubb and Hank Snow among them.

Robert Shelton lists five "influentials" in his book *The Country Music Story*—Roy Acuff, the Carter Family, Woody Guthrie, Hank Williams and Johnny Cash. Of these, all but Cash—who was too young—figured prominently in the development of "the Nashville sound." And all, including Cash, shared a background blessed by simplicity (however difficult it was for some). This was to influence the music they'd make.

Roy Acuff was the son of a judge who doubled as a Baptist minister in the Smoky Mountains of Tennessee. His early songs were sacred songs, although their titles might have confused; "The Great Speckled Bird," his trademark, got its title from the Bible, and "Radio Station S-A-V-E-D" had the Lord owning a radio station that presented "news direct from Heaven."

12

As a fiddler and singer, he sold more than twenty-five million records and became "The King of Country Music" by building today's powerful Acuff-Rose management, music publishing and record production empire. He was also C&W's goodwill ambassador, like Bob Hope taking his troupe of entertainers overseas for more than twenty years.

If Roy Acuff was ambassador and king, the Carter Family's function, and reputation, seemed to be that of innovator. This family of three—A. P. (Doc) Carter, his wife Sara and his sister-in-law Mother Maybelle Carter—was from the Blue Ridge Mountains in Virginia. In time, their offspring would join the trio, helping record more than 250 songs, many of them popping up years later as sung by Joan Baez, Doc Watson, the New Lost City Ramblers and Pete Seeger, or rewritten by Woody Guthrie and Bob Dylan. The Carter Family's closer-than-usual harmony for singing groups, use of the autoharp and guitar to accompany songs which earlier had been performed without accompaniment, and playing melodic as well as rhythmic accompaniment to their voices served as guides for many groups that followed.

Woody Guthrie is often bagged as a folk artist rather than a C&W voice, and perhaps the reason for this is his not going to Nashville as others had, traveling to California with thousands of his fellow Oklahomans instead. He was a composer of classic ballads and what Robert Shelton called "celebrations of the glories of America" ("This Land is Your Land," "Pastures of Plenty"). Of all Shelton's "influentials," Guthrie was the least influential within C&W, the most influential outside it.

Hank Williams was born in Alabama, the son of a shell-shocked veteran of World War I. He began playing guitar at seven and before he was 20 was the finest singer-songwriter in the history of C&W—writing songs so diverse in approach, and singing them so successfully, there was a tendency to think he was a product of Tin Pan Alley, not Nashville (signed to Acuff-Rose). "Cold, Cold Heart," "Hey, Good Lookin'," "I'm So Lonely I Could Cry" and "I'll Never Get Out of This World Alive" were among the 125

13

songs he wrote, many becoming classics in pop as well as in C&W. Hank Williams was born in a two-room log cabin and died twenty-nine years later (of alcohol, drugs and hard living) in the rear seat of one of his five Cadillacs.

Country music encompassed so much: from Gene Autry and Roy Rogers to Lester Flatt and Earl Scruggs, from songs for rounding up cattle to songs for driving trucks. And it was, as John Sebastian would write for the Lovin' Spoonful years later, all so simple. Nashville cats, he would sing in the song of that title, played as clean as country water, as wild as the mountain dew.

By the time Sebastian wrote this song, country music had merged with . . .

The blues. The other root. A peculiar by-product of black plantation life. (Partially.) No story tells this better than that of Muddy Waters, born McKinley Morganfield in Rolling Fork, Mississippi, in 1915 and raised on Delta farms by his grandmother. When folklorist Alan Lomax found him in the 1930's, he was working as a field hand in the cotton fields, playing guitar for weekend dances and country suppers. Then in 1942 he, like so many other blues musicians, left the South and went to Chicago to create in South Side whiskey joints something called "Chicago blues."

In Mississippi he had played in the Delta "bottleneck" style, wearing a smooth piece of bottle's neck or a short length of metal tubing on one finger of the left hand for some of the fretting. This gave his playing a high, whining or "singing" sound, and made it possible for him (and other bottleneck stylists) to slide from one note to another. In Chicago he augmented this style by trading in his acoustic guitar for an electric guitar and amplifier, recent innovations in the musical instrument field.

Waters also began playing in bands, merging his sound with that of other blues exiles. Probably the greatest of these was the late Little Walter, only 19 when he began recording with Waters (in the middle to late 1940's) and generally recognized as the most influential harmonica player Chicago has ever produced. Cupping his harp in both hands against the microphone, he created a new (distorted) tone, ex-

14

perimenting with rhythms and lines, and influencing nearly every harp player who followed him—from James Cotton to Junior Wells to Paul Butterfield.

Like Muddy Waters, B. B. King was a product of southern plantation life, born in Mississippi as Riley E. King and getting his famous initials after being called the Boy from Beale Street (in Memphis), the Beale Street Blues Boy, and Blues Boy King, thus B. B. The nicknames were appropriate, for King was (and is) the original master of the blues guitar. He obviously admired many earlier jazz guitarists, but where jazz had gone cool, then cold, in the middle 1940's, with bop, B. B. King's sound remained warm and exciting.

Still another singer and bottleneck guitarist from the Mississippi Delta country was Chester Burnett, the Howlin' Wolf. He was a stronger singer than Waters or King, and was known for slamming what were essentially field hollers up against an electric wall. He was also recognized for his songs—"Smokestack Lightnin' " and "Spoonful" among them.

These were only a few of the hundreds of Negro blues musicians in Chicago following the war, and with so much talent available, it was not surprising to find someone eager to transfer this sound to wax. So in 1946, the owners of a South Side nightclub, Phil and Leonard Chess, formed the Aristocrat label, following it with the Chess and Checker logos. Chess was begun with Andrew Tibbs, who was followed by Muddy Waters, then Howlin' Wolf, John Lee Hooker, Lowell Fulsom, Sonny Boy Williamson, Summerland Slim, Little Walter, Elmore James, Little Milton, Willie Mabon, and later, Bo Diddley and Chuck Berry.

Almost simultaneously, the late Sydney Nathan formed King Records in Cincinnati and Ahmet Ertegun started National Records (later Atlantic) in New York. Like the labels owned by the Chess brothers, these companies also became successful in a few years' time, building impressive talent lists. King had Hank Ballard & the Midnighters, Earl Bostic, Ivory Joe Hunter, James Brown & the Famous Flames, Little Willie John, Otis Williams & the Charms, and Billy Ward & the Dominoes . . . and National (Atlantic) produced records by Ruth Brown, LaVern Baker, Joe Turner, the Clovers, the Chords, the Drifters and many of the "bird" groups—the Ravens, the Flamingos, the Orioles, the Cardinals, the Penguins and the Crows.

In the early 1950's, vocal groups emerged as the major force in rhythm and blues, and any reason (or no reason) for forming one seemed acceptable. For example, Billy Ward, who had sung spirituals before organizing the Dominoes, picked the best singers in all Detroit—with Clyde McPhatter as lead vocalist and Jackie Wilson singing bass. (Ward wrote and arranged their songs, including "Sixty Minute Man," a two-and-a-half-million-seller.) At the other end of the "organization" chart were Otis Williams & the Charms, who merely happened to be knocking a softball around across the street from the King record plant when they were asked if they'd like to sing. (Sydney Nathan had just heard a song he liked, "Hearts of Stone," and he needed a group fast; it became the softball team's first hit.)

These were the "doo-wop" groups, adept at reducing vocal parts to a series of imaginative and rhythmic monosyllables. Songs would be introduced with a deep "doot-doo-doo-doo-doo . . ." (often with no instrumentation behind it) and harmony would be a series of "hum-mums" and "ooo-oooos."

During this time, rhythm and blues (R&B)—also called "race music" or "sepia blues"—was being produced solely by blacks and sold almost entirely *to* blacks. (Just as most country music sold only to those within *that* cultural borough.) Nevertheless, there were indications of approaching change in the audience, as noted by sociologist David Riesman, co-author of *The Lonely Crowd*. Interviewing youngsters in Chicago, he found a growing number who were rejecting the sound of Russ Morgan and Dinah Shore and listening to R&B. "Even in the field of popular music," he said, "there is always a minority channel over which less popular tastes get a hearing, eventually to become, perhaps, majority tastes."

By the time this forecast appeared, it had nearly approached reality, for in 1951, a Cleveland disc jockey named Alan Freed, who was white, began to include R&B, which was black, on his *Moondog House* show

16

on radio station WJW. (He had previously attempted to translate an earlier record show, *Request Review,* from radio to TV on Cleveland's WKEL-TV, so unsuccessfully he was soon hosting movies.) At the same time, Freed gave the "race music" he was playing a new name. To avoid (in his words) "the racial stigma of the old classification," he combined the two words that seemed most common to R&B songs of the day: *rock* and *roll*.

Bill Haley amplifies the story: "We started to make records in 1951, for Essex Records in Philadelphia, and the first rock and roll record was a thing called 'Rocket Eighty-Eight,' which was a reasonable hit for us then, in 1951. In 1952 we had 'We're Gonna Rock This Joint Tonight.' In 1952 I wrote a tune called 'Rock-a-Beatin' Boogie,' and the song started out with the lyric: 'Rock rock rock everybody/Roll roll roll everybody . . .' and a few years later Alan Freed was to use this and to coin the phrase rock 'n' roll . . ."

Apparently, Bill Haley has his dates crossed, but it matters not; he's underlined Alan Freed's point: there were a number of popular songs being written and recorded in this period using the words *rock* and *roll*. The same songs also were finding a changed audience. In 1951 Alan Freed staged his first rock show in the Cleveland Arena, turning away twenty thousand because there weren't enough seats. (The Arena has a thirty thousand capacity.) And the audience was racially mixed.

There were many reasons why young people (young *white* people) were turning to R&B (or R&R), and why groups like Bill Haley's Comets were being influenced by R&B. For one thing, it was danceable. So was Tony Bennett's "Because of You," another early 1950's hit, but by then the cheek-to-cheek bit was becoming more than a little old-fogyish. The whang of the electric guitar and the pronounced thump of the drums of rock, the four heavy beats to the bar and the raunchy lyrics, provided a musical drive and tension that complemented, rather than sublimated or ignored, youthful energies. (A few years later this rhythm would be reinforced by the invention of the electric

17

bass; during this time, the standup bass contributed little to rock.)

Rock 'n' roll songs also captured more accurately the attitudes and activities of the young record-buyer. Mainstream pop was jammed with apple pie and Mom, as pure (and bland) as mashed potatoes served at a D.A.R. lunch, to a waltz or fox trot "beat." For one thing, there was a total embargo on sex in the "acceptable" music, and how could someone who was worried about his mother finding a rubber in his wallet and the school cafeteria putting saltpeter in his lunch (or, getting knocked up or wondering how "far" to go) identify with Leroy Anderson's "Blue Tango"? So along came rock 'n' roll, dealing with sex point-blank.

There were probably hundreds of songs about sex recorded in the middle fifties. No one has made an accurate count, because most have been forgotten—thanks to little or no air play. (You have to hear something more than once to remember it.) Records often are banned from air-play even today, but present conditions are nowhere near what they were then, when rock 'n' roll was declared a public menace and songs were banned by the score.

> I need it
> When the moon is bright
> I need it
> When you hold me tight
> I need it
> In the middle of the night
> I need
> Your honey love*

That one was banned. Too suggestive. So were these:

> "Stingy Little Thing"
> "Too Much Lovin' "
> "I Want a Bowlegged Woman"
> "Work With Me Annie" (and the follow-up,
>   "Annie Had a Baby")

*"Honey Love" by Clyde McPhatter & J. Gerald, Copyright 1954 Progressive Music Publishing Co., Inc.

"Live Fast, Love Hard, Die Young"
"Baby, Let's Go Down to the Woods"
"Drill, Daddy, Drill"
"After the Lights Go Down Low"
"Baby, Let Me Bang Your Box"*

The R&B audience—David Riesman's minority group from Chicago—was growing, but still the record market was dominated by the clean, schmaltzy sound of white singers who'd long been established. This was a time when the record charts were ruled by Patti Page ("Tennessee Waltz"), Eddie Fisher ("Any Time"), Rosemary Clooney ("Come On-a My House"), and Teresa Brewer ("Till I Waltz Again With You"). And the only "black" artist consistently on the best-selling record lists was Nat Cole, whose "Pretend" and "Too Young" hardly could be considered very black.

It wasn't until 1954 that the popular music revolution gained its true momentum and there appeared for the first time something called "covers"—meaning white artists were taking songs previously recorded by R&B (black) artists and releasing them as their own.

The cover making the earliest—and for that reason alone, perhaps the most noteworthy—impact was "Sh-boom," originally recorded by an unknown black group, the Chords, released on an unknown label, Cat. Nonetheless, "Sh-boom" became a regional hit (in Los Angeles it was Number One for weeks). Then a white group, the Crewcuts, covered the song for Mercury. BINGO-BANGO-SMASH! It went zooming up to the Number One spot immediately.

That started the stampede.

In 1955 and 1956 there were dozens of successful covers made. Alan Freed had moved from Cleveland to New York to launch a nightly *Rock 'n' Roll Party* on radio station WINS, and he carefully avoided cover records, but there was no stopping the trend. Every

---

*This last song, by the Penguins (of "Earth Angel" fame), actually referred to a piano, but the "box" wasn't identified as such until the Penguins sang the last verse. Another interesting hit of the time (1951) was "Sixty-Minute Man," sung by Billy Ward and the Dominoes. It sold over two and a half million copies but was played on only a few R&B stations.

time a black artist or group recorded what seemed like hit material, white performers would cover it and go rocking and rolling to the bank with all the bread.

Black Performer	Song	Covered By
Spaniels	"Good Night Sweetheart"	McGuire Sisters
Moonglows	"Sincerely"	McGuire Sisters
Joe Turner	"Corrine, Corrina"	Ray Peterson
Drifters	"Ruby, Baby"	Dion
LaVern Baker	"Jim Dandy"	Georgia Gibbs
Flamingos	"I'll Be Home"	Pat Boone
Clyde McPhatter	"Seven Days"	Dorothy Collins
Hank Ballard	"Ko-Ko-Mo"	Perry Como
Chords	"Wheel of Fortune"	Kay Starr
Joe Turner	"Shake, Rattle & Roll"	Bill Haley & the Comets
Etta James	"Dance With Me, Henry"	Georgia Gibbs

This is progress? Yes. The black *could* have been saying: "They're stealing from me; therefore, I must have something good." That's progress. (It's 1954, remember.)

In time, a few artists broke the spell. LaVern Baker recorded "Tweedle Dee" in 1955. She was covered by Georgia Gibbs. Both versions were hits, but the original outsold the copy. The same year Pat Boone covered Fats Domino's "Ain't That a Shame," and Domino's version was the million-seller. The Penguins' "Earth Angel" also outsold a Crewcuts cover. LaVern Baker took the issue of covers to her congressman, who spoke out against the practice on the floor of the House of Representatives but was unable to do anything, since covers were legal. Death came to covers when the market demanded originals. By 1955, apparently, there was this demand.

This was also the year when the first "rock 'n' roll movie" was released. Frank Zappa of the Mothers of Invention wrote in *Life* magazine: ". . . I remember going to see *Blackboard Jungle*. When the titles flashed up there on the screen, Billy Haley and his Comets started blurching 'One Two Three O'Clock, Four O'Clock Rock . . .' It was the loudest rock sound kids had ever heard at that time. I remember being inspired with awe. In cruddy little teen-age rooms across America, kids had been huddling around old radios and

20

cheap record players listening to the 'dirty music' of their life style. ('Go in your room if you wanna listen to that crap . . . and turn the volume all the way down.') But in the theater, watching *Blackboard Jungle,* they couldn't tell you to turn it down. I didn't care if Bill Haley was white or sincere . . . he was playing the Teen-Age National Anthem and it was so LOUD I was jumping up and down. *Blackboard Jungle,* not even considering the story line (which had the old people winning in the end), represented a strange sort of 'endorsement' of the teen-age cause: 'They have made a movie about us; therefore, we exist . . .' "

Chuck Berry was one of the "new" artists of 1955 who said he'd agree with that: yeh, young people exist! He came to Chicago, and Chess Records, from St. Louis, and he brought with him the ability to play a driving guitar while laying down some lyrics that made sense. In other words, Chuck Berry was a singer-songwriter-guitarist who connected. His songs became rock classics, laced with humor and personal enough to strike emotional as well as musical chords. He wrote about things kids could identify with—cars, school, growing up and the music itself.

That Chuck Berry was one of the more articulate songwriters of the time tells you something about the popular I.Q. It also tells you rock was fairly simple lyrically, so simple in some tunes, in fact, critics of the "new music" (R&R) would use the words of a song as the focal point of their merciless attack.

One songwriter pinpointed for this peculiar assault (peculiar, really, when his lyrics were contrasted with those by the moon/June/spoon gang of songwriters) was Little Richard (Penniman), who introduced one of his early 1950's hits with: "Wop-bop-a-loo-bop/A-wop-bam-boom!/Tutti frutti/Oh rutti!"

Little Richard was on the scene for only eighteen months, during which time he sold an amazing thirty-two million records ("Ready Teddy," "Long Tall Sally," "Lucille," "Slippin' and Slidin'," "Rip It Up," "Good Golly, Miss Molly") and established himself as the pounding theatrical celebrant of rock . . . a king with greasy, processed hair, eye-whirling costumes, salmon-colored Cadillacs and what seemed to be a desire to destroy every piano in sight.

Eighteen months, that's all he had, and then he disappeared—into a seminary in 1958, tossing all his jewelry into a river, saying it didn't mean anything a'tall.

Bo Diddley was another classic of the time, in flashy-baggy suits and patent leather hair, wearing his electric guitar (red in color) almost at knee-level and slamming out an easily recognized shave-and-a-haircut-two-bits rhythm. He also had the brashness to write a song about himself ("Bo Diddley"), which became an instant and insistent hit, then recording "I'm a Man," "I'm Sorry," "Who Do You Love?" and "You Can't Judge A Book By Its Cover." Since then, the Animals, among others, have written songs about Bo Diddley, and nearly every one of his hits has been rerecorded at least once.

Ray Charles was working in bands in the South as a teen-ager when the first blues records were being cut in Chicago, developing his incredible talents as a pianist, organist, saxophone player, songwriter and singer. From the first song he recorded with his seven-piece band in Atlanta in 1954, "I've Got A Woman," to the most recent, this man's husky blues-gospel voice has served as a guide to hundreds of vocalists to follow (England's Stevie Winwood is one example). Rock critic Pete Johnson has appraised Ray Charles this way: "Whatever abuses the word 'soul' may have been subjected to, Ray Charles is its most perfect example and perhaps its definition." In later years, no matter what Charles recorded—soul music, blues, gospel, country-western, even Twist music—it sold millions of records.

One of the most important vocal groups of the time, the Platters, had its first hit in 1955, "Only You (And You Alone)," written by the group's manager, Buck Ram. Ram also wrote or co-wrote most of the Platters' later hits, including "The Great Pretender" (1955), "Heaven on Earth" (1956) and "The Magic Touch" (1956). The Platters were from Los Angeles and had in Tony Williams a lead singer whose voice became as well-known as that of Clyde McPhatter, who was singing lead in the Drifters in the same period. (Both would break from the groups for solo careers, but only McPhatter would find any success as a single.) On record, the Platters were noted for the subtle use of piano and string accompaniment, flecked in. Much of the R&B sound of the time was rough, the performances unpolished. Groups such as the Platters gave the field a softer ballad voice.

No compendium of rock greats of the middle 1950's would be complete without Fats Domino, a piano player from New Orleans whose first million-selling record, "The Fat Man," was an autobiographical song, like Bo Diddley's first. That was cut in 1948, and each year from 1952 to 1957, Antoine (Fats) Domino added at least one and as many as four equally successful discs to the list. There were seventeen gold records awarded Domino—"Bo Weevil," "Blue Monday," "I'm Walkin'," "Blueberry Hill," "I'm in Love Again" and "Ain't That a Shame" among them—before he took his barrelhouse piano-playing and smooth-as-scotch voice into the Las Vegas lounges and disappeared from the best-selling charts (his "comeback" of 1968 notwithstanding). Only two other rock acts—Elvis Presley and the Beatles—can match that boast.

With Chuck Berry, Little Richard, Bo Diddley, Fats Domino, Ray Charles and all the rest, the black performer had arrived. *Billboard,* an influential music business weekly, summarized 1955 as "The Year Rhythm and Blues Took Over the Pop Field."

With this first real proliferation of rock, road shows began to tour the country, and the country began to react. In Chicago, a radio station broke rock 'n' roll records over the air as daily ritual. In Houston, the Juvenile Delinquency and Crime Commission banned over fifty songs in one session. In New York, *Variety,* another trade paper, issued "A Warning to the Music Business," offering the somewhat questionable conclusion that "The most casual look at the current crop of lyrics must tell even the most naïve that dirty postcards have been translated into songs." And in Washington, a Senate subcommittee initiated a study into the correlation between rock 'n' roll and switchblade gangs.

It didn't seem to matter much. Everyone was leaping for the hay wagon now, as Frank Zappa wrote in *Life:* ". . . to make R&B acceptable, the big shots of the record industry hired a bunch of little men with cigars and green visors, to synthesize and imitate the work of the Negroes. The visor men cranked out phony white rock."

Less phony but no less derivative was the music of Bill Haley and the Comets, the man and group who helped introduce true rock to a mass audience, playing "Rock Around the Clock" in *Blackboard Jungle*. Haley, nearly 30 when that song hit in 1955, was something of a hillbilly singer when he started his career. He credits Red Foley and Hank Williams as his greatest influences of that time, but never having lived in the South, his sound was more "citybilly" than anything else, and the only following he acquired was a local one, in Hartford, Connecticut, where he played with a group called the Down Homers, and then in Chester, Pennsylvania, where he was musical director and leader of Bill Haley's Saddlemen, heard weekly on radio station WPWA.

As R&B became acceptable to a larger audience (working for a radio station helped Haley learn this), he adopted more of that sound as his own. And in the early 1950's, he combined the two, utilizing the blatting sound of an R&B saxophone with a driving country guitar, even a steel guitar for a while. (In truth, Haley took most of his sound from R&B; listen to an early Atlantic artist, Tommy Ridgley, who used horns and guitars in the same way.) Then, covering a song by Joe Turner, another Atlantic artist, "Shake, Rattle and Roll," Bill Haley and the Comets were on their way, becoming the first rock group to become popular for an instrumental rather than a vocal sound.

As this was happening, another contribution to rock was coming from farther south, from Memphis and Sun Records, a small company owned by Sam Phillips. Phillips had a number of young country-western artists on his label—Carl Perkins, Jean Shepard, etc.—and it was in 1954 when he signed still another, a former truck driver for the Crown Electric Company in Memphis, Elvis Aaron Presley. Presley said at the

24

time his favorite singers were Hank Snow, a C&W great, and Arthur (Big Boy) Crudup, a little-known Negro blues vocalist. It was Crudup who gave Presley much of his singing style, but the first records Presley cut were country-based ("That's All Right Mama," backed by "Blue Moon of Kentucky"). And it was on the country charts in Memphis that Presley made his first mark, going to the Number Three spot with that first disc.

In less than six months' time (following release of a second Sun record), Presley had been voted Number Eight among most promising new C&W singers and was touring the country circuit as "The Hillbilly Cat." Even so, his sound of the time was a blend, and building to a point where it would overlap all fields of popular music—pop, C&W, R&B, and rock 'n' roll.

Music black and white had merged at last.

2

The First
Rock Coronation

In 1956, just one year following the release of *Rock Around the Clock,* the first rock 'n' roll coronation was held, and the undisputed king was Elvis Aaron Presley, then just old enough to vote. (He would, that same year, endorse Adlai Stevenson, an act greeted by Democratic Party dignitaries with something less than ecstasy.) Other things rated higher on the Associated Press Top Ten Stories of the Year list—the Hungarians revolted, the United Nations established the first international police force to supervise a truce between Egypt and Israel, six U.S. Marine recruits drowned on a forced march at Parris Island and the first trans-atlantic telephone cable system went into use—but in the history of popular music and kindred social phenomena, no one person and one subject grabbed as many headlines, vicious attackers and energetic followers as Presley and rock 'n' roll.

Presley had come from country roots, from Tupelo, Mississippi, a village of only ten thousand when he was born there in 1935. As an only child (his twin died at birth), he was cosseted by his parents and given every opportunity his family could afford. "Even when I started to high school," he recalled years later, "my mama still walked me to school. I was 15 years old. My daddy was a common laborer. He didn't have any trade, just like I didn't have. He mostly drove trucks, and when he used to bring the truck home from the wholesale grocery, I used to sit in it by the hour. My daddy never made much money, but anything I wanted he would try and get me."

Presley's musical education was limited to listening to the radio and singing with his parents at camp meetings, revivals and the Assembly of God church. In high school (in Memphis) he acquired a guitar and began to sing for his classmates. His preferences were gospel blues and country music, logically, and so it wasn't unusual when he, like so many other hopeful young singers, approached Sam Phillips at Sun.

Presley cut his first record and went on the road with a country-western show. Roy Orbison, another young singer at the time, recalls what it was like: "Presley started touring with country shows that included Hank Snow and Johnny Cash. It was the same with me for the first few months because Bob Neal, my first manager, was Presley's first manager. Elvis'd appear in the southern states in a pink Cadillac, and in his lace, pink and black outfit. That outfit came from a men's shop in Memphis on Beale Street. They had all this wild gear. The colored guys were the first to wear those clothes. That was a big thing: to get those clothes, a diamond ring and a Cadillac. All the rockabillies got their clothes there."

Presley built his following quickly, however limited it might have been in its geographic base. He stood out from the other musicians and singers on the tours, didn't smoke and didn't drink, and appealed to the screaming girls. Then a disc jockey in Texarkana named Uncle Dudley spotted him and called a friend, a former carnival huckster named Colonel Tom Parker, then Eddie Arnold's ex-manager. "A kid named Parsley *(sic)* played to 800 folks in Boston, Texas," Uncle Dudley said, "and they went plumb crazy." When "Parsley" returned home, the Colonel was waiting.

If Parker seduced Presley with promises, the promises were soon fulfilled, and an incredibly unassailable team that continues to this day was formed. Within a year Presley was headlining his own jamboree, billed over Jean Shepard and Johnny Cash. He made weekly appearances on *Louisiana Hayride,* a radio show on KWKH in Shreveport, and the Colonel (an honorary title) bought additional radio time to plug his boy's records. He also sent Presley into the North with the Roy Acuff Show, and began to work on one of the major record labels, RCA Victor.

RCA was definitely interested, and when Parker had finished sweet-talking them, they agreed to pay an unprecedented forty thousand dollars for Presley's Sun contract, together with five unreleased masters and rights to Sun's earlier pressings. Sun retained the right to continue pressing copies of Presley's then-current hit—"I Forgot to Remember to Forget"—until the end of 1955, when it was to be released to RCA along with the other material.

Of course RCA Victor hadn't been alone in the bidding for Presley's larynx, but RCA had offered more, and the deal was closed at the annual C&W disc jockey festival in Nashville—during which Presley was named as the year's most promising new C&W artist—with Bob Neal (a Memphis disc jockey as well as Presley's early manager) giving Parker an assist. RCA promised to push Presley not just in the C&W market but in the pop and R&B markets as well. The song selected to launch this campaign, in January, 1956, was "Heartbreak Hotel":*

> Well, since my baby left me,
>   I found a new place to dwell.
> It's down at the end of Lonely Street,
>   it's Heartbreak Hotel.

*"Heartbreak Hotel" by Mae Boren Axton, Tommy Durden & Elvis Presley, Copyright 1962 Tree Publishing Co., Inc.

The bellhop's tears keep flowing,
   and the desk clerk's dressed in black.
Well, they been so long on Lonely Street,
   they'll never, never look back.

Another country-rock classic was released at the same time. This was "Blue Suede Shoes,"* written and sung by Carl Perkins on Presley's old label, Sun. This record finished second to Presley's in the race to the top of the record charts, but it was no less important, for it did much to establish the concept of the contemporary teen-ager:

You can burn my house,
Steal my car,
Drink my liquor from an old fruit jar,
But uh-uh honey, lay off-a them shoes.
Don't you
Step on my blue suede shoes.
You can do anything,
But lay off-a them blue suede shoes.

Perkins was drowned in the Presley push. His managers waited eight months before releasing another single. (Perkins was seriously injured in an auto accident, too, but there were other songs that could have been released.) Meanwhile, Presley was in the Number One slot.

"They laughed when Steve Sholes sat down to write out that $40,000 check for Elvis Presley's contract," a story in one of the trade papers began in April, 1956. "But this week the phenom from Mississippi was ringing up the cash registers to the tune of more than $75,000 daily in the retail record shops.

"Last November, Sholes, RCA Victor's specialty records chief, against the advice of Nashville's foremost taste arbiters, paid Sun Records that amount for the youngster's contract and also took over the discs he had cut previously for that indie label. There was considerable doubt whether, in Victor's more formal studio

---

*"Blue Suede Shoes" by Carl Lee Perkins, Copyright 1956 by Hi Lo Music.

atmosphere, Sholes could preserve the unique sound Presley had been getting both vocally and instrumentally.

"Now, apparently, Sholes and Victor have the last laugh. Presley's 'Heartbreak Hotel,' recorded under Sholes' supervision, has passed the million sales mark and this week was far and away the best seller in the country. Presley's album, also cut by Sholes, is one of the fastest selling albums in history, having sold 155,000 in two and a half months.

"In the pop singles field, Presley disks are selling at the rate of 50,000 a day, accounting for about 50 per cent of Victor's total pop business. They include six disks, five of which are reissues of original Sun masters. The LP's and EP's are selling at the rate of 8,000 a day. . . .

"Sholes flew to Nashville Friday [April 13] to cut some fresh wax with the lad. But Nashville will never be the same."

Nor would popular music ever be the same. When Elvis Presley and "Heartbreak Hotel" appeared—simultaneously—at the top of the retail, disc jockey and jukebox lists in both the pop and C&W categories and had the Number One LP on *Billboard*'s best-selling album chart, the recording industry realized once and for all that the musical barriers were down. A C&W artist had adopted R&B styling and then had made it in all markets. Said Paul Ackerman, *Billboard*'s executive editor: "Often the difference between a country side and an R&B side is merely the use of strings as against the use of horns. The Presley sound . . . might be called R&B without horns, but with strings."

And it seemed that rock 'n' roll was becoming more than a catch-phrase, a label that fit headlines easily; it was becoming a recognized musical form.

It is interesting, in retrospect, that so much of the reaction to rock 'n' roll generally and the Presley phenomenon specifically was hooked on morality and sex. Remembering the "Annie"-type songs of two years earlier and pondering in a clichéd Victorian fashion the pelvic gyrations of Presley and others, perhaps it seemed logical. But sex was, after all, only one of the many

29

subjects considered by rock 'n' roll songwriters and performers. (How "sexy" were "Heartbreak Hotel" and "Blue Suede Shoes"?) Then, as before and since, rock music was the music of vitality and youth, an integral part of growing up and developing a life-style, so naturally sex would be a part of it. Unfortunately, sex was emphasized by critics and the public at large, and when Presley appeared on *The Ed Sullivan Show,* what was remembered was not what he sang but what wasn't shown on the television sets at home: Presley, from the hips down.

Time magazine greeted Presley similarly, saying his movements suggested, in a word, sex, then added that Presley "was packing theaters, fighting off shrieking admirers, disturbing parents, puckering the brows of psychologists, and filling letters-to-the-editor columns with cries of alarm and, from adolescents, counter-cries of adulation." While *Newsweek,* actually placing Presley in their "Music" category, a subdivision of "The Arts" (he shared the page with a review of Frank Loesser's Broadway play *Most Happy Fella*), included in its report some "typical female comments," all including some reference to Presley either being a dope-peddler, a jailbird or looking like a snake. *Look* topped them all, saying Presley's success story was "overshadowed by a nightmare of bad taste. . . . On-stage," wrote Gereon Zimmerman, an editor, "his gyrations, his nose wiping, his leers are vulgar. When asked about the sex element in his act, he answers without blinking his big brown eyes, 'Ah don't see anything wrong with it. Ah just act the way Ah feel.' But Elvis will also grin and say, 'Without mah left leg, Ah'd be dead.' Old friends, like the Memphis *Press-Scimitar*'s Bob Johnson, advise him to clean up his 'dances.' Elvis listens and then goes out and does the same, very old things. His naïve intransigence threatens his future. Presley has taken the rock 'n' roll craze to new sales heights. He has also dragged 'big beat' music to new lows in taste."*

These self-appointed guardians of public morality,

*Gereon Zimmerman, "Elvis Presley . . . He Can't Be . . . But He Is," *Look* Magazine (Aug. 7, 1956). Copyright 1956 Cowles Communications Inc. By permission of the editors.

posing as reporters, were not alone in their attack. In Boston, Roman Catholic leaders urged the music be banned . . . and several cities did just that, among them San Antonio, where rock 'n' roll was banished from city swimming-pool jukeboxes because, according to the city council, the music "attracted undesirable elements given to practicing their spastic gyrations in abbreviated bathing suits." In New York, A. M. Meerio, associate professor of psychiatry at Columbia University, said, "If we cannot stem the tide of rock 'n' roll with its waves of rhythmic narcosis and of future waves of vicarious craze, we are preparing our own downfall in the midst of pandemic funeral dances." Even *The Encyclopaedia Britannica*'s yearbook called rock 'n' roll "insistent savagery."

It should not have surprised anyone that this sort of reaction to popular music occurred in America. Only the musical beat differentiated the attack that came thirty years earlier, when public reaction to jazz was, as in 1956 with rock 'n' roll, more "violent" than the music itself. At that time, the *Ladies' Home Journal* said jazz was definitely Bolshevik-inspired and that it constituted a replacement for sex and marriage that would reduce the birthrate. Articles of the period were titled "Does Jazz Put the Sin in Syncopation?" "The Jazz Path of Degradation" and "Unspeakable Jazz Must Go!" In 1956 the same public hysteria prevailed, far surpassing any alleged "hysteria" that existed among rock 'n' roll fans.

The criticism of rock is easily explained, even including the so-called "riots" that occurred when young people charged the stage, injuring each other and causing thousands of dollars in damage. True enough, the music was exciting, and often chairs seemed superfluous when dancing and movement seemed more appropriate than sitting, but when eight thousand youngsters are jammed into an auditorium designed for six thousand—as was often the case—there are likely to be scuffles, even if the attraction is a chamber quartet. At the same time, rock 'n' roll had the misfortune of arriving just when juvenile delinquency was getting more attention than ever before.

It is interesting, too, that *Look* magazine (a few

months before attacking Presley) quoted a New York psychologist as saying, "When the adolescent gets into trouble, the parent can blame it on 'that awful music.' It's a two-edged problem. The parent, by disliking the music so violently, only makes it more attractive to the child, who uses it as a symbol of his growing independence; and, of course, the more the child plays and dances to rock 'n' roll, the more the parent dislikes it." Said *Look:* "While adults cannot be asked to like rock 'n' roll, they may find tolerance to be the wisest course—tolerance allied with a memory long enough to bring to mind the fads of their own youth. Rock 'n' roll is a fad and eventually will be in the mainstream of American popular music. Is it music or madness? Perhaps it is a little of both. But it is no closer to insanity than those who attack it—or any form of musical expression—as morally bad."*

In Tennessee in 1956 an "Anti-Elvis Presley Club" was formed. There were fifty members of this organization, and they sent petitions to local disc jockeys saying, "It's getting to be sickening to hear him every time you turn on the radio. Let up, give us other music." The club fell apart two weeks after its formation under pressure (on the same disc jockeys) from irate Presley fans and the gathering momentum of rock.

Which is not to say "mainstream" pop music was dead. Presley was not alone on the record charts. Vic Damone had a hit that year ("On the Street Where You Live") and so did Doris Day ("Whatever Will Be, Will Be"), Perry Como ("More"), Gogi Grant ("The Wayward Wind") and Morris Stoloff ("Moonglow" and "Picnic"). Still, 1956 *was* Presley's year, and the year when a coronation was held. Besides releasing "Heartbreak Hotel," he had hits with "Don't Be Cruel" (the Number One single of the year), "Hound Dog," "I Want You, I Need You, I Love You," and "Love Me Tender," as well as a cover version of Carl Perkins' hit of earlier that year, "Blue Suede Shoes."

Colonel Tom Parker was running a tight and prof-

*George B. Leonard, Jr., "The Great Rock 'n' Roll Controversy," *Look* Magazine (June 26, 1956). Copyright 1956 Cowles Communication Inc. By permission of the editors.

itable ship in 1956, turning his king into gold. He convinced Ed Sullivan, using the William Morris talent agency to do his negotiating, that Presley was worth fifty thousand dollars for three appearances, and then asked NBC and CBS for three hundred thousand for two additional guest appearances and a special. (Three years later, when Presley completed a two-year hitch in the Army, Parker topped himself and asked *Life* magazine for three thousand dollars just to *photograph* Presley as he left the base!) And then Parker went to Hollywood, to sign Presley to Paramount Pictures for a long-range movie deal, a deal that would later guarantee "Elvis the Pelvis" a minimum of a million dollars per film.

Following in the Presley wake came a tide of country-based stars, who not only capitalized on his phenomenal acceptance but also made contributions of their own. By the end of 1956 and during 1957, white acts rooted in Nashville and Memphis, and later Texas, hadn't obliterated popular interest in black artists, but they'd certainly overshadowed them. Fats Domino, the Platters and Ray Charles continued to crank out splendid hit singles, but it was the C&W singer turned rock 'n' roll stylist who captured the interest, and dollars, of the record-buying public.

One of these was Jerry Lee Lewis, a piano-player from Ferridale, Louisiana, who in the eyes of Andy Wickham, an A & R man now working for Warner Brothers-Seven Arts Records, was a man who had a sneer "that made Presley look lush. Lewis wasn't like any of the others," Wickham recalls. "If they were wild, he was ferocious. If their music was sexy, his was promiscuous. Presley shook his hips; Lewis raped his piano. He would play it with his feet, he would sit on it, he would stand on it, he would crawl under it and he would leap over it, his shivery voice provoking goosepimples, his long crabby fingers assaulting the keys, his feet crashing the pedals like a speed-freak flooding the carburetor of a stalled Ferrari." Lewis made this sort of entrance with a song called "Great Balls of Fire":*

You shake my nerves,
    and you rattle my brain!
Too much lovin',
    that'll make me insane!
You broke my will!
Oh what a thrill!
Goodness gracious,
Great balls of fire!

Each line of his delivery was punctuated with a building four-note assault on the piano keys, until he was raping the ears of his audience while tearing off his jacket and vest and destroying his piano bench. With "Great Balls of Fire" and "Whole Lot of Shaking Going On," recorded a year later (in 1958), Jerry Lee Lewis elbowed his way into the rock 'n' roll classics list. It was only when someone learned he had married his cousin, the 13-year-old daughter of his drummer, that he was banished. (They remain happily married today, eleven years later, and Lewis continues to try for a well-deserved comeback.)

Jerry Lee Lewis was signed to Sun Records, as was another "new star" of the period, Johnny Cash. He was born in Depression poverty in a railroad shack in Arkansas and nearly died as a baby, until his mother stole some milk to nurse him to health. Even as late as 1947 the Cash family had no electricity. Cash was extremely shy, and it wasn't until Presley began to find some success on Sun that Cash screwed up the nerve to audition for Sam Phillips. When he signed the contract Cash had only fifteen cents.

Cash began touring and recording with a duo called The Tennessee Two (a guitarist and a bass player), making their first hits, "Folsom Prison Blues" and "So Doggone Lonesome," in 1955. Then in 1956, Presley's year, Cash recorded a mournful song he had written. "Sam kept tellin' me to pick up the tempo," Cash recalls. "I said it was goin' too fast. The first time I heard it on the radio I called Sam and begged him not to send any more out, not to release it. Sam said, well, let's go ahead and give it a chance." The record, "I Walk the Line," was on the charts for forty-four weeks and established Cash as a star whose audience would be like Presley's in that it crossed nearly all lines—folk, C&W, rock and pop.

Another act from the South (Kentucky) making its debut on the record charts in 1957 was an act that had been a part of the C&W and bluegrass scene for nearly a generation, the Everly Brothers, part of the long-established Everly Family. Don and Phil Everly had appeared on *Grand Ole Opry* a number of times by the time they were in their teens, and at the ages of 18 and 20 struck out on their own, recording for a new label formed by Archie Blyer of *The Arthur Godfrey Show*.

The Everlys had two hits in 1957, "Bye Bye Love" and "Wake Up, Little Susie." Each sold more than a million copies. (As "All I Have to Do Is Dream" and "Bird Dog" also would become gold discs the following year.) And in them was established a vocal style that, like others before, stretched one-syllable words into two or three, so that "love" became "lo-o-ove" and "sound" became "sou-ound." Their harmony was precise, always verging on loss of control but never doing so. The Everlys haven't had a million-seller since "Cathy's Clown" in 1960, but their styling has had its effect; as Chuck Berry and Bo Diddley and the blues guitarists of the 1950's influenced English groups of a decade later instrumentally, the "Liverpool sound" also owed a debt to the Everlys vocally.

In Texas, in the area adjoining New Mexico, is a stretch of flat cow country sometimes called "Tex-Mex," and it was here that several rock artists of the late 1950's were born. Buddy Holly was one of them.

In 1955-56 his records (for Decca) sold moderately on the C&W market; then in 1957, with Presley's all-market success established, Decca suggested an innovation: why not have Holly record on its subsidiary Coral label as a solo artist and with a group called the Crickets on another subsidiary, Brunswick—simultaneously!—with the product of both efforts aimed at the broadening rock market? Holly, anxious for his share of success and shy enough not to question the suggestions of men who seemed wiser, agreed. Thus, Holly soon had success coming two ways, as a part of a group and as a soloist. Nearly every record issued was a hit—"Words of Love," "Peggy Sue," "Heart-beat" and "Early in the Morning" recorded alone . . . and "Maybe Baby," "Oh Boy" and "That'll Be the Day" done with the Crickets.

Besides being good songs, they advanced the music of the time. Latin rhythms were being used by a number of artists in rock (Elvis Presley in "All Shook Up" and "Teddy Bear," Paul Anka in "Diana" and the Diamonds in "Little Darlin' "), but Holly introduced something new: rhythmic patterns with a Mexican flavor. He also established—with the help of Presley and Perkins before him—the role of the rhythm guitar.

Holly, like the Everlys, would influence the English groups to follow him (the Rolling Stones would record one of his songs, "Not Fade Away"), but he died before he could see it, in a plane crash in 1959. (The same crash took Ritchie Valens and the Big Bopper.)

Two others, Buddy Knox and Jimmy Bowen, followed Holly almost immediately—Knox with "Party Doll" and Bowen with "I'm Stickin' With You." Both took Holly's country sound closer to the mainstream of pop, and both, along with the Crickets who continued after Holly's death, soon disappeared. "Tex-Mex" had made its contribution and left.

Many of the songs of this era were written by the stars who performed them (Carl Perkins' "Blue Suede Shoes," Johnny Cash's "I Walk the Line"), a practice which later would make the traditional Tin Pan Alley type of songwriter nearly obsolete. In the early days of rock, however, there was one songwriting team that seemed perfect for all markets, Jerry Leiber and Mike Stoller.

"We were trying to get a record on a respectable label, a major, some kind of record our relatives might hear on the radio, a station they might be listening to," they told a radio station in Los Angeles. "I think we finally did . . . with the Cheers."

He wore black denim trousers
 And motorcycle boots
 And a black leather jacket
 With an eagle on the back*

*"Black Denim Trousers and Motorcycle Boots" by Mike Stoller and Jerry Leiber, Copyright © 1955 by Quintet Music Co.

Another song they wrote at the time was one that would be recorded first by Willie Mae (Big Mama) Thornton, later by Elvis Presley—"Hound Dog." Leiber and Stoller were young (only 18 and attending Los Angeles City College when "Hound Dog" was written), and they were the first independent rock 'n' roll producers, as well as first nonperforming composers to pay so much attention to the lyrics of rock. Often these words were nonsensical, especially when written for an R&B vocal group called the Coasters, who had come from the Robins when that group broke up. Probably the silliest was "Little Egypt," in which Little Egypt, a belly-dancer, "had a ruby on her tummy and a diamond big as Texas on her toe." Like Chuck Berry, Leiber and Stoller wrote about things the kids understood. "Charlie Brown" was humorous, but was also about a youngster who didn't get along in school ("Fee-fi-fo-fum/I smell smoke in the auditorium . . ."), and "Yakety-Yak"* probably was rock's first song about the generation gap.

> Take out the papers and the trash,
> Or you don't get no spending cash.
> If you don't scrub that kitchen floor
> You ain't gonna rock and roll no more.
> Yakety-yak.
> Don't talk back.

Popular music had changed, and two forms which previously had been unacceptable (C&W was too corny, too shrill, and R&B too gutsy, too rough), once married, were nearly in command of the entire market.

In Japan, a 19-year-old named Masaaki Hirao was being hailed as "the Elvis Presley of Japan's rockabilly set," and wearing not blue but yellow suede shoes. A report in the New York *Times* from Berlin said: "Here, just as in the United States, it looks like a rout of Dionysus; a mad chant, recognizable as delightfully comic German versions of Tin Pan Alley tunes, rises from the sweating throng." In Zakopane, Poland, blue-jeaned singers were belting what they called *ruck en*

---

*"Yakety-Yak" by Jerry Leiber and Mike Stoller, Copyright © 1958 by Tiger Music, Inc.

37

rullye. And in Boston, it was business as usual: one side saying rock was the sound of a nation dying, while the other was having fun—as when a Boston disc jockey offered seven strands of Presley's sideburns for the seven most ridiculous reasons for wanting one . . . and in one week there were over 18,400 contestants.

Whatever it was that Presley had done, he certainly had done it well.

"They all think I'm a sex maniac," he said at the time. "They're just frustrated old types anyhow. I'm just natural."

3

The *Other*
Philadelphia Story

In March, 1958, 9-year-old Pamela Miller of Van Nuys, California, taped a calendar to her bedroom wall, and for the next two years she crossed off the days. Elvis had gone to war.

Presley continued to have hits in his patriotic absence, but popular attention was diverted from his pelvis to something else as soon as he left. In fact, what came next in rock history already was underway when he reported for duty at Fort Chaffee. It began, if there must be an official starting date, six months earlier, on August 5, 1957, when ABC-TV introduced a Philadelphia-based record hop called *American Bandstand* and its affable, Ipana-grinned host, Dick Clark.

Clark had come to WFIL-TV (the ABC affiliate producing the show) and the City of Brotherly Love some time earlier, supplanting an earlier *Bandstand* host who had been charged with "improper activities" involving some of the young girls who danced on the show. According to a station publicity release, Clark was as clean as his grin. "To many mothers," the publicist wrote, "the afternoon show has brought a sudden, closer relationship with their children. 'He's sort

38

of a big brother who sets a good example,' one father commented, 'since *Bandstand* kids have insisted on wearing jackets and girls have cooled it on too-tight sweaters.' Parents applauded."

This was Clark's image all right. In his Utica, New York, high school he had been elected president of his class, and in his suburban Philadelphia home in the early *Bandstand* years (quoting rock critic Richard Goldstein), "There were no skeletons in his split-level closet; just a lot of two-button jackets and ties." In 1959, a different sort of scandal from that suffered by his *Bandstand* predecessor would hit, and Clark would be in the midst of it. Until then, Dick Clark, *American Bandstand* and what promotion men called Brotherly-lovesville were as good (and negotiable) as gold. And South Philadelphia, which had achieved some fame in earlier years as the birthplace of such diverse talents as Mario Lanza and Joey Bishop, became known, briefly, as the spot where the action was.

Dick Clark was born in Bronxville, New York, and was raised in the serene suburban comfort of Mount Vernon, one of the upper-middle-class villages north of Manhattan. His father was a sugar broker who, when the young Clark was in his teens, dropped out of the commuting bag and accepted a brother's offer to become sales manager of a radio station in upstate Utica. Clark says his father accepted the job because "he knew that, as young as I was, I wanted to go into radio someday."

From high school, where Clark excelled in just about everything, he went to Syracuse University, majoring in advertising, minoring in radio. "As a freshman I wasn't allowed to take radio courses, so I went to the manager of the student radio station and said, 'What kind of jobs do you have available for a guy who wants to learn?' He looked at me and said, 'Well, we need radio announcers.' I had done impersonations in high school, and when I tried out for that job, I simply did an impersonation of what I thought a radio announcer ought to sound like. Luckily for me, my impersonation sounded the way people who ran the radio station thought an announcer should sound."

After college he spent a year working as an announcer for a commercial station in Syracuse, then worked for his father's station, and then for a competing station. In May, 1952, he moved to Philadelphia as a staff announcer and disc jockey for WFIL.

In its inception, *American Bandstand* was a fluke, concocted to fill afternoon time. Two guys who are today anonymous merely got together to play games, show short films and persuade people to call in their musical requests. A studio audience was a part of this, and this is how teen-agers became a part of it; they were the only ones available at four o'clock (a high school was located nearby).

"They discovered that when they played recordings, the kids got up and danced," Clark recalls. "It became apparent that the show's future lay in getting on with the dancing. That's how *Bandstand* was born."

Clark, looking considerably younger than his 27 years, was the perfect host. (As an announcer, he had previously lost a beer account because he didn't look old enough to drink, let alone sell the stuff.) In a word, young people identified. The format was unimaginative, but it didn't matter; rock 'n' roll was popular, and *Bandstand* was the only show. So it shouldn't have surprised anyone when the network began to consider the program, and Clark, as product worthy of a national audience.

By April, 1958, Clark was an unparalleled smash, appearing on 105 stations and attracting a weekly audience of forty million (half of them adults), while drawing twenty to forty-five thousand fan letters a week and an income approaching half a million dollars a year. The show's Trendex rating nearly equaled the combined totals of the two rival networks. All across the country, teen-agers were vanishing from the streets after school hours. Some were even hitchhiking from as far away as Texas to participate. And in Miami, despite the temperature, young people were wearing heavy rolled socks and sweaters, because the kids on *Bandstand* did.

What had they come to see? No more than what looked like a bunch of kids in a garage, dancing to records. Occasionally a guest star would appear, to lip-sync (pantomime) to his or her current record release. Features were "Dick Clark's Top Ten," the ten songs Clark said were tops that week, and a bulletin board filled with photographs sent in by his following, all of them studied look-alikes. Candid, and often embarrassing, interviews filled in the spaces (as teen-agers and singers were asked to react to songs they'd just heard), along with Clark's bland etiquette and advice (later to appear in book form). (Perhaps because the time was bland, the show was bland; when a television show accurately reflects the times, its success is usually assured.)

With this success, *American Bandstand* quite logically became a launching pad for dozens of popular dances, songs and vocalists—the personalities and music forming the nucleus of the show, and the dances providing the "fill." It was, in fact, the novel dance steps devised during this period of rock that drew the audience and held it as much as the stars. (Being able to do the steps seen on Clark's show was important in Miami and Detroit.) And because there usually were only two or three guest stars on each ninety-minute show, unless the dances were variant, boredom might have set in.

Of course the record companies—well aware of the magnitude of Clark's audience—were anxious to promote dance crazes, too, for with each new dance step, there had to be those special records with words or rhythms to accompany it. Thus were the Fish, the Stroll, the Walk, the Madison, the Slop, the Circle, the Chalypso and the Philadelphia born.

The dances, lasting in popularity from a month to three months at best, filled a lot of television time and sold a lot of records. They also created minor-league stars, those show "regulars" who were in the dancing audience each day and, thanks to the consistent exposure, became nationally recognizable personalities. (Just as some of Walt Disney's Mousekateers later would develop their individual identities and become stars.)

Today, Denny Bruce is personal manager for a number of early Chicago blues musicians and 24 years of age. In 1962, he was a teen-ager and dancing on

Bandstand as often as he could find a ride to the studio from his suburban home in Willow Grove.

"Some of the regulars were written up in the fan magazines, just like the record acts," Bruce recalls. "Some were even paid to go to record hops just to dance. And they were always wearing new clothes. You see, these regulars were trend-setters; what they wore on the show on Tuesday was a national fad by Friday.

"It was really wild. The regulars understood how the cameras worked and they'd cling to the position that'd get them on-camera. They just watched the little red lights and when one went on, that meant that camera was on and those regulars were right in front of it, slopping and chalypso-ing their little brains loose. There were fights between the dancers, but you never saw them at home. Dick Clark was careful about that."

Denny and the other regulars on the dance floor were "stars" of one kind. Others born in this era came from equally mundane circumstances, but were "stars" in the truer sense. These were the recording personalities who were created overnight . . . and music had little to do with it.

There are a number of stories told to explain the "discovery" of Fabian Forte, but the most often told has Bob Marcucci, a personal manager in his middle-to-late 20's, rushing to the home of a South Philadelphia neighbor when he saw an ambulance drive up. A policeman named Dominic Forte had been hit with a heart attack, and as Marcucci offered his help, he noticed the cop's 14-year-old son, Fabian. Once it was established the elder Forte was okay and hustled off to the hospital, Marcucci is supposed to have asked the kid: "How'd you like to be a star?"

"You crazy?" the youngster is supposed to have answered, returning to the basketball court and football field at South Philly High and the six-dollar-a-week job he had working as a drugstore stock boy.

Marcucci didn't give up. He already had under his profitable managerial wing one recording star, Frankie Avalon (sort of a pubescent Frank Sinatra—although with stature and general appearance the similarity stopped), and he wanted to make it two. By 1959, two years after first seeing the boy, Marcucci is supposed to have won his campaign, convincing the somewhat round-shouldered, olive-skinned youngster with a duck-tail haircut that he, indeed, *did* have star potential.

Between winning the argument and winning the public, though, Marcucci sent the youngster to a voice teacher (several reportedly turned him away) and launched a massive promotional campaign. His first records were duds, but they provided a reason for his appearing on television programs (local *Bandstand* copies) all across the country. On tour, he also sang at high school record hops and signed autographs at neighborhood stores. At the same time, Marcucci was buying space in the music trade publications:

FABIAN IS COMING!
WHO IS FABIAN?
FABIAN IS HERE!

It worked, and Fabian (the surname was dropped at Marcucci's insistence) became a star. "Turn Me Loose" sold 750,000 copies and remained near the top of the best-selling charts for three weeks. A follow-up disc, "Tiger," sold more than a million. The boy was making as much as twelve thousand dollars a night. Perry Como and Ed Sullivan were extending their puzzled invitations. And Fabian was enroute to Hollywood with a thirty-five-thousand-dollar ten-week contract to make his first movie, "Hound Dog Man."

Flashback now to his beginnings and the manner in which others say he was discovered. This version skips the heart attack and Bob Marcucci and has Fabian discovered at a record hop. He just walked in and all the girls started screaming. "That was enough for us," Dick Clark is supposed to have said. "You don't look for a singer. The person who is the star has that magic thing, and that's all that counts." (Like the Monkees more recently, "singers" were sometimes exploited more for their looks and personality than for their talent.)

The late 1950's were peculiar years in the short history of rock. After a burst of creativity and vitality, rock began to atrophy. There were classic songs recorded in 1958 and 1959—"Stagger Lee," "Personality" and "I'm Gonna Get Married," all by Lloyd

43

Price; "All I Have to Do Is Dream" and "Bird Dog" by the Everly Brothers; "There Goes My Baby" by the Drifters; "Tears On My Pillow" by Little Anthony and the Imperials; "Smoke Gets In Your Eyes" by the Platters; "Since I Don't Have You" by the Skyliners; and the song that perhaps unintentionally parodied the hundreds of doo-wop groups, "Get a Job" by the Silhouettes. The Big Bopper sang "Chantilly Lace"; Phil Spector (who would later become a giant in the industry) cut his first record, "To Know Him Is To Love Him," as one of the Teddy Bears; and Elvis Presley continued his string of tasty hits with "Don't," "Hard Headed Woman," "A Fool Such as I" and "A Big Hunk O' Love."

Still it was Dick Clark's reign. Good singers, and good songs, may have sold records, but the *Bandstand* gang sold more.

As the elder son of Ozzie and Harriet, Ricky Nelson had been a star long before he learned how to play the guitar. He had, in fact, literally grown up in public, first on the Nelson family radio show (a fictional drama with a "real" family) and then on television's version of the same program.

At age 19 he had been a "singer" two years and had sold twelve million records, among them "Be Bop Baby" and "Poor Little Fool." Nelson usually had a superb band of studio musicians behind him on his records, but the weak lyrics and weaker voice did little to advance popular music and, sadly, represented his time. (He would, later, improve measurably and provide some listenable folk and country-flavored LP's.)

One of Nelson's compadres in rock was Frankie Avalon, Bob Marcucci's first creation. When *he* was 19 he had sold one and a half million copies of an acne'd plaint called "Venus." Avalon was one of the *Bandstand* regulars, and his dress was the Dick Clark uniform: neatly pressed if somewhat baggy pants, drape jacket (all buttons buttoned), white shirt and dark tie, and in a final grab for individuality, white buck shoes. Another of his hits of the time was, like the music of the period generally, "Ginger Bread." If the music of the period was gingerbread, it was also very sweet (read: saccharine), with a song by Bobby Vinton, "Roses Are Red," being typical. In the first verse, Vinton sang about how he signed his girlfriend's high school yearbook: "Roses are red . . ." and so on. So far, nothing but gingerbread. But in the following verses, the plot, as they say, thickens. The boy and girl drift apart, she finds someone new, finally writes a Dear John letter, then several years later they meet again. Now Vinton asks if the little girl with his old flame is her daughter. He says she looks like her daughter, and then says some day a boy will write in her yearbook, too, and probably will write: "Roses are red . . . ." This spongy little ditty was sung, of course, with all the appropriate sobs and gulps.

Other songs of this ilk were grimmer. "Teen Angel," sung by Mark Dinning, told the story of a girl who left the side of her steady date, went to retrieve his high school ring from the car he had stalled on the tracks, and was flattened by a northbound freight. Johnny Preston's hit, "Running Bear," had an Indian brave of that name leaping into angry rapids to swim to his Little White Dove, who jumped into the boiling river from the opposite bank to swim to him, and they drowned together. While "Tell Laura I Love Her," by Ray Peterson, had a stock car driver named Tommy entering a race to win money for a wedding ring and crashing; his last words form the title of the song.

These records sold in the millions.

Rock was hitting a low. Any given week it seemed at least half a dozen of the following were included in Dick Clark's Top Ten: "At the Hop" by Danny and the Juniors; "Lonely Boy," "Put Your Head on My Shoulder," "It's Time to Cry" and "Puppy Love" by Paul Anka; "Frankie," "Who's Sorry Now?" and "Lipstick On Your Collar" by Connie Francis; "Born Too Late" by the Pony Tails; "Dream Lover" and "Splish Splash"* by Bobby Darin; "Wild One" by Bobby Rydell; "Devil or Angel" by Bobby Vee (the Age of the Bobbys, someone called it); "A Teen-ager in Love" by Dion and the Belmonts; "Short Shorts" by the Royal

---

*"Splish Splash" is supposed to be the first record cut using an eight-track recording machine, a practice giving artists a chance to augment their sound amazingly. The eight-track machine is greatly responsible for changing musical history.

Teens (one of the members being a young Al Kooper); and "Kookie, Kookie (Lend Me Your Comb)" by Connie Stevens and Edd Byrnes. In nearly every case, teen-agers identified with these performers because (let's admit it) most couldn't perform any better than the kids could—and the kids knew it! Some, like Edd Byrnes, didn't even try to sing, proving stardom could come to someone who had mastered only the art of slicking back a restless pompadour, an art that was universal at the time.

While this was happening, Denny Bruce was learning drums, and as an aspiring group member (that would come later, in 1964, when he was one of the early Mothers of Invention) he viewed the music of the time carefully. Also very skeptically.

"The black groups were the only ones really worth watching and listening to," he said. "Most of them had a lead singer, backed by three guys who were basically dancers. They'd provide some backup voicing, but mostly they'd just do the latest dances.

"Then the white groups started copying the blacks. The Dovells are the best example. Tab shirts and a thin dark tie with a pearl tie-tack . . . four-button coats that buttoned up close to the neck, almost Edwardian . . . pointed patent leather shoes . . . and tight high-water pants, pants that stopped several inches up the ankle.

"I thought the white music was fabricated, but colored music turned me on sexually. As a beginning drummer, I was more interested in rhythm than to what Fabian was saying about some dumb tiger. It was a stale period for white musicians."

And Dick Clark was king.

Of course, Clark was not solely to blame for what was happening to rock; the record-buyer still had a choice. But Clark was the taste-maker, and although exposure on *American Bandstand* did not assure a hit, it certainly helped dozens of records reach the goal of one million in sales. "When I recorded 'Venus,'" Frankie Avalon told one interviewer, "Dick got behind it and it sold well over a million copies. He's the greatest."

Suddenly it began to smell of day-old fish, and Clark

was summoned to Washington. Congress was investigating something called "payola"—taking money from a record producer for guaranteeing that his record would be given air play—and the man who had done so much to clean up the image of rock was being charged with bribery. There was, as one writer put it, "the suspicion that he (Clark) was confusing aesthetic with financial interests."

Nearly a year earlier, Clark had been interviewed by Pete Martin of *The Saturday Evening Post*:

CLARK: Aren't you going to ask me more about that beef that I'm a dictator of popular music?

MARTIN: What am I supposed to ask?

CLARK: You might have mentioned to me that there are people going around proclaiming happily that a show very much like mine is being launched which will break Dick Clark's monopoly on the rock 'n' roll industry. These same people might tell you that, to a great extent, Dick Clark determines which rock 'n' roll song will become a hit. They might—and I have heard they do—spread the rumor that a songwriter or a manager must bring his song or singer to Dick Clark first. If not, these rumor-mongers say, Clark refuses to have anything to do with the artists as far as personal appearances on his program are concerned, and he will never play that song on his show afterward. Then, too, they continue, Clark has a number of traveling shows under his name which play the nation's big cities and feature only the artists who cooperate with him. I do have the traveling shows, of course, but the rest of it is nonsense.

MARTIN: I've never heard these accusations.

CLARK: That's because you're not involved in the music business. First you have to understand a little about the music business as such. It's a highly competitive, dangerous, lucrative, interesting business. Some people think it's a closed corporation; they're the ones who write songs and can't get them published. I've got more or less used to the unkind things the critics say about me and my show, but I haven't been able to take

47

being called dishonest gracefully. In far too many cases I am stupidly honest. My enemies claim that to be booked on one of my shows it is necessary first to pay me off or at least to kick back part of the fee the artist receives. It's got so bad that some of the people who interview me actually ask me if this is true.

MARTIN: That's pretty insulting.

CLARK: There's another canard. It is well known in the industry that I own three music publishing companies.

MARTIN: Do they publish sheet music or do they make records?

CLARK: Explaining it would be too complex. But I'll give it to you as briefly as I can. A music publishing company owns the copyright to a song in all of its forms; it's responsible for putting out the sheet music and licensing the recorded music for a song. There are people who say—and I take it they are honest in saying it—"Dick Clark won't play anything unless one of his three companies owns it." This is a stupid comment, because it's so easily disproved. I've been in the music publishing business for a year and a half, and in that time my three firms have had exactly two big sellers . . . I wish sometime you'd sit down and list the thirty or forty songs the *American Bandstand* plays in any one session. Then I wish you'd check back to see how many of those thirty or forty songs have been published by one of my companies. You'd probably come up with one out of forty. Actually that kind of ugly talk is easing up, but occasionally I still get someone who calls up and tells me, "I'd like to put an artist on your show. How much will it cost me?" I try to tell such people as clearly as possible what the real situation is, but even then they sometimes don't believe me.

Shakespeare once said something about "methinks he doth protest too much," and it was this attitude, apparently, the Congress took. Clark was one of several "disc jockeys" questioned, and a long succession admitted taking payments from music companies. (Alan Freed, the man who helped start it all, was charged with accepting thirty thousand dollars in bribes from six record firms; he resigned on the air, sobbing, breaking into "Shimmy Shimmy Ko-Ko-Bop" by Little Anthony and the Imperials.) Clark was one of the last called to testify, and he smiled and said he was clean. "I have never agreed to play a record in return for payment in cash or any other consideration," he said.

What Congress learned, however, was that Clark had numerous corporate holdings which included financial interests in three record companies, six music publishing houses, a record pressing plant, a record distributing firm and a company that managed singers. Thus, Clark had been in a position to give specific artists, music and records preference.

Did he? The Congressional committee's report indicated he did. It said, for instance, that in a period of twenty-seven months Clark devoted far less air time to Elvis Presley than to a newcomer named Duane Eddy . . . and Clark held stock in firms dependent at least in part on Eddy's success. The committee also pointed out that Clark owned 160 songs (as a publisher) and that 143 of them had come to him as outright gifts . . . and each time a song is played, the publisher shares a fee with its writer.

The investigation dragged on for weeks, showing how Clark had played one song, "Sixteen Candles" (by the Crests), only four times in ten weeks and it went nowhere . . . then once he owned it, he played it twenty-seven times in less than three months and it "took off like a rocket." It showed how he had received a "gift" of seven thousand dollars from the publisher of another song that became a hit after it was played regularly on Clark's show. It uncovered complicated investments in small record companies that resulted in Clark's earning thousands of dollars as a capital gain in a few months' time. And a songwriter named Orville Lunsford told how his record "All American Boy" got a fast ride to the Number Two position in record sales—but only, he said, after the Mallard Pressing Corporation, one of Clark's interests, got an order to print fifty thousand copies. "Almost immediately," Lunsford said, "I heard my song played every other day on Clark's show." At the peak of the investigation, "Clarkola" was even substituted in the headlines for "payola."

Even so, Clark emerged nearly unscathed, his Ipana grin intact. He had divested himself of all outside interests the preceding year (at ABC's insistence), he said.* He also received, during the course of the investigation, tremendous popular support. Teen-agers fanatic in their devotion to Clark filled the spectators' seats during committee hearings. The majority of mail received by ABC defended him. And (of course) many of the popular recording stars offered testimonials. ("I don't think anything is wrong with a man having one business, and an interest in another," said Frankie Avalon. "And why can't anyone give anyone a gift? I gave him a shirt, a pair of shoes.")

It was additionally pointed out that payola had been around since the days when Sullivan (before he joined Gilbert) got one of his songs performed by sharing the royalties with a leading baritone of the time . . . and that was over a century ago. Later, in 1916, the Music Publishers Protective Association reported that upwards of four hundred thousand dollars was being paid to musicians and singers to plug their songs; the publishers agreed to fine members who continued the practice, but the ruling was unenforced. More recently, in the late 1930's, a group of New York-based publishers retained an attorney to work with the Federal Trade Commission in drafting an anti-payola law. The plans died early.

With all this history, why, then, was anyone surprised?

Besides, to Clark (it seemed), the *Eleven O'Clock News*—on which he was featured prominently—was just another television show. All he had to do was smile and say "Shucks," and all was forgiven. Even Representative Oren Harris, the committee's chairman,

*It is interesting to note that given the same ultimatum by ABC, the show's producer, Anthony Mammarella, refused to give up his share of Swan Records and two publishing houses, and quit instead.

said, "You're not the inventor of the system or even its architect. You're a product of it. Obviously, you're a fine young man."

(Alan Freed had the explanation: "What they call payola in the disc jockey business, they call lobbying in Washington.")

When all was said and done, and after nineteen days of Congressional subcommittee hearings, the government issued its report, which said in part: "Fifty-seven witnesses were heard; they included disc jockeys and other programming personnel, network, and licensee executive personnel, phonograph record manufacturers and distributors, independent data processors, trade paper representatives, songwriters and publishers, and members of the subcommittee staff. Testimony appears to indicate that the selection of much of the music heard on the air may have been influenced by payments of money, gifts, etc., to programming personnel. In some instances, these payments were rationalized as licensing fees and consultation fees."

It was shown that station programmers received gifts of clothing, appliances and cars . . . that disc jockeys were retained by record companies as "consultants" . . . that advertising agencies and music publishing firms were established as "fronts." The means were varied, the end the same: pay-for-play.

Still, it didn't seem to matter. Many in the industry regard payola as part of their life-style; realists know it still exists. And so do most of those who were subpoenaed by Congress still exist; most are still in influential positions in the music world.

The Dick Clark era was a peculiar one in many ways, because while it gave rock its first "clean image" (skirts for the girls, jackets for the guys on *Bandstand*), along with its first true mass audience (TV) and a symbol of unification (Clark himself), it also marked a backward step in rock 'n' roll popularity. Rock suffered in the waning 1950's, thanks in part to the payola scandals, but also to the rapid decline in musical quality. In 1959, record sales reportedly dropped a whopping twenty-five percent. Buddy Holly, Ritchie Valens and the Big Bopper died in a plane crash. "Conflict of interest" and "morbidity" were the catchwords

51

of the day, and the epitaph on Philadelphia's pop tombstone. The hype had run out. Dick Clark's *American Bandstand* is still on the air—still on ABC, every Saturday—as if to challenge another network's Ed Sullivan in the television longevity (and blandness) race, but now Fabian and Frankie Avalon are actors (they say).

4

Meet Me
at Izzy's Place

It seemed that rock 'n' roll had gone down for the count when Dick Clark was called before Congressional investigators. It also seemed to some, who thought only of the Fabians and the music being customed to manufactured dance routines, that rock had exhausted its creative juices. (Even Elvis Presley, on his release from the Army, began to issue ballads rather than rock, and had long disappeared from the concert scene to join the cinematic sausage-factory crew in Hollywood.) Rock 'n' roll had begun to atrophy, and with much of the American record-buying public equating rock 'n' roll with payola—not to mention the continuing social attack—the time seemed appropriate for something new.

The something "new" that was introduced to and accepted by the mass audience was something really quite old, folk music. It was, apparently, a time to return to the roots. If the Big City (i.e., Philadelphia) was corrupt, the public seemed to say, well, let's go back to the country; let's get rid of tight pants, pompadours and electric guitars and bring out fiddles, gingham dresses and wagon wheels. It wasn't quite that cut and dried, but the "down-home honesty" of folk music seemed a proper antidote to everything that ailed popular music.

There had been earlier popular interest in folk music, of course, most recently in the 1940's (concurrent with the emergence of Southern blues artists in Chicago) when Huddie Ledbetter, better known as Leadbelly, came out of Louisiana State Prison to write and perform "Midnight Special" and "Good-night Irene" . . . when Woody Guthrie, one of the great folk balladmakers of this century, introduced among the one-thousand-plus songs in his bag "So Long, It's Been Good to Know You," "Pastures of Plenty" and "This Land Is Your Land" . . . when Josh White and Big Bill Broonzy were acquiring some of the acclaim they were long due . . . when, as Robert Shelton wrote in *The Face of Folk Music,* "a period of national stress (World War II) directed attention to our democratic heritage and our celebration of minorities' contributions were similarly being heralded." This constituted the first major urban folk revival, when folk music moved out of the backwoods and into the city streets.

The 1940's revival was also the time when Pete Seeger formed the Almanac Singers with Guthrie, Millard Lampell and Lee Hays. ("In the country," said Hays, "a farmhouse would have two books in the house, a Bible and an almanac. One helped us to the next world, the other helped us make it through this one.") A few years later, Seeger would form another folk group, the Weavers—with Hays, Ronnie Gilbert and Fred Hellerman—dedicating this second quartet to Leadbelly and becoming the first group of its type to reach the best-selling record charts, with songs like "Good-night Irene," recorded with Gordon Jenkins in 1950; "Kisses Sweeter Than Wine"; and "On Top of Old Smokey," a hit in 1951 with Terry Gilkyson.

Together, Woody Guthrie and Pete Seeger are generally credited with fathering the second urban folk revival as well, which began in 1958.

Woodrow Wilson Guthrie was born in Okemah, Oklahoma, spent his childhood in an oil boom town, drifting to California in the "Okie" migration that came midway through the Depression, when dust storms destroyed the farms. He made a living—barely—singing in saloons, performing occasionally on country-oriented radio shows and for union meetings, political rallies, rent parties, and dance and theater groups. Seeger's background was somewhat more formal, coming from a musical family (his father, Charles Seeger, was an "ethnomusicologist" at Harvard and later, with his wife, taught classical music at Julliard), but his music was no less "real." Seeger was playing tenor banjo in his high school jazz band the same year Guthrie headed west from Oklahoma, but shortly after that got turned

54

on to folk music while attending a square dance in Ashville, North Carolina. From that time on, his commitment was to folk music, fostering and encouraging many of the later-successful folk-oriented endeavors—the influential People's Songs (a publishing firm that markets records and books to schools) and *Sing Out!* (a folk magazine still being published monthly). He also helped reorganize the annual Newport Folk Festival, which had been abandoned for a while. It was for good reason Seeger was called "America's tuning fork" and "The Pied Piper of American Folk Music."

Folk music had gone through several stages, or transmutations, by now: from ethnic folk (the "ethnic," or original, folk song sung by the original artists) to traditional folk (traditional songs sung by nearly anyone, but sung traditionally) to the folk of the traditional translator (traditional songs sung, again, by nearly anyone, but now with the individual singer's interpretation thrown in) to urban folk (new songs sung by new singers, adhering to a basically traditional structure or "sound"). The day of the olden ballad dolefully presented to hushed reverence was gone. In times past, as Herbert Russcol wrote in *High Fidelity* magazine, "It was all a chaste scene preserved in amber, as fixed a tableau as that of the bewigged lover serenading his lady on a French tapestry. The repertory was as unalterable as an Ambrosian chant, unless the folklorist had come up with an authenticated ditty twanged out for him in the Appalachian hills by a pipe-smoking eighty-seven-year-old mammy who had heard it from her granny. The singer would not have dreamed or dared to sing his own song: that was heresy. His listeners wanted him to be not a creator, but a curator."

When folk music entered the pop music scene in 1958, this was no longer true, and although many of the "old-timers" were quite evident, it was the newcomer who represented the urban revival and who is remembered today. The Seegers and Guthries and "eighty-seven-year-old mammys" provided the tradition and the youngsters provided the sound. The times they were a-changing (as one of the youngsters, Bob Dylan, would sing), and the first to signify this change were Harry Belafonte and the Kingston Trio.

Belafonte was a handsome Negro actor who couldn't get work and had opened a tiny Greenwich Village hamburger stand to augment his even smaller earnings as an occasional vocalist. Like the Weavers before him, he knew of the illiterate former convict named Huddie Ledbetter, and he admired his powerful material. He had been trying to sing blues and pop, but after attending a memorial concert to Leadbelly at New York's Town Hall (Leadbelly had died of a withering bone disease), Belafonte returned to the folk originals. He also abandoned the idea of accompanying himself on guitar and met an agent named Jack Rollins, who recognized "star material." He was booked into the Village Vanguard, the press was asked to view Rollins' new "discovery" and Belafonte took off like a shot.

Then when it came time to record his first album for RCA Victor, he met a composer named Irving Burgie, who had traveled with a West Indian woman named Louise Bennett as Lord Burgess and His Serenaders. Burgie showed Belafonte some of the West Indian songs he had written (actually, rewritten, as many had been traditional melodies in public domain), songs like "Lindstead Market" and "Jamaica Farewell." Now Belafonte discarded his American folk material and made a West Indian record instead, thereby introducing the "calypso" sound.

"Day-O," Belafonte's first hit, smashed its way to the top of the record charts in 1957, and was followed by "Banana Boat Song," by the Tarriers. Soon, millions of homes were bouncing with the calypso beat, and the music trade papers were saying: "Rock 'n' Roll Dead; Calypso Takes Over!"

The announcement was a bit premature (reflecting the writers' and editors' long-standing paranoid fear of rock), for this was in 1957, when *American Bandstand* stopped being a local record hop and first was given a national audience. The Dick Clark era was just beginning, and still the names on nine and a half out of ten records were those who sang rock, not calypso or folk. Nonetheless, folk music had made an impressive debut, beginning a slow ascent that would accelerate in a few years time. And Harry Belafonte, displaying excellent taste in an acceptable (i.e., neatly dressed) style, was laying the groundwork for a group that would put folk music in the Number One spot, the Kingston Trio.

At the time, there were no contemporary folk groups "making it." The Tarriers, and several others, including the Weavers, were on the scene, but a single hit (in the Tarriers' case) and several hits several years earlier (Weavers) did not a successful recording group make. Thus the Kingston Trio was born—taking its West Indian name from Belafonte's flash success.

Two of the members, Bob Shane and Dave Guard, began their careers strumming ukuleles while attending Punahou High School in Honolulu (also developing a comedy diving act popular among their fellow students). Guard then went on to Stanford University and Shane went to Menlo Park (California) Business School, where he met Nick Reynolds. Following college the three tried singing together. "We batted around some college hangouts singing for cakes and coffee," Reynolds said later, "until we met Frank Werber from San Francisco, who became our personal manager. He really put us through the hoops. 'You listen to your voice on tape,' he said, 'and you go to a vocal coach, and you practice your instruments . . .' Eventually, we didn't sound quite as bad as we did."

The first song the trio recorded (for Capitol) was a traditional folk song, "Tom Dooley," a song Frank Warner (another folk giant from years past) had sung at that Leadbelly memorial in New York. The song went right to the top.

Other songs, recorded later, would also reflect their folk heritage (Pete Seeger's "Where Have All the Flowers Gone," etc.), but all would have a contemporary feel. "When we find something we like, we adapt it," Dave Guard said. "It may not be ethnic when we get through with it, but after all, what's ethnic? Why should we try to imitate Leadbelly's inflections when we have so little in common with his background and experience?"

"Tom Dooley" was an immediate hit in 1958, and for the next five years the Kingston Trio remained exactly where they were when they started: on top (avoiding the years of "paying dues" in the basket houses that were to follow, where the entertainers took

what was collected in a basket or hat in lieu of salary).
Only one of their single releases, "Tom Dooley," was
rated a million-seller by the Record Industry Association of America, but during that period a dozen more
sold almost as well, and eleven of the trio's sixteen
albums reached the Top Ten on the *Cash Box* and
Billboard charts. Some of the material—so little variety, spread so thin over so few years—was weak, but
much of it was excellent. They hadn't the punch of
some other folksingers of the time, yet one song,
"Merry Minuet," was strong enough to make a point,
even if it was cloaked in a humorous delivery. The
song started with a catalog of catastrophe—rioting in
Africa, starving in Spain, etc.—and worked its way up
the disaster ladder, all the way to the mushroom-
shaped cloud. With several laugh-lines (jokes) along
the way.

Although this song was not a hit single for the
Kingston Trio, no one song better captures the spirit
of the time. In the late 1950's, what sociologists called
"The Silent Generation" was being replaced by what
nearly everyone was calling "The Beat Generation";
there were growing numbers of disaffiliated youth, feeling alienated from society. The majority of young people may not have joined this generation and gone "on
the road," but with the passing of the witch hunts of
the Joe McCarthy era and an increased interest in civil
and human rights, young people felt the pangs of social conscience again. The Kingston Trio presented the
message in a format programmed for laughs, and no
better format could have been created then. (At the
same time, Mort Sahl and Lenny Bruce and half a
dozen satirists and comedians were making *their* names
known for the first time, too.) It was "cool" and "in"
to dig jazz in this period, but the jazz renaissance of
the late 1950's was remote and folk music was more
emotional, more fun.

Another reason the Kingston Trio became a success
was evidenced in the packaging. Like Belafonte, the
three boys represented folk music cleaned up some and
citified. The denim workshirts and the no-foolishness of
the country originals (alien to urban audiences) had
been replaced by matching red-and-white-striped but-

ton-down shirts and carefully rehearsed patter and repertoire. Listening to their records now, the modern folk fan may agree with those who preferred "ethnic" as opposed to "commercial" folk music then, finding the Trio's approach a bit coy, a bit too show biz. But they did have an infectious enthusiasm and dedication to making the man on the street aware of the wealth of folk songs that America possessed (recording "This Mornin', This Evenin', So Soon" by Carl Sandburg, "M.T.A." by Bess Hawes of the Lomax family, "Colorado Trail" by Sandburg and Lee Hays, etc.). Popular music was seeking an antidote to rock, it seemed, and if the pill was sugar-coated, that just made it all the simpler to swallow.

(Of course, folk music was more than a soothing pill to ease the ills of rock. We know now that it was just one more form, or type, of music entering—again— the popular stream, later to be part of the blend of today. But at the time, it achieved craze proportions, seeming to provide the answer to everything.)

The Kingston Trio did much for folk music. Besides introducing many of the real folk classics to a mass audience, the success of this trio served as the inspiration for many other fine groups—the Limeliters, the Brothers Four, the Cumberland Three, the Chad Mitchell Trio, the Gateway Singers, the Highwaymen, the New Lost City Ramblers, the Rooftop Singers, the New Christy Minstrels, the Back Porch Majority, the Travelers, the Serendipity Singers, Peter, Paul and Mary, and countless others. And with increased interest in folk music generally, second-level popularity came to other young people in the field—Casey Anderson, Hoyt Axton, Ian and Sylvia, Leon Bibb, Sandy Bull, Judy Collins, Logan English, Lisa Kindred, Jim and Jean, Carolyn Hester, Phil Ochs, and two unknowns who later would command the attention of uncounted millions worldwide, Joan Baez and Bob Dylan.

Much of the focus of this era was in the neighborhood in New York long established as the section where the avant-garde lived, Greenwich Village. Here the "new" popular music developed around the fountain in Washington Square Park and in small, barely-commercial basket houses such as Charley Washburn's

Third Side, the Four Winds, and the Cafe Basement, where Steve Stills (much later of the Buffalo Springfield), John Sebastian (of the Lovin' Spoonful), David Crosby and Jim McGuinn (of the Byrds) and Larry Taylor (of Canned Heat) would literally sing for their supper. In the Village, young folksingers lived together and worked together, trading songs as much earlier singers and songwriters had done for decades before them.*

One of the places the folksingers met to sing and swap songs was the Folklore Center on MacDougal Street, owned by Israel Young, an ex-pre-med student who "just happened on the Village" in his student days, dropped out of school and moved there to open his music shop in 1957. Almost immediately, "Izzy's" became a clearinghouse, and Izzy became the unofficial mayor of the community.

The interior of the Folklore Center was simple then (it has since moved to another location), only ten feet wide and five or six times as deep. On the left wall were personal notices listing apartments for rent, instruments for sale, lessons being given; farther along was a pay phone, the only phone in the place. Along the opposite wall were shelves of books over racks of record albums. "I have albums of over two hundred and fifty different folk artists," Izzy said at the time. "If I don't have something you want, I can probably get it for you. There are no stereo albums in the racks. Almost no Villager owns a stereo set." In the back was a small room with a fireplace and what John Sebastian remembers as "at least a dozen busted guitars lying around." It was here the folksingers gathered to pick and sing.

Izzy was also a personal manager for a time (two weeks), helping the young John Sebastian organize the Even Dozen Jug Band. "He was a nice guy," Sebastian recalls, "a lot like the people who were younger than

*They also swapped members, from one group to another, as when John Stewart left the Cumberland Three to replace Dave Guard in the Kingston Trio when Guard left to form the Whiskeyhill Singers; when Erik Darling of the Tarriers left to replace Pete Seeger in the Weavers and later to form the Rooftop Singers; and Lou Gottlieb left the Gateway Singers to join Alex Hassilev and Glenn Yarbrough to form the Limeliters.

he was. You have to understand this was a time when we were running around, discovering the world for the first time, trying drugs and politics and finding there were others who thought as we did. Izzy was sympathetic. I think we reminded him of himself when he was younger."

Izzy was also an early activist, leading the folksingers against the city of New York when the parks commissioner, in 1961, decided guitar-pickers were a threat and banned singing in Washington Square Park. "We're fighting for our freedom," he sang. "We shall not be moved/We're fighting for our freedom/We shall not be moved."

Around Izzy's were the coffee shops and small night-clubs that were created to provide a platform for this "new" music. One of the most successful of these (though not at first) was Gerde's Folk City, a tavern and cabaret that featured bluegrass groups, where the young Bob Dylan played.

In the immediate vicinity of Gerde's were the Gaslight, the Village Gate, the Bitter End, the Kettle of Fish (really just a bar, but one of the folksingers' favorites), the Playhouse and the Night Owl. While elsewhere in the country—for the folk craze spread far and wide and fast—there was the Ten O'Clock Scholar in Minneapolis, the Second Fret in Philadelphia, the Club 47 in Cambridge, the Gate of Horn in Chicago, the hungry i and Purple Onion in San Francisco, Cosmo Alley and the Unicorn in Los Angeles. In all these places, and more, the folksinger headed the bill.

It should have surprised no one, then, when a television network displayed some interest in this musical form, and in the autumn of 1962 (a year when the Kingston Trio, Joan Baez and Peter, Paul and Mary had best-selling albums) the American Broadcasting Company debuted a show called *Hootenanny,* with Art's boy Jack Linkletter as host. The show lasted two seasons (about the same length of time ABC-TV's rock show *Shindig* was to run in a later time), and this marked the end of the folk craze. Before the craze was over, though, there were two magazines called *Hootenanny* on the stands, cut-rate guitars and songbooks for sale, and "hootenanny" boots for sale.

61

There was also a raging controversy over whether or not Pege Seeger was a Communist. Seeger had been called to testify before the House Committee on Un-American Activities in 1955, and two years later was indicted by a grand jury for contempt, but the conviction was reversed in 1962. This was the same year *Hootenanny* appeared, yet Seeger was blacklisted from appearing on the show. The irony was that Seeger, more than anyone else, had been responsible for the "hootenanny" feeling that prevailed and thus was actually responsible for the show being on the air. Judy Collins and Carolyn Hester led a boycott of the program in defense of Seeger, but the show continued without them.

Popular music took several tentative turns in the early 1960's, but few new stars were born outside the folk field, and most of the non-folk personalities were those who'd appeared before or during the Dick Clark era. Elvis Presley continued to appear on the charts and so did the Everly Brothers, Duane Eddy, Marty Robbins, Connie Francis, Frankie Avalon, Ricky Nelson, Paul Anka, Brenda Lee, Sam Cooke, Brook Benton and Bobby Darin. Some of the songs were exceptional—such as "Cathy's Clown" by the Everlys, "Shop Around" by the Miracles (the first real hit of the then-fledgling Motown-Tamla empire), and "Only the Lonely" by Roy Orbison. Still, most of the rock records issued then reflected the intellect and charm expressed in the title of Brian Hyland's hit of 1960, "Itsy Bitsy Teenie Weenie Yellow Polka Dot Bikini."

The same year, a young former chicken-plucker from Philadelphia who called himself Chubby Checker (a play on Fats Domino) had a freak hit called "The Twist." The following year he had another hit that was customed to another peculiar dance step, called "Pony Time." They were "freak" hits because it wouldn't be until another year passed, in 1962 when folk music was reaching its zenith on ABC-TV, that dances swept the country again. In 1962, Checker's "The Twist" was a hit for the second time, and this time was followed by "Peppermint Twist" (Joey Dee and the Starlighters, who served as house band in a New York nightclub called the Peppermint Lounge),

"Mashed Potato Time" (Deedee Sharp), "Twistin' th.
Night Away" (Sam Cooke), "Locomotion" (Little
Eva), "Dear Lady Twist" (Gary U. S. Bonds), "Twist
and Shout" (Isley Brothers) and a horrible exploitation
quickie called "Monster Mash" (Bobby "Boris" Pick-
ett). Even Ray Charles issued a popular album called
"Do The Twist With Ray Charles." It seemed that
Hank Ballard, who had originated the Twist, and his
Midnighters were the only group *without* a hit version
of a dance.

Like the dance crazes of the Dick Clark era, these,
too, died a rapid death, to be replaced momentarily by
surf music and hot rod songs. The Beach Boys started
the trend in 1962 with "Surfin' U.S.A.," "Surfer Girl,"
and "Surfin' Safari," and this last song, written by two
of the Beach Boys (Brian Wilson and Mike Love),
inspired another surfing group's name, the Surfaris, and
in practically less time than it takes a surfer to wipe out
(crash), *that* group had a hit by that name ("Wipe
Out") and surf music was bigger than the sport itself.
Jan and Dean appeared just one wave behind the Beach
Boys with "Surf City," and with each succeeding tidal
swoop came more—Dick Dale and the Deltones, the
Ventures, and the Sun Rays to name three, all California groups—and each had the same loud, direct
harmonies and the double-speed, screaming guitars.

There's a "woody" mentioned in the lyric of "Surfin'
Safari" (usually an old station wagon with wood sides,
thus the name), and this was only one of many vehicles
honored in lyric and melody then, as Jan and Dean
sailed from surfing to hot-rodding, scoring with "Go
Little Cobra" and others that sounded, really, like surfing songs—usually with the sound of exhaust pipes
thrown in.

Only the Beach Boys survived this plunge into the
surf, and no one representing either the Twist era or
hot rod music is here today, except peripherally. It
was folk music that dominated popular music at the
turn of the decade, and it was folk music that gave
rock 'n' roll a personality equally as influential as Elvis
Presley had been. His name was Bob Dylan.

Dylan had been born Robert Zimmerman in Duluth,
Minnesota, and was a runaway when he was 10. He

...edly worshiped Woody Guthrie in his forma-
...ears, singing many of Guthrie's songs. Then he
...n to write his own, and his unique lyrics soon
...racted an avid, if limited, following. His style varied
from mumbled lyrics with slurred guitar chords to
clearly enunciated words accompanied by crystal-clear
notes. "A poor man's Jack Elliott," someone said.

How Dylan emerged from the hundreds of youngsters
who arrived in Greenwich Village illustrates as well as
anything else what the scene of the time was like. Like
so many other new arrivals to New York's folk mecca,
Dylan appeared (without pay) at the Monday night
"hoots" at Gerde's Folk City. Two of three men important to what came next were there one night—Roy
Silver and Albert Grossman, both of them young
(thirtyish) personal managers. The third, Arthur Mogull, worked uptown for the publishing arm of Warner
Brothers, and when either Silver or Grossman found
someone with "promise," they took him (or her) to
Mogull.

"Those two guys had the Village locked up," says
Mogull, who is today the president of Tetragrammaton
Records. "They were on the street seven nights a week.
There wasn't a kid who came to town they didn't hear.
So when Roy heard Dylan, first he got Dylan to sign a
management contract and then he brought Dylan to
me. I gave him a thousand dollars in advance and
signed him to Whitmark Publishing for three years,
exclusive. That thousand was the most we'd ever paid
anyone, and anyone includes Richie Havens, Judy Collins, Bob Gibson, Phil Ochs, Dave Van Ronk, Ian and
Sylvia, Odetta, Will Holt and the Reverend Garry
Davis. We weren't taking advantage. That was what the
scene was like then."

Mogull, who had previously served as publisher for
the Kingston Trio, says that during the course of
Dylan's three-year contract, Dylan earned royalties to-
taling "about three million dollars, and Warner Brothers made almost double that."

Before all this money and success arrived, however,
Silver went to work for Grossman giving Grossman 10
of his 20 percent interest in Dylan, and then sold his
remaining 10 percent for twenty-five hundred dollars.

(Silver did not consider throwing himself in front of a fast-moving truck when Dylan finally hit, because by then he had found an unknown Negro comic named Bill Cosby, whom he also took to Mogull and Warner Brothers.)

With Grossman, Dylan found success. Albert Grossman had come to New York from Chicago, where he had been co-owner of the Gate of Horn and doubling as an economist for the Federal Housing Administration. With him he brought his first act, Odetta. Then he found Peter, Paul and Mary. (Also taken to Mogull, who signed them.) Then—in 1963—Peter, Paul and Mary recorded one of Dylan's songs, "Blowin' in the Wind." The rest, as they say in all those awful stories, is history. "Blowin' in the Wind" immediately went to the top of the charts.

Almost overnight there were fifty-eight different versions of the song on the market (as singles or included in LP's), ranging in style from that of gospel's Staple Singers to Marlene Dietrich. And Dylan became the musical spokesman for the entire civil rights movement (actually turning up in Mississippi and in the 1963 March on Washington). At one point, *Newsweek* challenged the authorship of this song, also revealing Dylan's real name, but Dylan survived—because he *had* written "Blowin' in the Wind," and his fans felt if a man wrote that, who cared if his name was Blind Boy Grunt (a name he used in jest to make an early recording).

By now, of course, Dylan had signed with a major label, Columbia, to produce one album a year, as was customary for most "doubtful" folk artists. (His "discoverer," John Hammond, offered him a two-year contract before ever hearing him.) Dylan wouldn't have a hit single of his own for some time, but he was long before then considered one of the best songwriters in the business—in the tradition of Woody Guthrie and Pete Seeger, writing songs of social consciousness ("protest," although it wasn't called that then), combined with a sort of free-form poetry. Dylan was anti-authoritarian. There were freedom fights to be won (in the Deep South and elsewhere), and the folkies and activists elected little Bobby Zimmerman king.

Joan Baez was their queen, of course. She had left Boston University's Fine Arts School of Drama in 1959 and debuted at the Newport Folk Festival the same year. Unlike Dylan, she was an interpretive artist, not a creative one—working with others' songs—with a magnetic sort of soothing intensity. Her voice was clear and sweet, like cider, but she sang of things that bothered her, of man's inhumanity to man, as if her voice had begun to turn to vinegar.

In 1962 she joined the boycott of ABC's *Hootenanny* protesting the network's blacklisting of Pete Seeger; in 1963 she was with Dylan in the civil rights March on Washington; in 1964 she appeared at Sproul Hall in Berkeley to give the Free Speech Movement her message ("Do this thing with love and you will win").

Rock hadn't been forgotten with the arrival of folk music, but it *had* taken a back seat. A lack of imagination (complacency), the taint of bribery (payola), and perhaps half a hundred other factors had caused rock to contract a horrible malaise, the symptoms being fatigue and ennui. In part, this came as "product" of the Eisenhower years, when America stopped living and played golf.

Then, in 1960, John F. Kennedy was inaugurated, and with him came challenge and change. The civil rights movement caught fire, and the voices of Bob Dylan, Pete Seeger, Joan Baez and the Freedom Singers were linked in concert in New York, as the hopes of the black man were joined hundreds of miles to the south. Folk music, and folksingers, seemed as if "designed" for this cultural and sociological reawakening. So folk music filled a gap, returning popular music to its roots (blues and C&W), almost as if laying some sort of lyric and melodic foundation for a revitalization of rock (soon to come).

That's the way some people explain it.

Regardless of what folk's role in history might be, there is no debating the effect many folk artists had on rock, once they had, like their blues and C&W forebears, discovered electricity. (And the label-makers created "folk-rock.")

The urban folk revival also presaged another trend: the album's rise to prominence over the single release. In *Cash Box*'s compilation of the best-selling records of 1963 and 1964, there were only four folk singles listed —"Puff, the Magic Dragon" and "Blowin' in the Wind" by Peter, Paul and Mary, "Walk Right In" by the Rooftop Singers and "Don't Let the Rain Come Down" by the Serendipity Singers. In the same period there were sixteen folk albums on the list—by Peter, Paul and Mary, Joan Baez, the Kingston Trio, the Smothers Brothers and the New Christy Minstrels. Many of the LP's even made the Top Fifty lists both years.

Then came the biggest act in pop history.

5

England's Challenge:
Beatles Rule!

The story has been told often, and well.*

In 1956, the year Elvis Presley released "Heartbreak Hotel," John Lennon and five others, all in Teddy Boy clothing and Presley pompadours, had formed a group called The Quarrymen (sort of a skiffle band— banjo, washboard and all of that); the following year George Harrison and Paul McCartney joined the group, replacing some members who'd dropped out. Like so many beginning groups, the band changed its name often, becoming the Rainbows and the Moondogs, then the Silver Beatles. For the most part they appeared in their native Liverpool, journeying twice (in 1960 and 1961) to Hamburg, Germany. Then in October, 1961, came a kind of turning point, when 18-year-old Raymond Jones walked into a Liverpool record shop man-

*It is interesting to note that the best book of several about the Beatles, Hunter Davies' official biography, *The Beatles*, contains so little which hadn't previously appeared in print—not because Davies wasn't a fine researcher, but because by the time the book appeared (in 1968) so much had already been written about the quartet.

aged by Brian Epstein to buy a record, "My Bonnie," recorded by the Beatles in Germany. Epstein had never heard of the record *or* the Beatles, he said, but he made a note to himself: "My Bonnie. The Beatles. Check on Monday."

Epstein talked with friends, went to hear the boys at the Cavern (a local club where the boys played regularly), liked their enthusiasm (hated their sloppy stage presence), requested a meeting, and by year's end had signed them for personal management.

Whether or not the Beatles would have made it without Epstein is a point that is moot and unimportant. Probably they would have succeeded, but there is no questioning that Epstein's tidy sense of organization and genuine enthusiasm played a great role. The Beatles were beginning to weary of limited recognition, and signing with this proven businessman apparently gave them the hope they needed.

The environment was also right. Since 1956, when Bill Haley and the Comets appeared in *Rock Around the Clock* (released in Britain nearly simultaneously with its American release), this new form of music called "rock 'n' roll" had enchanted and excited young Britons. Ian Whitcomb, a schoolboy at the time and later a popular singer ("You Turn Me On" was his hit in 1965), remembers the "rocker" era vividly: "Jackets hung low and had velvet lapels, ties were black bootlace, shirts had huge checks, slacks were a bit baggy. The members with motorized mounts (with sidecars for the birds) wore leather jackets, whilst the bus travellers sported British-made jeans made by Tex-Sun and Lee Cooper and black vicious shoes with curling, pointed toes dubbed 'winkle-pickers.' Their manifest was not written down. It can only be experienced by soaking in the sights, sounds and smells of a stage show by one of their idols—either Jerry Lee Lewis, Fats Domino, Little Richard, Bill Haley, or Gene Vincent. Or the records and memorabilia of the Rocker martyrs Buddy Holly, Eddie Cochran, Johnny Kidd, the Big Bopper. Tommy Steele and Cliff Richard emerged as superstars from this musical merry-go-round. Others flashed temporarily but now are names to mention only when you want instant recall of the British Pop Fifties. We were all forming skiffle groups then."

Whitcomb goes on to name the "all-time Rocker Top Ten": Bill Haley's "Rock Around the Clock"; Jerry Lee Lewis' "Great Balls of Fire"; Elvis Presley's "Hound Dog"; the Big Bopper's "Chantilly Lace"; "Hoots Mon" by Lord Rockingham's Eleven; Chuck Berry's "Sweet Little Sixteen"; "That'll Be the Day" by Buddy Holly and the Crickets; Fats Domino's "Ain't That a Shame"; "Tutti Frutti" by Little Richard; and Eddie Cochran's "Summertime Blues." These songs, he says, molded English rock.

So English youngsters were listening. They had bought the records and they had greeted the visiting American stars with adulation that topped even the enthusiasm the performers had received in America. With them these "rocker superstars" brought a form of music that had developed in the colonies, the blues. (Bob Wooler, a Liverpool disc jockey, had written in *Mersey Beat* in 1961: "Why do you think the Beatles are so popular? They resurrected original rock 'n' roll music, the origins of which are to be found in American Negro singers . . .") So while rock 'n' roll in America was "progressing" through the Dick Clark era and beyond, the English lads were studying the roots. In America in the late 1950's, popular music strayed from the blues. Now, with the Beatles and half a hundred other groups that would soon find success, the interest in the blues was rekindled.

In 1962, the year Bob Dylan cut his first album for Columbia and America was twistin' the night away, Ringo Starr replaced Pete Best as drummer and the Beatles released their first English record, "Love Me Do." It went to the Number Seventeen spot on the British charts; by the next year England was theirs. In November they were summoned by royalty, appearing at London's Prince of Wales Theatre, sharing the Command Performance bill with Marlene Dietrich, Flanders and Swann, and other top acts. (They had also by now established their irreverent approach to success: "People in the cheaper seats, please clap," John Lennon told the audience. "The rest of you just rattle your jewelry.")

The same month *Newsweek* gave the Beatles half a page, saying they provided a sound that "is one of the most persistent noises heard over England since the air-raid sirens were dismantled." The Beatles had sold over two and a half million records that year (unprecedented in English pop history) and their concerts were always sold out, with thousands of screaming fans causing bobbies to be called in force. "This is Beatlemania," said the *Daily Mail*, adding rather plaintively: "Where will it all lead?"

Where it all led, of course, was right back to America, from whence the blues had come. In 1964, one hundred and eighty-eight years after George Washington and his boys had kicked the redcoats out of America, the British invaded (and conquered) the United States.

Julius Fast wrote in his book *The Beatles: The Real Story:* "On Friday, February 7, 1964, the U.S.A. foresaw another crisis with Cuba: Castro had cut off the Guantanamo water supply . . . London and Paris agreed to build a rail tunnel under the English Channel, an almost dreamlike feat of engineering, while in Jackson, Mississippi, the case against the accused killer of black civil rights leader Medgar Evers went to an all-white jury. In fashions, the Paris Spring look was in, and the decision was that the ideal woman for the spring ahead would be 'soft, feminine, and young, but not a giddy teen-ager.' Skirt hems were kept primly at the kneecap. And that same day, at Kennedy International Airport in Queens, New York, three thousand teen-agers stood four deep in the upper arcade of the International Arrivals Building to give a screaming, hysterical welcome to four English boys. Airport officials termed the reception 'Incredible. We've never seen anything like this before, not even for kings and queens!' "

Top Forty radio stations began clocking the time in "Beatle minutes before (or after) the Beatle hour" and reported the temperature in "Beatle degrees." (All part of a huge promotional campaign launched by NEMS, the Beatles' company.) When the "fab four from Liverpool" appeared on *The Ed Sullivan Show,* an astonishing seventy-three million people were watching—nearly forty-five percent of the entire population!—and the next day *The Washington Post* said in its columns: "Don't knock the Beatles; during the hour when they were on Ed Sullivan's show, there wasn't a hubcap stolen anywhere in America." Even evangelist Billy Graham said he'd violated his rule and watched television on the Sabbath, just to see them.

So in demand were tickets to their concerts, that when they appeared at Carnegie Hall, David Niven and Shirley MacLaine were turned away. (Lauren Bacall and Mrs. Nelson Rockefeller got in.) In Washington, so many fans greeted them so noisily, policemen covering the concert stood through the performance with bullets stuck in their ears. (England's prime minister, Sir Alec Douglas-Home, was due to arrive in Washington the same day, but he delayed one day to avoid the Beatle melee; when he did reach the capital, President Johnson said, "I liked your advance party.")

Of course the businessmen were there, too, for Beatlemania meant Bucks. The week they arrived in the country, two hundred thousand "official Beatle sweatshirts" were shipped; official Beatle wigmakers were already half a million orders behind; Beatle dolls, Beatle posters, Beatle buttons ("I Love Paul," "I Love Ringo," etc.), Beatle tee-shirts, Beatle hats, Beatle egg cups (?), Beatle nightshirts, Beatle ice cream (??), Beatle magazines, Beatle pants, and Beatle soft drinks were well beyond the planning stage; and Gene Shacove, a Beverly Hills hair stylist, had created a Beatle cut that was "so simple the girls set on five rollers and comb out!"

Nor were the Beatles themselves, or Capitol Records, unhappy; less than a month following the Beatles' arrival in the United States, besides the incredible concert grosses, the boys took home to England two hundred fifty-three thousand dollars, their royalty share of the two and a half million records sold in just four weeks.

The tour was considered a success.

There were, of course, those who said it would pass. Billy Graham, after watching the lads on *The Ed Sullivan Show,* said, "All are symptoms of the uncertainty of the times and the confusion about us. They are a passing phase." And the *Herald Tribune* in New York reported they were "75 percent publicity, 20 percent haircut and 5 percent lilting lament."

As the decade, and the Beatles, progressed, the few denigrators would be proved wrong, and higher (and more sophisticated) accolades than those received in 1964 would come to the four sons of workingmen. For good or evil, their hair style and manner of dress, as well as their thoughts on religion ("we're more popular than Jesus"), drugs ("I thought LSD rather nice, and beneficial") and meditation ("it's better than drugs") would influence uncounted millions internationally. And their music would develop to combine nearly everything from madrigals and Bach to random electronics, and their musical precision and nearly impeccable taste would push hundreds of other pop groups to do as well . . . thus pushing rock music ahead. (One of the many things the Beatles would give rock was the concept that groups should evolve and grow—developing musically—rather than stand in place and merely continue to issue dozens of records that sounded like those that preceded them.) "When people ask to recreate the mood of the sixties," Aaron Copland wrote in *Look* magazine in 1968, "they will play Beatle music." Copland, one of the world's highly acclaimed composers and conductors of classical music, was not referring to nostalgia alone.

In 1964, the Beatles weren't quite that great—not musically, anyway. At first, their music was merely simple and fresh. The complex melody lines (complex for rock 'n' roll, that is) and the subtle lyricism would come later. Initially, there was only good, clean fun, and the message was no more complicated or controversial than "I Want to Hold Your Hand" (the Beatles first Number One hit in America), so innocent and infectious that everyone (parents included) accepted them immediately.

The early lyrics of the Beatle songs were simpler than words on Valentine's Day cards, punctuated with shouts of "yeah, yeah, yeah." The songs were repetitious, to the point of taking a line from one song—"Let me be your man" from "I Want to Hold Your Hand"—and changing the words and tempo only slightly to form another song on the same album, "I Wanna Be Your Man."

The Beatles appeared then in pencil-thin, collarless suits and great pudding-bowls of hair, seeming almost asexual. Yet, they were taking the blues into middle-America, presenting it so it was acceptable (just as the Kingston Trio "cleaned up" folk music). The long hair? Well, that was a slight aberration, excusable because, after all, they just wanted to hold hands . . . and that was fine with mom and dad, what mom and dad wanted to see, in fact. According to the Beatles, they didn't even want to hug or hold anyone tight, they just wanted to dance all night.

Many of the songs recorded by the Beatles then were songs of the blues-rock past: "Twist and Shout" (an Isley Brothers hit in 1962); Carl Perkins' "Honey Don't" and "Everybody's Trying to Be My Baby"; Chuck Berry's "Rock and Roll Music" and "Roll Over, Beethoven"; and Little Richard's "Long Tall Sally." Other songs, originals, paid no less homage to those who had created a style and sound then nearly forgotten in America. It is ironic that some of those who originally sang what became known as "Beatle songs" were then banished in America.* And it is no less ironic that it would take a rock 'n' roll band from England to make Americans aware of their own rock 'n' roll greats.

Following their initial success, the Beatles could easily have settled into the pattern established by those who had preceded them in rock. Like Elvis Presley, they could have continued to crank out hits, seldom altering their sound, while making a movie or two.

The Beatles selected a different path—perhaps to keep from growing bored, or in keeping with a "plan" —and it is not important why. What is important is that they chose to use their incredible popularity as a basis for nearly immediate growth.

Under the guidance of their producer, George Martin (whose name appears first on *The Beatles' Second Album*), they softened their twist-and-shout singing style and experimented with more interesting har-

---

*Chuck Berry had been jailed on a narcotics charge, remember, and Jerry Lee Lewis had been written off when he married his 13-year-old cousin.

monies. For a time, however, their lyrics remained as basic as they'd been initially. Yeah, yeah, yeah.

A Hard Day's Night (the film and the album, both released the same year, 1964) probably marks the end of the Beatles' "early" period of development. This can only be seen in retrospect, however, for only later would the Beatles develop their talents to an extent where critics would begin dividing their production into "periods." At the time, it all—especially the film, one of the all-time boxoffice champs—seemed merely a part of Beatlemania.

Of course the Beatles were not alone on the record charts in 1964. (They *controlled* them, that's all, at one point appearing in four or five of the top ten positions on the singles chart, two or three in the top five on the album chart.) And with them were a few fellow Englishmen, the first of the deluge that was about to begin—the Dave Clark Five ("Glad All Over"), Billy J. Kramer and the Dakotas ("Little Children"), Peter and Gordon ("A World Without Love"), and Dusty Springfield ("Wishin' and Hopin' ").

This was also the year when Roy Orbison continued his string of country-rock hits on the Monument label (he had earlier been on Sun) with "Oh, Pretty Woman," and the Kingsmen recorded an unimaginative song called "Louie, Louie," a record that was so basic, so popular and so uninspired, it joined the slang of rock, as in "I used to be in a Louie-Louie band, before I knew how to play or sing." (Later, when lyrics of popular songs would come under renewed attack, it would be said that if "Louie, Louie" were played at sixteen r.p.m.'s, it was "dirty"; actually all this did was make an unintelligible lyric even more unintelligible.) The Four Seasons, featuring the falsetto voice of Frankie Valli and commercial songwriting talent of Bob Gaudio, were introduced the same year, with "Dawn" and "Rag Doll," and the Drifters, still popular after so many years, cut the classic "Under the Boardwalk." While Elvis Presley's soundtrack album from his umpteenth drive-in movie, *Fun in Acapulco,* sold about as well as the soundtrack from *Lawrence of Arabia.*

This was also a time when two of the most significant

forces in rock shifted from first to second gear, beginning to establish "the Spector sound" and "the Berry Gordy (later Motown) sound," named for those who created them.

Phil Spector was then just 21, a Los Angeles boy who had been a founding member of the Teddy Bears, a group that had had a hit record in 1958, "To Know Him Is To Love Him" (inspired, Spector says, by the inscription placed by his mother on his father's grave). In 1959, he had retired as a performer and turned to producing, becoming the first to orchestrate rhythm and blues heavily (in the Drifters' "There Goes My Baby" the same year). With Jerry Leiber, he wrote "Spanish Harlem," which became a hit for Ben E. King. He started his own publishing company, Mother Bertha (named for his mother, who was listed on the payroll as a bookkeeper and later signed a number of classically funny advertisements about her son in the music trade papers), and started his own record label, Philles (named for himself).

With a young arranger named Jack Nitzsche, he developed a "wall of sound" and became known as one of the first men in the business to allocate as much as ten thousand dollars on the production of a single song, using as many as thirty instruments. Spector claims even his first hit, as one of the Teddy Bears, was created with "a million overdubs." Now he was topping even that, laying down track after track after track for the Crystals, beginning about 1962, recording "Uptown," "He's A Rebel" (written by Gene Pitney), "Da Doo Ron Ron" and "Then He Kissed Me." Other acts projecting Spector's sound included Bobb B. Sox and the Blue Jeans, the Alley Cats, Darlene Love and the Ronettes. (This last group took its name from its lead singer, Veronica, who later married Spector.)

Not bad for someone who'd been voted Least Likely to Succeed by his classmates at Fairfax High School (in Los Angeles) a few years earlier.

The Motown (short for Motor Town—Detroit) dynasty of Berry Gordy, Jr. was begun in 1958 when he found Bill (Smokey) Robinson, then still in his teens and a leader of a group called the Miracles. Before that Gordy had owned a record shop (which failed), had worked as a chrome trimmer in a Ford assembly plant, and with one of his sisters, Gwen Fuqua, had written several hits for Jackie Wilson—"Reet Petite," "To Be Loved," "I'll Be Satisfied," "That's Why" and "Lonely Teardrops" among them. With royalties from these songs he started his record company, and in 1961 produced and co-wrote (with Robinson) Motown's, and the Miracles', first national Number One hit, "Shop Around."

In 1962 Mary Wells had her first Motown hit ("The One Who Really Loves You") and so did another Gordy act, the Contours ("Do You Love Me?"). In 1963, Gordy introduced Little Stevie Wonder, the "12-year-old genius," singing and shouting and playing bongo drums ("Fingertips") and Martha and the Vandellas merely singing ("Heat Wave"). By 1964, when the Beatles hit, Gordy had recorded the Supremes ("Where Did Our Love Go?") and Marvin Gaye ("Can I Get a Witness?").

In a few years' time, Gordy had collected one of the more formidable rosters of talent in pop history. (Adding to those already mentioned: the Four Tops, the Temptations, the Marvelettes, Gladys Knight and the Pips, Junior Walker and the All Stars, among others.) At the same time, he had established himself as a man who could turn out hit records the way his former employer produced automobiles.

Early this year Phil Spector was given a "blindfold test" by KHJ, a Los Angeles radio station then preparing a forty-eight-hour-long history of rock 'n' roll. The first record he was thrown was the Four Tops singing "Reach Out." In his reaction to the record, Spector said, "If you listen to this record carefully, you'll notice Motown has the same thing Volkswagen has. They have a style, and it's never really going out of style and as long as it continues to sell . . . they'll go on . . . it's like the old joke about Motown: Motown is the same record recorded with different lyrics every three weeks."

Spector added: "Realistically, they're very creative."

The "Motown sound" was planned, constructed and polished by Gordy with the assistance of three songwriters—Eddie Holland, Bryan Holland and Lamont

76

Dozier. Sheets of brass were added to the rhythm and blues foundation. The instrumentation was massive (like Spector's, but generally heavier in brass and percussion, where Spector liked strings), and the vocal parts were usually gospel-based. The finished product was always slick and, an estimated seventy percent of the time, successful. (The industry average was well under thirty percent.)

Still, 1964 was the Beatles' year, with single records being issued in the United States by three different companies (Swan, VeeJay and Capitol), albums on two (Capitol and United Artists), until Capitol acquired the rights to all the group's material. (Capitol had originally turned thumbs down on the Beatles, later buying the competing firms' masters when corporate minds were changed.) Singles released included "I Want to Hold Your Hand," "Can't Buy Me Love," "A Hard Day's Night," "I'm Happy Just to Dance With You," "And I Love Her," "Do You Want to Know a Secret?" "Love Me Do" and "Twist and Shout." Every one was a hit.

If it was English in 1964, it was good. If it was from Liverpool, it was great.

Frank Zappa says of that period, talking of his own band's early days: "There was always the hope held out that if you stick together long enough, you'll make money and you'll get a record contract. It all sounded like science fiction then, because this was during the so-called British invasion, and if you didn't sound or look like the Beatles, you didn't get hired."

6

America's Response:

Everything á Go Go

In 1965 rock came in a tidal swoop; the entire nation was awash. Hundreds of millions of records and transistor radios were sold that year (along with tens of thousands of electric guitars), and if young people weren't listening or dancing to rock, they were performing it, in thousands and thousands of groups. The English "invasion" doubled and tripled in intensity, and the inviolate law of physics held true: for every action there is an equal reaction; thus, for every new English group to arrive on American shores, one new American act was there to welcome it. (And letting its hair grow long.) There were television shows devoted to rock, dozens of magazines devoted to rock, hundreds of nightclubs devoted to rock. It was as if Bill Haley's shout of ten years earlier—"Rock Around the Clock" —had finally, and irrevocably, come true.

The Beatles arrived on the first wave and behind them—once it had been determined that the audience, and the dollar, was there to be claimed—came half a hundred other acts—all exciting, all "with-it," all "mod" and "fab" and "gear," all British. Centuries of British tradition were dashed as England's capital became not the site of a famous bridge, a famous clock and a famous palace, but "swinging London," a foggy city that surrounded Carnaby Street. And to the north and west was Liverpool, where "it" definitely was at, home for dozens of top groups and mecca for millions of fans.

On ships and planes there arrived almost daily in New York, to fan out across America, the Searchers, Herman's Hermits, the Seekers, Freddie and the Dreamers, the Zombies, Gerry and the Pacemakers, Wayne Fontana and the Mindbenders, the Animals, the Kinks, the Moody Blues, the Rolling Stones, Chad and Jeremy, the Hollies, the Who, Manfred Mann, the Nashville Teens, the Yardbirds, and Them. (To name just a few of the "chartbusters.") Even at the time, it boggled the mind, causing many to wonder if there were anyone under 25 years of age in England who *didn't* sing or play a guitar. The Beatles had created not only "Beatlemania" but "group-mania." There were a number of soloists arriving, too—Georgie Fame, Marianne Faithful, Tom Jones, Cilla Black, Donovan, Ian Whitcomb, Sandie Shaw and Petula Clark—but groups carried the weight, claiming most of the record sales, and fans.

78

Probably the most important of these groups—forgetting for the moment the Fab Four from Liverpool—was that comprised of five young men who took their collective name from an old Muddy Waters song, "Rolling Stone Blues," and their sound from the same place: blues. But the Stones, more than most others, remained deep in the blues—gutsy, aggressive, sensual, economical, honest.

The Rolling Stones released two best-selling albums in 1965 (*Rolling Stones, Now!* and *Out of Our Heads*) and two others (*12 × 5* and *The Rolling Stones*), and in all four they stuck close to the musical styles they admired, those of Chuck Berry, Muddy Waters and Bo Diddley. Like the Beatles, they recorded material written by Chuck Berry ("You Can't Catch Me" and "Around and Around"), but unlike the Beatles, when they performed their own material it was not music to smile by. The Beatles were innocent and playful. The Stones were not. Rolling Stones songs were twentieth century working-class songs.

"Satisfaction" was *the* song of 1965 (lodged in the Number One spot for six weeks in July and August) and the song that probably more than any other captured most precisely what rock 'n' roll was about—before, during and since. The group's lead singer (and co-author of "Satisfaction" as well as nearly all the Stones' original material), Mick Jagger, was (and is) a perfect vehicle for rock. His voice was natural, gutty and raw, and his delivery was threatening. He panted and he grunted and belted the words, mimicking those he admired, yet taking them onto some other plane.

The Stones also looked the part they played—wearing grab-bag clothing, hair longer than most groups had, sneeringly sexy expressions. Jagger stood on one lean leg, jerking and twitching the other one, mouthing his harmonica as if he were in love with it, poking his tongue between thick lips, peering at his audiences through eye-slits that communicated only one thing. The Beatles asked teen-aged American females for their hands; the Stones asked for their pants.

Even before "Satisfaction" became a hit, there were many who said the Rolling Stones were (at the very

79

least) in questionable taste. Perhaps they were; it depends upon *your* taste, not theirs. Actually, they merely cared not a damn about anyone's tastes, while assaulting what were generally pinpointed as "middle-class sensibilities," and if the middle class objected, tough luck. "Something is happening and you don't know what it is, do you, Mr. Jones?" Bob Dylan sang.

Middle class: tough luck!

Dylan started something, too. In 1964, when the Beatles arrived, he was America's leading folk hero. In 1965, he was America's leading rock hero. The transition was easier than most remember it to be. Much has been written about the night in 1965 in Forest Hills, New York, when Dylan appeared for the second half of his concert backed by an electric band (organ, bass and guitars). After each number, folk purists in the audience shouted, "We want Dylan, we want Dylan," summoning their old hero, the work-shirted, cloth-capped troubadour who used to sing at civil rights rallies in the South. To no avail. Dylan had gone electric, publicly. And apparently his fans had forgotten that several songs on his album *Bringing It All Back Home*—which had been released somewhat before this concert—had had electric backing.

"I had this thing called 'Subterranean Homesick Blues,'" Dylan explained. "It just didn't sound right by myself. I tried the piano, the harpsichord. I tried it as blues. I tried it on the pipe organ, the kazoo. But it fit right in with the band. I haven't changed a bit. I just got tired of playing the guitar by myself."

Thus, rather innocently and naturally, was born folk-rock, a label that was soon to be pasted on any American singer and musician who'd once played acoustic guitar but now used electricity. Dylan was credited with starting it—something he'd later deny—and soon several former "folksingers" would be joining him in the transition. *Life* magazine, and others, called the new wave of popular American singers—Sonny and Cher, Barry McGuire, the Byrds, etc.—"the children of Bobby Dylan," but they weren't truly that. They often sang Bob Dylan songs, and they, too, had traded in acoustic guitars for electric guitars, but it all happened at once. Dylan was a force, a talent, but he cannot take credit for something he did as naturally as he said, when so many others were doing the same thing.

Dylan's longest electric single release (and perhaps all of rock's longest single, too—more than six minutes) was directed at young people who were on the street, those who were like he had been so recently—"without a home . . . a complete unknown . . . like a rolling stone." And then Dylan gave one of his songs one of the puzzling titles he was famous for—"Rainy Day Woman No. 12 and 35." The song had very little to do with women or the weather. "Everybody must get stoned," he said. Folk-rock was the thing, the label that seemed to fit. Folk music had been a music of protest before (Seeger and Guthrie sang about the fledgling union cause and were active politically, remember) and so was the music of rock in 1965. It all fit together. Or seemed to. And in midsummer of that year, the Number One song was one that had been inspired by Bob Dylan, "Eve of Destruction," written by P. F. Sloane and sung by Barry McGuire (who'd come from the New Christy Minstrels). If the button is pushed, McGuire croaked, there was no running away.

Others in the "protest" bag weren't so concerned about weighty matters such as the bomb, but regarded instead the problems young people had in dressing and looking the way they wanted. One of the most popular of these was "Laugh At Me," written by Salvatore (Sonny) Bono, a former record promotion man who found himself being teased by fellow customers at a Los Angeles restaurant and went home to write about how people get their kicks from making fun of the clothes he wore. Sonny, with his half-Indian wife Cher, grossed four million dollars that year. Cher said she didn't own a dress (preferring frilly, colorful bell-bottom trousers, and thereby setting a trend), and Sonny said he didn't own a tie (preferring bobcat vests and flowing shirts, thereby setting a trend or two of his own). (Yes, they did offer their names to a clothing manufacturer.) Sonny and Cher were the public lovers of pop in 1965 ("I Got You Babe" was another million-seller), and their bag was loving protest.

81

"Folk + Rock + Protest = Dollars," the headline in *Billboard* read.

More meaningful was the music of the Byrds, five young men to whom music came first, controversy and protest somewhere farther down the list. The leader of this group—if ever it truly had one, for personality conflicts would plague the Byrds through a dozen personnel changes in the ensuing years—was Jim (now Roger) McGuinn, son of a journalist, prep school graduate, backup musician for the Limeliters and the Chad Mitchell Trio, guitarist for Bobby Darin. After which he went out on his own, meeting Gene Clark at a Los Angeles folk club, with whom he decided to play and sing, "sort of like Peter and Gordon." Clark had come from Missouri, grew up in Kansas farm country, had sung with a variety of country groups before joining Randy Sparks' New Christy Minstrels for fifteen months. The third, David Van Courtland Crosby, was raised in Hollywood, also graduated from a prep school, spent five years with singing groups (including Les Baxter's Balladeers) and as a solo artist in Greenwich Village basket houses. The fourth, Chris Hillman, was a surfer and guitar and mandolin player in country bars, who'd also worked with the Randy Sparks groups. Michael Clarke was a conga drummer Crosby found in Big Sur.

According to legend, the Byrds were formed by McGuinn, Crosby, Clark and Jim Dickson (a record producer for Elektra who became the Byrds' manager) after they'd all seen the Beatles in *A Hard Day's Night*. As the story goes, some were pulling for a folk sound, others were tugging for rock. The blend (precise and near-brilliant on record, erratic at best in a club) was made and a record was released.

"Tambourine Man" went to the top, taking with it a sound that was better than nearly all other current rock. McGuinn's twelve-string guitar playing had been acclaimed highly in his acoustic period, and under electric amplification it seemed as if he were playing half a dozen instruments at once. A tight and danceable drumbeat, fine rhythm guitar work from Crosby, Hillman's agile bass line, and the smooth mesh of voices (McGuinn, Clark and Crosby) created a sound that was so intricate it seemed simple, always an explanation for brilliance and one of the secrets of success.

Popular acceptance of the Byrds, and "Tambourine Man," established several things. For one, it was now evident that an American group could attract as many fans as an English band could. (The Byrds were almost *that* popular.) For another, it also established Dylan as a songwriter to be used as a launching pad. Two years earlier, Peter, Paul and Mary had had a hit with Dylan's "Blowin' in the Wind," but in 1965 nearly everyone either duplicated their success or tried to. Forty-eight Dylan songs were recorded in one month —"It Ain't Me Babe" by the Turtles, "All I Really Want to Do" by Cher *and* the Byrds (they shared the hit), "Ballad of a Thin Man (Mr. Jones)" by the Grass Roots among them. Even groups who didn't record Dylan material acknowledged his influence. "He's a force on our music," said one of the Lovin' Spoonful. "Just like 'The Star Spangled Banner,' we've all heard it."

"Tambourine Man" was also purported to be a song about a drug-dealer in Greenwich Village ("Take me for a trip . . ."), and thus it came to represent what seemed to be a lyric trend: songs about dope. The Association, another Los Angeles group stuck in the folk-rock bag, had a hit with "Along Comes Mary," which was supposed to be about marijuana. Donovan sang of a "violent hash eater" in "Sunny Goodge Street." And a favorite nightclub was called The Trip. Parents and grown-ups generally reacted as they might have been expected to react: in horror.

Of course all this really meant was that young people were doing what they'd always done—they were singing about what they did. The best popular music seldom does more than reflect its own environment, and when it ceases to be timely, it ceases to be successful or relevant. Just as the Beach Boys had shown in their songs a youthful interest in surfing in 1962-63 and Jan and Dean had mirrored a similar fascination in hot-rodding ("carburetor soul"), the music of 1965 was merely reflecting that which occupied the thoughts and activities of young people of the time. Drugs were a part of life, and so naturally the music

83

included it. In other words, young people began experimenting with drugs before they began singing about
it.

They also continued to sing about the music itself.
Trying to explain magic, according to one popular song
of the time, was like trying to tell a stranger about
rock 'n' roll. Either you believed in both or none.

"Do You Believe In Magic" was written by the
leader of the Lovin' Spoonful, John Sebastian, the son of
a classical harmonica player. He'd grown up in Greenwich Village, where he had played in jug bands and as
a backup harmonica or autoharp player for other folk
acts. (He played harmonica for Dylan in Gerde's Folk
City, for Tim Hardin on his first LP.) With Zal
Yanovsky (formerly singing and playing in the Mug-
wumps with Denny Doherty and Cass Elliott, later of
the Mamas and Papas), Steve Boone and Joe Butler,
he rehearsed in the cellar of New York's Albert Hotel,
blending folk, rock, jug and ragtime into what he called
"goodtime music."

Funny enough, even adults began to call it that,
too—despite their feelings about long hair and drugs
and the growing anti-war attitude, all expressed in the
songs. Grown-ups were beginning to follow in their
children's dancing footsteps.

Certainly this was motivated at least in part by
"adult" America's eternal quest for youth, but curiosity
probably contributed. ("This was a time when people
in neckties started coming to see the 'freaks,' who were
the dancers, who turned out to be called go-go girls,"
Barry McGuire's record producer Lou Adler recalls.)
Rock 'n' roll hadn't gone away—these are the grown-
ups talking now—and, uh, well, we really ought to go
see for ourselves . . . I mean, uh, we did do the twist
and that was fun.

Enter the go-go scene.

But flashback first to 1964, when Lou Adler found
himself on LaCienega Boulevard in Los Angeles, standing in line to get into a club to see a black comedian.
He saw another club nearby.

"There was no line at that club and I though we'd
go there and wait," Adler recalls. "It was Gazzarri's,
and inside was Johnny Rivers, in a suit, with a drummer.

There was this strange feeling in there: Something was happening. It was like an adult Dick Clark show. Nobody had been dancing in California. I'd seen a little of it back East with the twist, but nothing here. At Gazzarri's they were dancing.

"Johnny came up to me after the set and introduced himself. He said he was thinking it might be a good idea to cut a record live at the club and he wanted to know if I'd be interested."

The album was recorded, and then re-recorded in a studio. ("The strange thing was, when we finished it, we found most of the noise I'd heard on the dance floor I'd really *seen*. People waving their arms, dancing, moving around . . . take that away and the noise level seems to go 'way down. Next time you're in what you think is a noisy club, close your eyes and see if you don't hear the noise level drop.") The album was finished, and quickly rejected by the man Adler was working for. Legal complications followed that, and the album was never released. As a result, the first "live" nightclub album of this time came not from Johnny Rivers but Trini Lopez, and was recorded at another Los Angeles club, PJ's.

One of the owner's of PJ's then was an ex-Chicago cop named Elmer Valentine, who soon thereafter sold his interest in the club and went to Europe for a vacation. Among the cities he visited was Paris, where he saw a nightclub he thought should be imported to America. It was something called a "discothèque" and named Whisky à Go Go.

"I ran into Elmer one week before the Whisky was to open," Adler says. "He needed an act and I suggested Johnny Rivers. So a week later, I took another recording truck out to the Whisky, to try the album a second time."

That album, *Johnny Rivers at the Whisky à Go Go,* was recorded January 15, 1965, the night the Sunset Strip club opened. It became an instant hit, as did the club in which it was recorded, and together the album and the club started the go-go trend. Soon there were between two and three hundred people each night lined up around the block to get in, while those who *were* inside were jammed together like college students in a phone booth; reporters from *Time* and *Life* had to be sneaked in through the kitchen. There had to be places for all the new groups to perform in, so the Whisky à Go Go became a chain, stretching from Los Angeles to Atlanta, while hundreds of other clubs followed along. There was the À-Go-Go in Aspen, Colorado; the Bucket à Go Go in Park City, Utah; the Frisky à Go Go in San Antonio; the Champagne à Go Go in Madison, Wisconsin; and the Blu-Note à Go Go in Whitesboro, New York. ("Everything à go-go," said *Time*, telling several "à-go-go" jokes, a short-lived fad that used visual word pronunciation gimmickry like *Van Gogh à Gogh Gogh* and *escargot à got got*.) Discothéques—all over! At one point, Manhattan claimed twenty-one of them. And nearly everywhere, half the customers were young, half were old enough to be the first half's parents, and probably were.

"Nothing is sacred any more," one teen-ager moaned appropriately for *Time* magazine. "I mean we no sooner develop a new dance or something and our parents are doing it."

Ah, the dances. For every dance Dick Clark had introduced, the go-go scene devised two. There was the Pony, the Frug, the Watusi, Walkin' the Dog, the Shimmy, the Hully Gully, the Swim, the Freddie (the only dance to come from England), the Mashed Potato, the Jerk, the Monkey, the Locomotion and the Shake, to name a few. One group, Cannibal and the Headhunters, had a hit with "Land of a Thousand Dances," and another group, the Gentrys, told everybody to keep on dancin' and a-prancin'. And in every club there was at least one go-go girl, high in a glass cage over the dance floor, dressed in a short fringed dress that shimmied and shook when she did. The idea was for the customers to do what she did—the Pony, the Watusi, etc. Most of the middle-aged customers watched very closely.

The adults were flocking to the beat. As *Time* reported in May, 1965, "No debutante cotillion or country-club dance is complete these days without a heavy dose of rock 'n' roll. At a charity ball on the roof of the St. Regis Hotel, some of Manhattan's highest society wiggled around the dance floor doing the Mule, flapping their hands like mule's ears to the thudding beat of Lester Lanin's orchestra. 'It's good for your health,' says Lanin, who beefs up his society band with a rock 'n' roll trio called the Rocking Chairs. Even evangelists have adapted to the new beat. A group of Episcopal students from the University of Maryland, armed with electric guitars and bongo drums, have been celebrating with great success a big-beat 'rejoice' Mass at several churches in the Washington-Maryland area, including a service that President Johnson and Lady Bird attended. In London, the Salvation Army has formed a rock 'n' roll group called the Joy Strings, whose repertoire includes such numbers as 'We're Going to Set the World A-Swinging.' 'Our square approach,' explains Drummer Captain Joy Webb, 'wasn't getting us anywhere.' "

And of course there was a television show, *Shindig,* which became so popular so quickly, it split amoeba-like into a hundred shows. *Shindig* was begun as a country-western show, with an Englishman named Jack Good as producer. The pilot film, produced for ABC-TV, was good, but something wasn't quite right. So a second show was videotaped, and this one emphasized rock. Two weeks after it debuted, hundreds of television stations across America were introducing their own low-budget versions, half-hour and hour-long shows that offered lots of up-tempo rock, a line of Watusi dancers in skimpy dress, a fast-talking master of ceremonies (usually a popular disc jockey) and commercials for chewing gum and acne cream. "Hi-de-hi, Shindoggers," Jimmy O'Neill said after participating in *Shindig*'s final Stridex spot, "remember . . . rock on!" Of course Dick Clark was there, too, with *American Bandstand* on Saturday (still) and with *Where The Action Is* Monday through Friday afternoons.

While all this was happening, rock 'n' roll had begun to grow up. The maturation was rough in spots, but no longer was rock 'n' roll in elementary school.

For one thing, the Beatles had abandoned "yeah yeah." In December, 1965, Capitol Records released *Rubber Soul,* and thus the Beatles once again altered the course of popular music: the four moptops ceased being moptops, to adopt the stance of artists. *Rubber*

Soul differed from anything the Beatles had done before. For the first time, the Beatles experimented with offbeat instrumental sounds: those of the harmonium, fuzz bass, electric piano and sitar. (This was the first time Indian music appeared as an influence.) The lyrics became elliptical, candid and moody. In "Norwegian Wood," for example, not only did the Beatles begin playing with time (from 4/4 to 5/4 and 11/4), but they also introduced a new and sometimes puzzling lyric structure.

In another song from the same LP, "Run for Your Life," the Beatles showed a change in attitude regarding the opposite sex. Whereas it once was hand-holding and simple Valentine emotion that occupied the boy-girl songs of the Beatles, now it was a different story. "I'd rather see you dead, little girl, than to be with another man," the Beatles spat melodically.

Nor were the Beatles developing in a vacuum. Right along with them were several others—among them the Beach Boys, Simon and Garfunkel, and the Mothers of Invention.

The development of the Mothers of Invention closely parallels that of the Beatles, for as the Beatles began experimenting with electronic music and atonal effects and nodding toward classical precedents (in *Revolver,* in the summer of 1966), so did Frank Zappa and his Mothers; Zappa's first album, *Freak Out,* was released within six weeks of *Revolver.* Zappa was deep into rhythm and blues, but with this first LP he would begin to establish himself as a part of the pop avant-garde.

A major difference between the Beatles and the Mothers existed, and that was radio air-play and general acceptability. The Beatles' songs were always played; the Mothers' never were. Too intellectual. Or some such thing. Besides, the records were either "weird" (like the Mothers themselves) or "controversial." Some of the song titles proved that: "The Return of the Son of Monster Magnet," "Help, I'm a Rock," "Hungry Freaks, Daddy" and "Who Are the Brain Police?"

In 1965 the Mothers of Invention appealed to a

small, freaky cult in Southern California, and musicians and composers everywhere.

The Beach Boys, meantime, had abandoned surf music, keeping the Four Freshman-type harmony and singing first about hot-rodding ("Little Deuce Coupe" and "409") and then chauvinism of one sort or another ("Be True to Your School" and "California Girls"). And then in 1966, the Beach Boys created *Pet Sounds,* an album that had taken Brian Wilson about four months to compose and arrange, and "Good Vibrations," a song that was considered at the time to be the most advanced rock release of all time. In these records, Wilson had utilized a number of new sounds, including that of a theremin in "Good Vibrations" (which became Number One even in England, burying the Beatles) and dogs barking at the end of the album (Wilson's dogs; therefore: *Pet Sounds*). And because he had stopped traveling with the Beach Boys, he had more time to experiment in the studio with overdubbing (singing and playing all the parts himself).

Within a year's time, Brian Wilson would be declared a "genius." (Anybody who lives in Bel Air, paints his house purple, covers the floor of one room with sand, pitches a tent in another and moves in . . . he has to be a genius, right? And after he spent so many thousands of dollars on *Smile* and then burned the tapes because he thought it was "fire music" that would, if released, cause the city of Los Angeles to burn to the ground . . . well!) There was even a summit meeting arranged: Brian Wilson and the Beatles got together to toe the floor and look at each other timidly.

Paul Simon and Art Garfunkel were two New York City-bred college graduates who sang about alienation, the communication breakdown, mindless conversation and insecurity—all universal themes usually ridden with clichés, but when considered by Simon (the writer of most of their material), made successful through understatement rather than vilification.

The sounds of Simon and Garfunkel, the Beach Boys and the Mothers of Invention were different. So, too, were the sounds of other groups and individuals of the time. Roger Miller sang an amusing country-western "King of the Road" (and Jody Miller answered with

"Queen of the House"); Sam the Sham and the Pharaohs pushed a repetitious "Woolly Bully" into the Number One position and held it there six weeks in a row; Barbra Streisand sang a haunting "People"; the McCoys told everybody, between beats of the chewing-gum jaws, to "Hang On, Sloopy"; the last overdubs were placed in Phil Spector's "wall of sound" as he produced two hit singles ("Unchained Melody" and "You've Lost That Lovin' Feeling") and two hit LP's for the Righteous Brothers; Herb Alpert's synthesized mariachi band, the Tijuana Brass, was peddling *Whipped Cream and Other Delights;* modern soul was emanating from the Stax-Volt recording studios in Memphis and the throats of Wilson Pickett ("In the Midnight Hour") and Otis Redding ("Respect"); the Shangri-Las were falling for "The Leader of the Pack"; and half a hundred others were making different sounds.

Rock 'n' roll had grown up and grown out, following whatever drummer could be heard, splitting indiscriminately (amoeba-like), then splitting again, until there were so many "sounds" that what was called pop music encompassed nearly everything. The short eighteen-month-or-so-long period started with a reaction to the Beatles (folk-rock) and closed with an incredible diversity and maturity. Folk-rock had come to be used to describe nearly everything that hadn't been labeled before, providing those who are neurotic about categories with some sort of huge umbrella; and in the end, it was, indeed, only a large umbrella, shielding a thousand people and nearly as many sounds.

7

Love, Drugs & Soul

In 1965, when it was like it is supposed to be now, when San Francisco really was the City of Love, before the Haight-Ashbury had become a mecca for social misfits, before "hippie" had become a household expletive, before young people with long hair and colorful clothing began to believe their own press notices and act like the mass media said they did . . . back then, young musicians began to collect on warm evenings in weathered Victorian houses in this old section of the city near Golden Gate Park. Guitar players and organists and drummers and singers wandered from house to house, rehearsing together and apart, organizing and folding and reorganizing bands, listening to records and smoking or swallowing dope. The music of rock groups practicing in garages and behind drawn shades filled the air of the neighborhood.

Only a few San Francisco bands were working then. The Charlatans were whooping it up in the Red Dog Saloon across the Nevada border, in Virginia City. The We Five ("You Were On My Mind") and the Beau Brummels ("Laugh, Laugh") had songs on the record charts. But that was about it. It was still mid-English invasion. The young musicians in the Haight-Ashbury continued to rehearse and get high.

The same time, a frustrated actor named Bill Graham was serving as business manager to the San Francisco Mime Troupe, a theater group strongly identified with the radical political community in Berkeley. Their minority views guaranteed them minimal work, and so on November 6 a benefit was held, which combined several of the arts: Lawrence Ferlinghetti read poetry; one of the new San Francisco bands, Jefferson Airplane, rotated sets with the Fugs, a radical band from New York, and John Handy's jazz group; and Allen Ginsberg led the three thousand present in chanting mantras.

(A few weeks earlier a former Texan named Chet Helms and his creative business commune, The Family Dog, staged the first "psychedelic" dance at the Longshore Hall—with Jefferson Airplane and the Charlatans.)

In December a second benefit for the mime troupe was held, this time in the Fillmore Auditorium. This huge hall was in the center of San Francisco's black ghetto, but by nine-thirty, as Ralph Gleason reported in his *Chronicle* column, there was a double line around the block outside. Bands playing that night were the Grateful Dead, the Great Society and the Mystery Trend, all from San Francisco.

The next month novelist Ken Kesey asked Graham to produce his Trips Festival, a three-day mixed-media attempt to recreate an LSD experience without the LSD. The first day of the festival was described by *Realist* editor Paul Krassner as "a ballroom surrealistically seething with a couple of thousand bodies stoned out of their everlovin' bruces in crazy costumes and obscene makeup with a raucous rock 'n' roll band and strobo-scopic lights and a thunder machine and balloons and beads and streamers and electronic equipment and the back of a guy's coat proclaiming 'Please don't believe in magic' to a girl dancing with four-inch eyelashes, so that even the goddam Pinkerton Guards were con-tact high." The bands playing were San Francisco bands.

"The Haight-Ashbury era began that weekend," Tom Wolfe wrote in *The Electric Kool-Aid Acid Test*.

And the pop music-pop culture revolution had be-gun afresh. The discothèque was OUT and the cav-ernous dance hall was IN. Indirect lighting was re-placed with "psychedelic" (literally, mind-manifesting or mind-expanding) blends of stroboscopic lights, liq-uid color blobs, black light, moires, films and slides. Poster art was reincarnated to advertise the dances. Brothers Ron and Jay Thelin opened The Psychedelic Shop on Haight Street and started a new look in mer-chandising and a market for the peculiarly useless prod-uct. ("Useless" in the sense that you couldn't "use" incense and posters to keep your head dry or your stomach full—very groovy otherwise.) Two former Harvard instructors, Drs. Timothy Leary and Richard Alpert, were founding their religion, the League for Spiritual Discovery, with LSD serving as a contem-porary substitute for bread and wine. (Sign from the Trips Festival: ANYBODY WHO KNOWS HE IS GOD, GO UP ON STAGE.) Even staid old journalism was being altered, as the "underground" newspaper began its first proliferation. (Begun in 1964 in Los Angeles, much of what the underground press was then, and is now, con-cerned popular music; in fact, most underground news-papers have fairly consistently paid their printing bills with advertising income from record companies.) Underground radio appeared, a maturation in broadcast sound that seemed to come when Top Forty radio didn't grow up with its audience.

Everything was changing. The puddles of projected light; the smell of sandalwood mixing with that of pot; guitar amplifiers turned all the way up to ten; body painting; *The San Francisco Oracle;* Robert A. Heinlein's *Stranger in a Strange Land* (and groking); psychedelic twelve-bar blues; paisley; Winnie the Pooh buttons; the Vietnam Day Committee; lots of guitar feedback—it all began to run and flow, becoming an amorphous mass of sight and sound that stretched to the far horizon and beyond.

Through it all was pop music. Music finally had become a part of the environment, and the environment had become a part of the music. It was all One. Hip togetherness.

San Francisco became known as "America's Liverpool," as not one or two but dozens and dozens of groups began to attract serious attention—besides Jefferson Airplane, the Charlatans, the Great Society, the Grateful Dead and the Mystery Trend already mentioned, the most popular included Quicksilver Messenger Service, Big Brother and the Holding Company, Moby Grape, Loading Zone, Country Joe and the Fish (from Berkeley), Lothar and the Hand People, Chocolate Watch Band, the Grass Roots, the Sopwith Camel, 13th Floor Elevator, the Great Pumpkin, Heavenly Blues Band, and the Sons of Champlin.

Most of these bands not only rehearsed and played together, but also lived together, forming communal cells in the Haight. Jefferson Airplane, the band that would come to serve as the city's best-known band, was no exception. "This is in early '66 now," said the group's drummer, Spencer Dryden. "The Haight was heaven for anybody with long hair. About eight hundred dyed-in-the-wool hippies and that's it. It was a family thing. No tourists. Everybody *did* live together and *did* help each other out."

A life-style was being formed. By the San Francisco bands and their friends.

And the anthem seemed to have been written by a

23-year-old former carnival worker then in jail on a marijuana conviction—Dino Valente—and sung by the Youngbloods, a group from the East who'd come to San Francisco when they'd heard the "vibrations" were good. It was time, Valente and the Youngbloods said, to smile on your brother, get together, love one another, right now.

Jefferson Airplane's first hit single that summer was "Don't You Need Somebody to Love?" and the buttons the group had made said "Jefferson Airplane Loves You"; Marty Balin told *Time:* "The stage is our bed and the audience is our broad. We're not entertaining, we're making love." Bumper stickers proclaimed: GOD IS LOVE and MAKE LOVE, NOT WAR. It was called the Love Generation and by January, 1967, weekends had been declared obsolete and replaced with refreshing neo-tribal free-form gatherings called Love-Ins. Young people had renounced their political (imperialistic), economic (warlike) and cultural (hung-up) heritage and were embracing a passive and pacific alternative.

"What the world needs now is love, sweet love . . ." Jackie DeShannon had sung in 1965 in her only Number One hit. Now the world was getting it.

Of course there were those who said the Love Generation was immoral, irresponsible and irreverent; for many on the far side of the generation gap, love had become a four-letter word. This charge was answered by J. I. Simmons and Barry Winograd in their book, *It's Happening,* in this fiery, youthful plaint, directed at adults: "Look at you, blowing up whole countries for the sake of some crazy ideologies that you don't live up to anyway. Look at you, mindfucking a whole generation of kids into getting a revolving charge account and buying your junk. (Who's a junkie?) Look at you, needing a couple of stiff drinks before you have the balls to talk with another human being. Look at you, making it with your neighbor's wife on the sly just to prove that you're really alive. Look at you, hooked on *your* cafeteria of pills, and making up dirty names for anybody who isn't in your bag, and screwing up the land and the water and the air for profit, and calling this nowhere scene the Great Society! *And you're gonna tell us how to live?* C'mon, man, you've got to be kidding!"

The life-style was *against* Vietnam and *for* marijuana, *against* Lyndon Johnson and *for* dancing, *against* hypocrisy and *for* ecstasy, *against* the draft and *for* meditation, *against* police and *for* sex, and on and on and on. And nowhere were these positions better demonstrated, explained, shouted, chanted, cried, crooned, cajoled and ordered than in the popular music. Once again the music reflected, or mirrored, the thought and activity of young people . . . absorbed and distilled the "message" or attitude, then spat it into the hinterlands on acetate, converting a youthful audience everywhere.

Time to meet the leading messiahs.

1. *Jefferson Airplane.* One of the first "Haight-Ashbury bands," one of the first to sign a record contract (with RCA Victor for a reported twenty-five-thousand-dollar advance) and the first to get a national hit record, "Somebody to Love." Thus this band came to represent a city and a generation's commitment to Something Else.

Jefferson Airplane was begun when a new nightclub needed an opening act. Owners of the club, the Matrix, asked Marty Balin, a folksinger, if he would find a group. What Balin did suited the meaning of the word *matrix*—"something holding, or capable of holding, embedded within it, another object to which it gives shape or form." Instead of finding a group, Balin created one, taking its name from one of its members, Jorma Kaukonen, who had been playing a guitar in a Berkeley folk club, using the name Blind Thomas Jefferson Airplane. Paul Kantner played another guitar in the group. Kaukonen's peculiar friend from Washington, D.C., Jack Casady, played bass. The first drummer was Skip Spence. Sharing vocals with Balin was Signe Andersen.

On August 13, 1965, a Friday, the Matrix opened its doors and the Airplane made its debut. A friend took this "birthdate" and prepared the band's astrological chart, predicting an "opportunity to be of service to others, perhaps engage in social change (and) a most harmonious and beautiful influence," mentioning music, the arts and interests psychic and mystical. It was as if the astrologist were reading the future of San Francisco.

"I can remember when we started and we joked about let's be the top rock group in the country," Marty Balin recalls. "We talked about that because we were convinced we'd never get out of the Matrix. Everything we joked about came true. It happened very fast."

No longer was San Francisco a secret; an entire nation was beginning to look west by now, and the bands were in the center ring.

"We played two or three months at the Matrix, and thousands of record companies came in to see us," Paul Kantner remembers. "It was really easy for us. We didn't have to play second-billed to other groups, or anything like that. Everybody liked us because we didn't have any competition really. Companies kept bidding for us, and we picked RCA somewhere along the line because they just happened to be the high bidder when we decided to go with a company."

While this was happening, Grace Slick was singing in another group, the Great Society, a band she and her husband had formed when they'd heard and seen Jefferson Airplane at the Matrix. Grace says today she didn't know how to read music very well in those days, nor had she ever sung before publicly. No matter. The group was together and jobs were being offered. Sometimes the Great Society and Jefferson Airplane would even play together in the same club.

So when the Airplane lost its girl singer (to motherhood) and it seemed the Great Society was breaking up, Grace merely changed bands, as if she were changing clothes. It was a little more complicated than that, but not much. Because the two groups had played together, Grace knew most of the songs anyway.

It was at this point that the Airplane began to take off—just as that obvious phrase *(Jefferson Airplane Takes Off)* had been the band's first album title. Grace's voice provided something additionally unique to the Airplane's sound, and the second album, *Surrealistic Pillow,* the first album on which she participated, earned the band a gold record for one million dollars in sales.

Jefferson Airplane had two hit singles from that second LP, one romantic ("Don't You Need Somebody to Love?") and the other allegedly "psychedelic" ("White Rabbit"). And this is what Jefferson Airplane was for its audience—six people living on love and drugs. For a member of the Love Generation, there wasn't a formula any better than that.

2. *The Grateful Dead.* This band was different from Jefferson Airplane. The members of this band had been a central force in Ken Kesey's early acid tests. (The group's guitarist, Jerry Garcia, was known as Captain Trips.) If the members of the Airplane were the cocky, electronic prep school kids of rock—a fair description, even if it does slight their impressive musical talents—members of the Grateful Dead were the Hell's Angels of rock: greasy, outrageous, comic, tough. What they called "stone(d) freaks."

As such, they created music you entered slowly, almost tentatively, relaxing defenses slowly, while the sound built until you were either totally committed or totally lost. If you got inside and the rhythms took you along, you knew once and for all what "psychedelic" meant. If you got lost, you probably were bored to death.

The words didn't seem to mean very much in the Dead's music; the rhythms were the thing.

3. *Country Joe and the Fish.* From Berkeley. The most overtly political group. (Originally called Country Mao and the Fish, the fish a reference to a Mao Tse-Tung quotation: "Every fish in the sea is a potential convert.") This group made and marketed their first records themselves— a seven-inch LP that included two of the band's anti-Johnson songs called "I-Feel-Like-I'm-Fixin'-to-Die Rag"* and "Superbird." "Superbird" reappeared later on the group's first (and best) album for Vanguard, *Electric Music for the Mind and Body;* the other on the second LP.

> 1-2-3 What are we fightin' for?
> Don't ask me—I don't give a damn
> Next stop is Vietnam

*"I-Feel-Like-I'm-Fixin'-to-Die Rag" by Joe McDonald, Copyright 1967 Tradition Music Co.

And it's 5-6-7
Open up the pearly gates
Well, there ain't no time to wonder why
Whoopee!
We're all gonna die.

The first album included a romantic side, too, with songs like "Not So Sweet Martha Lorraine" and "Grace" (for the Airplane's Grace Slick). Joe McDonald had a pleasant folk voice and a sardonic writing talent; this set the style. The others in the group were excellent singer-musician-songwriters, and together they provided the best electric message rock of the period.

4. *Big Brother and the Holding Company*. Something else. Like Jefferson Airplane, this was a band of guys fronted by a girl vocalist. There the resemblance stopped. For the lead singer in this group, Janis Joplin, was not like Grace Slick, who was really that: slick . . . enervating and pleasantly shrill, alive and sexy, but finishing-school cool. (Grace had gone to Finch.) Janis Joplin was Texas blues—knuckled and whiskeyed, all pounding flesh, lusty and explosive. In time, it would be Janis—not Grace—who would emerge from San Francisco as The Star, the Judy Garland of the hippie set.

Big Brother was Janis Joplin, a white Big Mama Thornton, a honkie Billie Holliday, backed by a competent band (that she would, in 1968, leave). She had the power to lay several notes on top of one another simultaneously, in harmony with herself, while tossing a full mane of hair and pounding one booted foot up and down in frenzy. She was (and is) a rather dowdy chick, but one of the sexiest in the business.

The differences between the four bands can be likened to sexual approach: Jefferson Airplane wanted to seduce its audience; Janis and Big Brother wanted the fuck the audience; the Grateful Dead wanted to rape the audience; and Country Joe . . . well, he wanted to *talk* about it.

Were there similarities? Sure, but not so many as a number of writers and critics insisted there were. For one thing, there was no "San Francisco sound," just as there was no real "Liverpool sound." Most of the bands in the San Francisco Bay area projected some melodic ambiguity, a jerky sort of stream-of-consciousness (sloppy?) approach to lyrics, noisy electronic effects and atonal touches, feedback . . . but the description is too broad to say there was a single sound produced. The life-styles were closer than the sounds.

Oh, you could assert that all San Francisco bands were loud. If you wanted to.

Looking back, it is rather astonishing to realize that considering how much attention San Francisco got, very few hit records came from there. Jefferson Airplane had "Somebody to Love" and "White Rabbit" and that was it, really.

Two reasons for this: (1) the bands of San Francisco were designed to perform rather than record, and when the bands did record, everyone agreed they sounded better live; and (2) the bands were making a contribution that was difficult, if not impossible, to measure in record sales—as was evidenced when Jefferson Airplane visited Bobby and Ethel Kennedy in their New York home and found a white rabbit poster in the game room, with the message "Feed your head."

No . . . the hits were coming from outside the San Francisco pack, mostly in Los Angeles, where such diverse groups as the Monkees, the Mamas and Papas, and the Doors all were becoming Super Groups.

The obvious motivation for the Monkees was cash and the inspiration of the Beatles' first film, *A Hard Day's Night*. The Monkees were designed to cash in on Beatlemania, organized as a weekly half-hour television show with the same hand-held camera and frenetic directing and editing techniques the film offered. The Monkees were designed to look like the Beatles, sing like the (early) Beatles, act like the Beatles.

In time, the Monkees (along with a number of other groups which were initially mediocre) would develop beyond generally bright, happy and totally inoffensive songs like "Last Train to Clarksville," but in 1966 they were pure bubble gum, aimed at the hearts (and piggy banks) of the youngest rock 'n' roll fans.

The Doors appealed to an older audience and represented something akin to a neo-Freudian response to England's Rolling Stones. The band's vocalist, Jim Morrison, a high-ranking naval officer's son, became a leather- or lizard-clad sex symbol, chanting and grunting peculiar poetry to the tight, somewhat hypnotic rhythms of Ray Manzarek's jazz-based organ, Robby Krieger's guitar and John Densmore's drums.

> The time to hesitate is through
> No time to wallow in the mire
> Try now, we can only lose
> And our love becomes a funeral pyre.*

In another song, Morrison wrote and sang of Spanish ships' captains jettisoning horses in the middle of the Atlantic, to lighten the cargo in an attempt to recapture the wind:

> When the still sea conspires an armor
> And her sullen and aborted
> Currents breed tiny monsters,
> True sailing is dead.†

In the Doors' music, there was poetry in "End of the Night"‡ ("Realms of bliss/Realms of light/Some are born to sweet delight/Some are born to sweet delight /Some are born to the endless night"). There was satire in "Twentieth Century Fox's"§ "No tears/No fears/No ruined years/No clocks/She's a Twentieth Century fox"). In "The End,"‖ Morrison walked on down the hall and threatened, "Father . . . I want to kill you. Mother, I want . . ." and in "When the Music's Over," he shouted the battle-cry of a generation: "We want the world and we want it now!"

Jim Morrison became a sort of Peck's cute li'l Bad Boy of Pop—getting arrested for ad-libbing an "obscene" poem in New Haven, reaching into his leather pants to play with himself in Chicago, urinating on an amplifier in Seattle. By mid-1968, there were no less than ten cities in which the Doors couldn't play. Their records sold millions, and Morrison said he'd rather be back at the Whisky à Go Go, where they started.

The Mamas and the Papas were called folk-rock because they had previously sung in folk groups, converging in Greenwich Village during the folk boom, dropping out (fleeing to the Virgin Islands) and re-surfacing in Los Angeles with Lou Adler (who earlier had produced hit records for Jan and Dean, Johnny Rivers, Barry McGuire) as their record producer. This combination, made the Mamas and the Papas enormously successful, America's first real Super Group. First there was "California Dreamin' " and then "Monday Monday" and then, as Top 40 radio shouted between records, the hits kept coming.

John Phillips became one of the most impressive songwriters and vocal arrangers in contemporary music, but apparently there was just so much he could do as (nominal) leader of the group; personal conflict and what they themselves called "one great big party" caused the Mamas and Papas to collapse like a harpooned dirigible. They burned themselves out: drinking, doping and . . . kaput.

Before they disappeared, however, John and Michelle Phillips, with Lou Adler and a few others, organized and produced a festival that was to provide an unprecedented high in pop music entertainment, in Monterey, California. The following acts performed at that festival, waiving all payment for undertermined charity: Eric Burdon and the Animals, the Association, the Beach Boys, Big Brother and the Holding Company, the Blues Project, Booker T and the MGs, Buffalo Springfield, Paul Butterfield Blues Band, the Byrds, Canned Heat, Country Joe and the Fish, Electric Flag, Grateful Dead, Jimi Hendrix Experience, the Impressions, Jefferson Airplane, the Mamas and Papas, Hugh Masekela, Scott McKenzie, Steve Miller Blues Band, Moby Grape, Laura Nyro, the Paupers, Quicksilver Messenger Service, Lou Rawls, Otis Redding, Johnny

Rivers, Ravi Shankar, Simon and Garfunkel, Dionne Warwick, and the Who.

Never again would so impressive an array of contemporary musical talent be gathered together on one field in open celebration. The bumper stickers had promised "Music, Love and Flowers" and that's what the festival delivered. Even the police, seldom high on teen-agers' favorite people list, were called "Flower Fuzz."

There were a number of stand-out acts at Monterey, one of the most memorable being that of Jimi Hendrix burning his guitar. Later Hendrix was recognized not just for his theatrics, but for his guitar-playing, which, most musicians and critics agreed, put him in the Number One or Two position internationally (vying with England's Eric Clapton).

It was logical that Hendrix (and Clapton and half a hundred more blues guitarists) would happen. White rock had always relied heavily upon the blues form and upon vocal and instrumental techniques of the traditional black musicians and singers. From the middle 1950's to the present, despite all the profound changes which had occurred, the traditional sound and style had remained the focus and foundation of rock. In other words, if there hadn't been a Muddy Waters, there wouldn't have been an Eric Clapton.

The blues revival began on two fronts in 1967: black and white.

Many said white blues was a contradiction of terms. They said Eric Burdon, Stevie Winwood, Eric Clapton, Paul Butterfield, John Mayall, Mike Bloomfield and Steve Miller couldn't play real down-home blues; they were honkies and faking it.

The musicians themselves disagreed. John Kay of Steppenwolf, for example, believed that the young, urban whites were becoming heirs to the blues tradition because many blacks either couldn't or wouldn't sing blues any more. And, he said, "Now that white musicians really have something to sing the blues about, like the bomb and Vietnam—all the destruction crippling lives on both personal and sociological levels—they have a valid reason for creating a few blues standards of their own. Previously, white musicians

102

could only reproduce second-rate versions of Negro blues, but the current world situation has changed all that. Now everyone has something to cry about."

Coinciding with the explosion of white blues bands (Canned Heat, Cream, Jimi Hendrix Experience, Fleetwood Mac, Jeff Beck Group, Young Rascals, Steppenwolf, etc.), there was a revived interest in those to whom these bands were paying musical tribute. Sharing the bill at the Fillmore East and West (Graham opened a second concert hall in New York eighteen months after beginning his weekly dance concerts in San Francisco) with some of these newer groups were the blues originals—Chuck Berry, Bo Diddley, B. B. King, Albert King, Buddy Guy, Otis Rush, Albert Collins.

And something the label-makers called "soul." Black writer Claude Brown described it: "Soul is sass, man. Soul is arrogance. Soul is walkin' down the street in a way that says, 'This is me, muh-fuh!' Soul is that nigger whore comin' along . . . ja . . . ja . . . ja, and walkin' like she's saying, 'Here it is, baby. Come an' git it.' Soul is bein' true to yourself, to what is *you*. Now, hold on: Soul is . . . that . . . uninhibited . . . no, *extremely* uninhibited self . . . expression that goes into practically every Negro endeavor. That's soul. And there's swagger in it, man. It's exhibitionism, and it's effortless. Effortless. You don't need to put it on; it just comes out."

There was soul in songs sung by Arthur Conley ("Sweet Soul Music"), Sam and Dave ("Soul Man") and Aretha Franklin ("Baby I Love You" and "Respect") in 1967 and half a hundred artists in 1968.

Soul was pigs' knuckles and Malcolm X; the Shing-a-ling and the Boogaloo and the Funky Broadway; Nina Simone and Muhammad Ali; Motown (sometimes) and Stax/Volt (always); learning Swahili and wearing a Free Huey button. "Soul music is music coming out of the black spirit," said the militant black poet-playwright LeRoi Jones.

The Beatles were less than silent during this increasing diversification of rock, surpassing nearly everyone in terms of rock complexity and taste when they spent four months (nine hundred hours in the studio) and ninety-five thousand dollars recording their twelfth album, *Sgt. Pepper's Lonely Hearts Club Band*. (After hearing it, Jefferson Airplane went back into the studio, apparently ashamed of spending only ninety hours on their third LP, *After Bathing At Baxter's*.) The Beatles had shown an experimental interest in sound effects, gospel, country music and baroque counterpoint in *Rubber Soul* (released in December, 1965), and since then had grown measurably . . . through *Revolver*, which showed powerful elements of classical structure and Eastern influence . . . with *Sgt. Pepper* being nearly universally hailed as a contemporary masterpiece.

No longer were the Beatles' primary influences the Everly Brothers and Chuck Berry. Now they included two electronic composers, John Cage and Karlheinz Stockhausen, and a classical Indian sitarist, Ravi Shankar. The electric guitars and Ringo's drums were present for the recording sessions, of course, but so was a forty-two piece orchestra, mostly made up of members of the Royal Philharmonic.

The approach to lyrics had developed, as well, with the Beatles singing about how many holes it would take to fill the Albert Hall. Not to mention tangerine trees and marmalade skies.

The diversity of the period boggled the mind. Besides those records already mentioned, in 1967 Bobbie Gentry croaked a saccharine C&W-flavored "Ode to Billie Joe"; the Mothers of Invention introduced a complex, multi-layered avant-garde album construction called "We're Only In It for the Money"; the Young Rascals (soon to drop the Young in the name) sang about boys and girls "Groovin' "; Phil Ochs resolved the nettled Vietnam controversy—at least for himself —by singing "The War Is Over"; the Who emphasized a hard rock instrumental sound (in "Happy Jack" and "I Can See for Miles") and then destroyed their instruments on stage at the close of every set; Donovan, the Beach Boys and the Beatles, among others, paid tribute to the Maharishi Mahesh Yogi and other people and things Eastern; the Buffalo Springfield combined country and rock better than anyone had and still didn't have a real hit; Motown slipped from a 1966 peak in record sales, but still churned out hits by the Supremes (who became Diana Ross *and* the Supremes: "Reflections," "The Happening" and "Love Is Here and Now You're Gone"), Stevie Wonder ("I was Made to Love Her"), Tammi Terrell ("There Ain't No Mountain High Enough"), and Martha and the Vandellas (who became Martha *Reeves* and the Vandellas: "Jimmy Mack" and "Honey Chile"); the Lovin' Spoonful scored the film *You're a Big Boy Now;* Paul McCartney wrote the theme music for *The Family Way;* and Simon and Garfunkel agreed to provide some background music for a film called *The Graduate.*

Something for everybody, the man said.

As the rhythms, harmonies and melodies became freer, so too did the audience become freer, more experimental. No. It was the other way around. Popular music—rock 'n' roll—was still reflecting the action and philosophy of youth.

When Haight Street residents "buried" the hippie, they announced the birth of the Free Man.

Dancing became free-form expression. No rules.

The music said Fuck Rules, too.

Theater became a part of rock (Doors, the Who, Crazy World of Arthur Brown) and rock became a part of the theater *(Hair).*

Filmmakers incorporated the talents of pop musicians and pop musicians became filmmakers *(Magical Mystery Tour).*

People on the music scene began to ask: What's next?

No one answered.

PART-2:

Some Of The Scenes

8

The Story of a Hit

On February 25, 1967, "I Never Loved a Man" by Aretha Franklin made its first appearance on the *Cash Box* rhythm and blues chart (Number twenty-six). This was Aretha's first record on the Atlantic label, following five years of pleasant but directionless recording for Columbia. The record was quite different from anything she had done before, and the same week *Cash Box* named it a "Pick of the Week":

Here's a groovy lid from Aretha Franklin that promises to do lots of action in both the sales and spins areas. Top side, "I Never Loved a Man the Way I Love You," is a high-powered ballad which is likely to see pop and R&B action. "Do Right Woman, Do Right" is a real lowdown blues session.

On March 4, this record went to the Number Eight position on the R&B chart in *Cash Box* and made its debut on the Top One Hundred chart, Number Seventy-three with a bullet, meaning it had taken a significant jump. (Most new records first appear in the eighties or nineties on the chart.)

By March 11, "I Never Loved a Man" had reached the Number One spot in the R&B market, a position it would hold for seven consecutive weeks (until late April), and jumped to Number Forty-five on the Top One Hundred, with a bullet.

March 18 in the Top One Hundred: Number Twenty-eight, with a bullet.

March 25: Number Twenty, with a bullet.

April 1: Number Sixteen, with a bullet.

April 8: Number Fourteen with a bullet. (As records approach the top of the charts, a jump of only two or three places is considered significant.)

April 15: Number Ten, with a bullet.

That's as high as it went in the Top One Hundred, and as it began to drop, Aretha's second single release for Atlantic, "Respect," made its debut at Number Fifty-six! "Respect" would go to Number One, and both records would be certified within a month or so as million-sellers by the Record Industry Association of America (RIAA).*

Aretha Franklin was born in Memphis, Tennessee, in 1942, one of five children of the Rev. C. L. Franklin, now the pastor of the 4,500-member New Bethel Baptist Church in Detroit. (Her brother Cecil is an assistant pastor now.) This is a church in the Deep South holy-roller tradition, where, as *Time* reported, "the preaching is so fiery . . . two white-uniformed nurses stand by to aid overwrought parishoners."

Aretha grew up in Detroit, not far from the black East Side ghetto which would be the scene of some of the country's bloodiest racial uprisings. Growing up in the same neighborhood with Aretha were several other singers-to-be—all three of the original Supremes, all the Four Tops, Bill (Smokey) Robinson of the Miracles, and several more who would in the early 1960's become part of the Motown sound.

There was also a gospel sound in Detroit as Aretha was growing up. Billy Ward had sung spirituals be-

*The *Cash Box* charts have been used over *Billboard*'s here to avoid any confusion with what are called "turntable hits," meaning the records are played on the radio heavily but don't sell very well. *Billboard*'s charts are based on sales *and* air-play, while *Cash Box* compiles its weekly list of top records solely on the basis of sales.

fore organizing the Dominoes, an early R&B group that featured the voices of Clyde McPhatter and Jackie Wilson. An even greater influence was Aretha's own father, whose friends included Clara Ward, Mahalia Jackson, James Cleveland and Mava Staples. They visited the house often and Clara even sang at a family funeral.

Aretha's first solo performance was in her father's church, when she was not yet in her teens. Later, the entire family (including her sisters Carolyn and Erma, the latter now living in New York and traveling the pop music circuit) went on the road—barnstorming the Midwest and South with their father, preaching and singing praises to God.

Sam Cooke, another gospel singer from Detroit who was one of Aretha's best friends, left gospel for popular music and found success fairly easily. This moved Aretha to try for the same brass ring, leaving home for New York. She was 18.

In 1961, she found a personal manager (Mrs. Jo King) and a record deal (Columbia), leaving the gospel circuit behind and moving toward the jazz club circuit. Her records, meanwhile, were a variant lot—the material ranging from blues ("Muddy Water" and "Trouble in Mind") to folk ("If I Had a Hammer") to Broadway ("Once in a Lifetime" from *Stop the World —I Want to Get Off*) to standards ("Look for the Silver Lining" and "Love for Sale") to jazz ("This Could Be the Start of Something"). The records were excellent, but sold only moderately. Aretha had no real image, no direction.

Her five-year contract expired in the autumn of 1966. "Rock-a-Bye My Baby" had made an appearance low on the charts and so had a song called "Sweet Bitter Love," but there hadn't been artistic satisfaction (or sales) enough to prompt Aretha (or Columbia) to renew. Clive Davis, the president of Columbia, admits: "We just didn't know what to do with her."

In 1966, Aretha Franklin was a smallish (five-foot-five), chunky Negro girl with a four-octave range. She could sing and she could sing well. She had been named in *Down Beat* magazine's international jazz critics poll as the "new star female vocalist." It was a label that didn't quite fit.

Jerry Wexler is nearly twice Aretha's age, a record producer also serving as executive vice-president of Atlantic Records. "I always thought she was by far the best soul singer, and I was in hopes that when her contract ran out, we'd have a shot at it," Wexler says.

He is a balding, bushy-browed man, deeply tanned, with full sideburns gone gray and a thick gray-and-black goatee topping a stocky frame. He is from New York, and his voice carries the inflection peculiar to Brooklyn and the Bronx.

He has been producing successful R&B records for nearly twenty years (most of the early ones with Ahmet Ertegun, Atlantic's founder-president)—including "Sh-Boom" by the Chords, LaVern Baker's "Tweedle Dee" and the Drifters' "Money Honey," stretching forward to Wilson Pickett's "Midnight Hour" and "Mustang Sally." It was apparent he'd liked to have added Aretha Franklin to the impressive list. His position of executive responsibility within the company practically dictated he produce only those that he *must* produce. Aretha seemed to be one of them.

Wexler explains that he and Aretha had a mutual friend in Philadelphia, a gospel disc jockey named Louise Williams. "I happened to be in Muscle Shoals [Alabama] on a Wilson Pickett session and she called me—Louise—and she said call this number, it's Aretha Franklin. I'd never spoken to her at that point. Louise said, 'She's ready to talk to you.' So I called her. It was midnight and that was my introduction to Aretha.

"She was in Detroit, at home. I said, 'How do we get this into posture, who do I talk to?' She said, 'Well, you can talk to my husband,' Ted White, who was her manager at that time. Which was arranged, and they came to New York a few days later and we sat down and negotiated a contract."

This was sometime in the fall of 1966. Shortly after that Aretha and Wexler had two meetings to discuss what material might be recorded. They met at Wexler's comfortable home outside New York, on Long Island.

"Aretha and I had two very long—day-long—meet-

110

ings prior to going to Muscle Shoals to record. I brought in my song bag and she brought in hers. Together we agreed upon a cadre of songs from which we would select the actual songs to be recorded. In other words, from maybe forty or fifty ideas, we resolved it to twenty, and without firming it up any more than that, we knew from the twenty we could certainly get what we wanted."

They arrived at these songs in three ways: (1) by playing songs that had been recorded by songwriters on what are called "dubs," demonstration records; (2) by going over typewritten lists of known songs; and (3) by Aretha's playing and singing songs she had been working on—her own and songs written by writers she knew.

"She played 'I Never Loved a Man,'" Wexler recalls, "a song that Ronnie Shannon had brought to her, a young Detroit writer, and Aretha had her whole conception of it. She played it and I thought that was probably the best of the original songs to do on the first session."

During these same "daily skull drills" (Wexler's description), Aretha also played piano and sang her own readings of a Rolling Stones song, "Satisfaction," and a hit by Otis Redding, "Respect." Both would later be hits for Aretha—in her own style. Aretha was what Wexler called a "contributory artist," someone who can take someone else's material and make it nearly her own.

The third "character" in this story is a town, Muscle Shoals, one-fourth of a four-city complex that straddles the Tennessee River near the Wilson Dam in northernmost Alabama, about 120 miles east and slightly south of Memphis, collective population about one hundred thousand—what Wexler calls "one hundred thousand *souls*."

Wexler, and Atlantic, had "discovered" Muscle Shoals in desperation. Atlantic had been cranking out R&B hits for a long time when, as Wexler put it, "it became clear to me in the Sixties that all our records had a studio stink on them." Looking around, Wexler found the Stax/Volt operation in Memphis and arranged to cut some of his future product there. Stax and Volt, two blues labels then behind Atlantic in sales, had developed the "workshop" method of recording, and this changed Atlantic's sound, once Wexler had moved in, taking a "house producer" named Tommy Dowd with him. (Dowd was engineering records for Atlantic in the late 1940's and early 1950's—including "One Mint Julip" by the Clovers and "Wheel of Fortune" by the Cardinals—with Ahmet Ertegun producing.)

"This Stax/Volt thing came along like a revelation, an epiphany," Wexler recalls. "The Stax/Volt rhythm section, y'know, has Booker T. and the MGs and the workshop. Here are four guys who, y'know, come to work every morning, take off their coats and start to blow. Whatever the project is, that's what they address themselves to. Just a minimum of mystique and bullshit and attitudinizing, and here we are, who's up? Carla Thomas, Pickett, y'know, Otis is comin' in; let's go to work and play—every day."

Wexler says he and Dowd produced a sound that was a synthesis of Atlantic's old R&B sound and the Memphis blues of Stax/Volt. He took Wilson Pickett there (with Dowd as his engineer) and recorded "Midnight Hour" and "Don't Fight It," and a number more—copping, as he put it, the "way they voiced their horns, their bass line . . . their workshop approach." At the same time, he and Dowd added their own "curleycues" (often in terms of harmony), and Dowd often stayed on in Memphis to engineer several artists for Stax/Volt. The Atlantic "sound" remained apart from that of Stax/Volt, but as Wexler puts it, "it was a first cousin, no denying it."

In time, however, the Stax/Volt operation became so successful, Wexler and Atlantic were asked to leave; Stax/Volt just couldn't spare Atlantic the studio time. In desperation, Wexler says, he looked to Muscle Shoals.

"I had taken a few masters from Rick Hall [who owned the Fame Studios there]," Wexler recalls. "I'd never met him. We were telephone pals. But I knew there was such a thing as studios out there in the boon-

ELVIS PRESLEY

Bill HALEY AND THE COMETS

THE BEACH BOYS

THE EVERLY BROTHERS

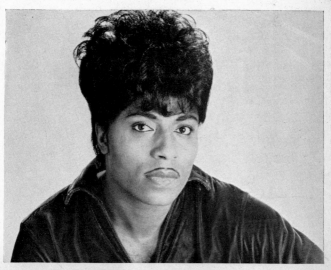

LITTLE RICHARD

CHUCK BERRY

BUDDY HOLLY

PHIL SPECTOR

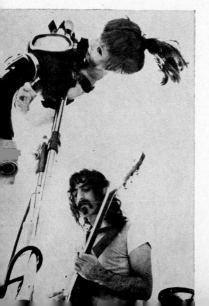

FRANK ZAPPA

THE BEATLES

MICK JAGGER

BOB DYLAN AND THE BYRDS

BOB DYLAN, DONOVAN, AND MARY
TRAVERS OF PETER, PAUL & MARY

COUNTRY JOE AT THE LOVE-IN, 1966
Golden Gate, San Francisco

JANIS JOPLIN

docks of Alabama and that there were some pretty good sounds coming from them."

There were two studios in Muscle Shoals at the time—Rick Hall's and Quin Ivy's. (There are now four.) Jimmy Hughes and Joe Simon had done records there. Joe Tex recorded his first hit for Dial (an Atlantic subsidiary), "Hold On to What You Got," in Muscle Shoals. So had Percy Sledge, with "When a Man Loves a Woman."

So Wexler took Pickett there, to cut "Land of a Thousand Dances" and "Mustang Sally." The studio seemed all right.

"I liked it for several reasons," Wexler says. "First of all, I like to be away from New York and all the tangential influences and unnecessary stimuli, the hang-ups you get in New York. I also liked it because I like the sound of Rick Hall's four-track studio. To me, it's maybe the very best studio in America for a soul sound. And then I liked it because they have a terrific cadre of musicians there, who work in this woodshedding, ad-lib, head arrangement type of method, which is very akin to the Stax/Volt thing."

When Aretha and Wexler talked, it was agreed they'd record in Muscle Shoals.

Assembling all the elements for a million-selling record is little different from collecting parts for an automobile.

"I Never Loved a Man" now had an artist (Aretha), a producer (Jerry Wexler, working in the booth; Tommy Dowd working in the studio with the band), an engineer (Rick Hall, owner of Fame Studios), a studio. The next elements were backup musicians.

"At that time the rhythm section that was available was in my opinion probably the best R&B rhythm section I could ever imagine getting together in one studio," Wexler says. That was Roger Hawkins on drums, Tommy Cogbill playing bass, Chips Moman on lead guitar, Jimmy Johnson on rhythm guitar, and Spooner Oldham sharing electric piano and organ with Aretha.

"Their entry into this was not via progressive rock or acid music. These are Southern country people who have sort of turned away from country music and to-

113

ward the blues, which doesn't mean they've abandoned country, but rather that they've turned from the tedium of the Nashville grind and have gone into this more creative R&B thing, which stirs them. When they play the blues, they don't have to sit down and memorize seventy-five Robert Johnson records. These people are the roots.

"It's a matter of some astonishment to a lot of people to learn that the band on 'I Never Loved a Man' happened to be all Caucasian people . . . and it's maybe the smokiest and funkiest of her records. I know Tom Jones almost fell over when I told him that."

There were also horns present at the session, with Charley Chalmers on tenor saxophone, writing whatever haphazard chord charts might be gotten up. The rest was strictly ad-lib.

Everyone arrived in Muscle Shoals the night before, stayed at the Downtown Hotel in Florence, across the river from Muscle Shoals. It was the only hotel around. ("You have your breakfast there at the hotel and you go to the studio, and the only other thing you do is go to the bootlegger for whiskey, because Alabama's dry.")

They arrived at the studio the next day about noon. The control room Wexler and Hall worked in was small, the studio itself much larger—rugs stained with use, cigarette burns in the piano top, the room otherwise immaculate.

The first thing: Aretha played and sang "I Never Loved a Man" for the assembled musicians. This was the first time they'd heard it.

They nodded and verbalized their approval. A "heavy" song, they said. Then Tommy Cogbill began to generate a bass line, which, according to Wexler, is almost always the first concern in getting a record together. "And the bass line comes fast and easiest when it's set up by Aretha's playing on piano with her left hand."

Then there was some shifting around, as musicians found their way into the song. It was decided Spooner Oldham would open the record on electric piano—for the introduction (eight bars). Aretha would then

114

come in on piano. Everybody else had their parts down. No charts. No real guidance. More than anything else: a "feel."

It was all happening at once; Wexler doesn't remember there being a "lot of geeing and hawing." In Muscle Shoals, it's TCB—taking care of business.

Soon after beginning, Spooner wrote out what passed for chord charts for the rhythm section. Then Charley Chalmers went upstairs into Rick Hall's office to scratch out the horn parts. About two hours into the session—about two-thirty or three—they began to tape.

"We began taping at the point when there was something worth playing back, either because it was very good or very bad," Wexler says. "We did the whole thing in five hours, horns and all."

There were no breaks taken in this session. Aretha remained seated at the piano, her solid frame remaining motionless during pauses and moments when tape was being rewound for playback. Then when she played and sang, her face opened up, reflecting the pain and joy of the song, actually living the story the song told:

> You're no good,
> Heartbreaker.
> You're a liar
> And you're a cheat.
> I don't know why
> I let you do these things to me.
> My friends keep tellin' me
> That you ain't no good.
> Wo-oh-oh, but they don't know
> That I'd leave you if I could.
> I guess I'm uptight
> And I'm stuck like glue
> 'Cause I ain't me . . . I ain't never
> I ain't never . . . no-no-
> Loved a man
> The way I love you.

Aretha's tone was always so pure, ranging over the

*"I Never Loved a Man" by Ronnie Shannon, Copyright 1967, 14th Hour—Pronto Music.

four octaves, her dynamics so unique, Wexler says the effect had producers, engineers and musicians alike rushing from studio to control room to hear every play-back.

Some time ago I thought
You would run out of fools.
But I was wrong;
You got one that you never lose.
The way you treat me is a shame.
How could you hurt me so bad?
Baby, you know that I'm the best thing
That you ever had.
Kiss me once again.
Don't you never, never say that we're through
'Cause I ain't never, never, no-no-
Loved a man
The way I love you.

I can't sleep at night,
And I can't eat a bite.
I guess I'll never be free,
Since you got your hooks in me.
Wo-oh-oh
I ain't never loved a man
I ain't never loved a man
I ain't never loved a man
Hurt me so bad . . .*

The song slowly faded.
". . . her piano playing!" Wexler wrote in the liner notes to the album containing this song. "The inevitable comparison is to Ray Charles, whose singing and arranging concepts flowed with and around his inspired piano statements." And thus it was during Aretha's first session for Atlantic. Always the specter of Ray Charles was there, but as an influence, no more.

In the control room, Wexler's stocky frame was positioned behind Rick Hall's new stereo equipment. He had urged Hall to buy a four-track machine, but three tracks were as many as he wanted at first. This was the break-in recording session, and minor bugs oc-

*Ibid.

116

cupied the engineer's and Wexler's attention as minor musical changes were discussed and learned in the studio.

There weren't plans for excessive overdubbing on this record. None, in fact. And the only overdub that was added to the original track was one little vocal trick suggested by Spooner for one of the breaks. The rest of it was recorded straight through. Everybody'd wind up and let go.

"The fantastic thing about Aretha is you think it's a great take, you're knocked out with it, and she says, 'No, no good, I have to make another one.' Y'see, there are some notes she's got in her head she didn't make. You don't have a clue as to what she's thinking of. She'll go and try for them again. That's the only thing that changes vocally: Aretha constantly striving and shooting against some ideal phrasing that's known only to her. She's a genius. She and Ray Charles are the two geniuses we know about in the popular music business. They're the two we know of for sure."

They completed "I Never Loved a Man," broke for supper ("barbecued ribs and Brunswick stew across the street"), and went back into the studio to record the record's second side, a song called "Do Right Woman." They recorded only the bass, drums and electric piano parts before the session blew up. Circumstances prevented any more being done at that time and Aretha went back to Detroit, Wexler and Dowd to New York.

"I was terribly excited, I was really turned on to this record," Wexler says, "so when I went home for the weekend I brought a dub home with me and I got on the phone and I called all the key R&B disc jockeys around the country that I knew to play it for them on the phone.

"They were ready for Aretha, all the jockeys. The word was out: Look out! Aretha's on Atlantic! Look out! The jockeys had a tremendous acceptance of her. They were really ready.

"So I started playing this record on the phone and I bent everybody outa shape, they were going mad: When can I have it? So all of a sudden a whole big

117

scam starts on this record and I don't have a second side. I can't release it."

Wexler telephoned his disc jockey friends all day Saturday and Sunday. Monday he had a number of additional dubs made, sending them to many of the deejays he had talked with the day before. The following Monday Aretha came to New York to finish—almost single-handedly—the record's B-side.

First she recorded a piano track, then she doubled on organ. Next she added the lead vocal. She only had one sister with her, Carolyn, and together they did all the background harmonies. Bam-bam-bam.

"When I sent the record back to Chips Moman, he almost fell down." He wrote that song with Dan Penn:

> Take me to heart
> And I'll always love you
> And nobody can make me do wrong.
> Take me for granted,
> Leaving love unshown,
> Takes will power
> And temptation strong.
> Woman, don't let your mind . . .
> You should understand
> She's not just a plaything
> Just flesh and blood
> Just like her man.
>
> If you wanta do right all days, woman
> You've gotta be a do right all night man.
>
> Yeah yeah yeah—
> They say that it's a man's world,
> But you can't prove that by me.
> And as long as we're together,
> Show some respect for me.
>
> A woman's only human
> If she could only understand.*

The record was a hit. It was selling between one hundred twenty-five and one hundred forty-five thou-

*"Do Right Woman—Do Right Man" by Dan Penn and Chips Moman, Copyright 1967, Press Music Co., Inc.

118

sand copies a week at its peak, sold well in excess of a million in eight. It appeared first on the R&B charts, as do most of Aretha's records (only because the R&B markets usually get the record first) and immediately crossed over into pop.

"I Never Loved a Man" made this crossover for an interesting reason. It has to do with the climate that existed (and continues to exist) when the record was released. This is the climate of soul.

"Today a very strong R&B record will always go pop," Wexler says. "Without question. This is not true of country songs today. Even the monster country songs won't cross over. This is a turnaround from what was happening ten years ago, in the days of Marty Robbins and Buddy Holly and Buddy Knox and all the others, when country songs did cross. Now that's all changed. We've parochialized the music—a country record, a jazz record, an R&B record. The crossover thing very rarely takes place in any field—least of all in jazz, next least in country, right?

"And it used to be that that would be your goal: If you got a good record in whatever field, you would try to get some pop play, always hoping for the miracle. Today it's not a question of miracles, or whether or not it will cross over, if you have a good R&B record. There's no question that it won't!"

This helped make "I Never Loved a Man" a hit. But mostly it was the music itself, and the voice of a plain Negro woman in her middle 20's who would come to be known as "Lady Soul."

Soon after "I Never Loved a Man" was certified a million-seller by the RIAA, Aretha Franklin had become a top attraction at college concerts and was booked into Carnegie Hall. She appeared on all the top television shows and toured Europe, where she was hailed as the new Bessie Smith.

In two years' time she released nine single records. All but one of them sold at least a million copies. *Billboard* and *Cash Box* called her the Top Female Singer of 1967, an honor that was repeated in 1968. She was awarded two Grammies (the music industry's Oscar), for the Best Rhythm & Blues Recording and

Best Rhythm & Blues Solo Vocal Performance (for her cover of Otis Redding's "Respect").

She set a new record in 1968, earning more gold (million-selling) records than any other female artist in record-business history (eleven). Six of those gold records were released in that year, setting a record for the period. (Actually tying with the Rascals, who also had six gold records on the Atlantic label in 1968.)

Two years earlier she had been just another underrated, overlooked singer. One hit record changed it all.

9

We're Only In It
for the Money

FROM THE SOUNDTRACK OF *Don't Look Back,* IN WHICH BOB DYLAN'S MANAGER, ALBERT GROSSMAN, SPEAKS TO AN ENGLISH PROMOTER REGARDING DYLAN'S APPEARING ON ENGLISH TV: "Now, what kind of money do you think? How far do you think we can push them?"

FROM AN ADVERTISEMENT IN 16 MAGAZINE (CIRC: 1,250,000): "Please send me *Monkee Private Picture Book.* I am enclosing a one-dollar bill."

FROM AN INTERVIEW WITH BILL GRAHAM, OWNER OF THE NATION'S TWO LEADING ROCK CONCERT HALLS, FILLMORES EAST AND WEST: "When we held a benefit for the Delano grape strikers, I didn't do a whole number about how great a guy I am for giving the strikers my hall for a night. But somehow Herb Caen [a popular San Francisco columnist] heard about it, right? And he heard about my driving a truck full of food we bought with the money down to Delano, right? The word gets out. It's like when Martin Luther King got shot in Memphis. Somebody there had to put him in a box, right? That somebody didn't go around saying, 'Casket by So-and-So.' But the word gets out and the next time some Memphis cat dies, he's going to get his box at the same place. That sounds like bad taste, I know, but that's the way it is. It's good business to give things away."

FROM A STORY IN *Rolling Stone* CONCERNING THE SIGNING OF QUICKSILVER MESSENGER SERVICE AND THE STEVE MILLER BAND TO CAPITOL: "Quicksilver's contract calls for a forty-thousand-dollar advance, a ten thousand bonus and four-year options. The last two years, if the options are picked up, will cost Capitol one hundred thousand each. Miller's group picked up a fifty thousand advance, a ten thousand bonus and four-year options with a cumulative total of seven hundred and fifty thousand . . ."

FROM AN INTERVIEW WITH SIR JOSEPH LOCKWOOD, CHAIRMAN OF ELECTRIC & MUSIC INDUSTRIES (WHICH INCLUDES CAPITOL AND THE BEATLES): "I'm not crazy about pop music. I like it because it sells."

FROM THE FIRST BEATLES PRESS CONFERENCE HELD IN AMERICA, FEBRUARY 7, 1964, IN NEW YORK: *Question:* Do you hope to take anything home with you? *Answer:* Yeah, Rockefeller Center.

FROM *Billboard*'s 1968-69 INTERNATIONAL BUYER'S GUIDE OF THE MUSIC-RECORD INDUSTRY, THE FOLLOWING RECORD LABELS: Pieces of Eight, Silver Dollar, Gold Standard, Money, Kash, and Security.

FROM *Billboard*'s WORLD OF SOUL YEARBOOK, THIS HEADLINE, TOPPING AN ADVERTISEMENT FOR STEREO TAPES: "Sell Your Soul!"

The only thing that should have surprised anyone about *Forbes* magazine putting the record business on its cover in 1968 was that it took the editors of this business publication so long to do so. From 1956, when Elvis made his RCA Victor debut, to 1966, when Jefferson Airplane appeared on the same label, retail sales of records in the United States alone jumped from three hundred twelve million to over seven hundred million dollars. A year later, in 1967, sales were estimated at eight hundred million, and although the 1968 total hasn't been tallied as this is written, conservative estimates add still another hundred million. While John M. Wiley, director of research for Columbia Records, insists that annual sales already exceed one billion dollars. This doesn't rival the yearly grosses recorded by General Motors and Standard Oil, but it should have been obvious to any businessman why *Forbes* gave rock its good bookkeeping seal of approval.

Forbes' consideration of "The Record Business: Psychedelic Billions" also captured precisely the feel and approach to rock 'n' roll taken by most rock businessmen—concert promoters, personal managers, booking agents, publicists, rack jobbers, or any of a hundred other types of commercial alchemists whose job it is to turn rock into gold. The point made repeatedly was that rock 'n' roll was the twentieth century's answer to Sutter's Mill: "Listen, Dad [said *Forbes*]: This is now an industry where an investment of next to nothing can make a man a millionaire practically overnight."

Nor has *Forbes* been alone in making this statement. The business editors of *Newsweek*, nearly three years earlier, devoted their Spotlight on Business to "Records: The Whole Funky Grown-up Bit." "Given the small amount of money needed to make and distribute to disc jockeys a 45-r.p.m. single (five thousand dollars will do the trick), anybody could grab an unknown rock group and get into the record act . . ." the editors of *Newsweek* said.

Newsweek then did what *Forbes* was later to do: march out the "overnight success" stories. Among the tales rather shabbily told were those of Dunhill (begun on seventy-five thousand, sold two years later for three million to the company that provided the original backing), A&M (started in a garage in 1962 by Herb Alpert and Jerry Moss, now selling about fifty million dollars in records yearly), Motown (founded by a Detroit factory worker who used a production-line technique to market the Supremes, the Temptations and the Four Tops, among others), and Philles (introduced by Phil Spector, who was on the government's millionaire list by the time he was 21). In each of these stories, the editors' tone seemed at best to be one of grudging respect. *Forbes* quoted Larry Newton of ABC Records as saying Dunhill's leading group, the Mamas and the Papas, were "four animals." And *Newsweek* considered Spector only as "a 24-year-old sprite whose shoulder-length locks and bizarre, dandyish dress rival those of any of the oddball rock performing groups . . ."

Another point to be made springs from the style in which the *Forbes* and *Newsweek* stories, along with others, were written. *Newsweek* began its report: "It's wiggy, baby, wiggy. That's the record business. There's all these wiggy adults—maybe like 100,000 of 'em—out there scraping, scrambling, tummeling—for hits. Over a thousand record outfits. A couple, oh, 5,000 writers, singers, A&R men. Ten thousand—yeah, easy—10,000 retailers, radio stations, one-stoppers, rack jobbers, distributors, platter pushers, disc jocks. Who knows how many clerks and dial twisters. Man, there they are. The whole funky grown-up bit out there combing the country, stalking the beat, the message, the *sound* that'll set the teen-agers moving and grooving. It's what's happening."[4]

It was as if *Forbes* took its cue from *Newsweek:* "It sends parents screaming into the night, eardrums splintering: so who cares? It sends the kids from 8 to 18, and that's what counts. It's a sound, a *sound,* a SOUND. Don't call it noise, Dad. Try to dig it. For it's really the sound of music, today's and tomorrow's; and what's more, it's the sound of money, maybe $2 billion worth."

Of course this is consistent with how adult businessmen approach nearly anything that is born of, and represents, youth. The Twist, the Nehru jacket and sideburns are only three of countless symbols of youth that have been hastily adopted by adults who suffer from that peculiar American malaise, the Ponce de Leon complex.

The overwhelming reach of the popular music industry must be recognized along with its prevailing attitude. Here is a partial list of components, compiled from information provided by England's Electrical & Musical Industries Ltd. (EMI), the largest music organization in the world, and Henry Brief, executive director of the Record Industry Association of America, Inc. (RIAA):

*Excerpted from "Records; The Whole Funky Grown-Up Bit," *Newsweek* (Oct. 11, 1965). Copyright Newsweek Inc., Oct. 11, 1965.

Number of record manufacturers: 13 major, 40 significant size, several thousand very small

Number of record labels: about 1,700 in all, of which 200 periodically reach the charts*

Number of retail record outlets (discount stores, record shops, rack locations, etc.): about 150,000

Number of phonographs: about 50 million

Number of juke boxes in operation: about 500,000

Number of radio stations: 4,117 AM, 1,631 FM

Record playing time on radio: 80 percent (Approximately 18,000 disc jockeys program popular records)

Radios in use: about 250 million (99.3 percent of homes have one or more radio; average American listens 17.5 hours per week)

Music publishers: 5,050

Music trade associations: 92

Piano, organ, musical instrument sales: $955 million

Sheet music sales: $40 million

Prerecorded tape sales (not including cassettes): $106 million

"Measure any aspect of the business," said EMI, "and the numbers are *large*. Sounds wonderful, and it is in many ways—until one realizes that the competitive situation in the U.S.A. is probably the keenest in the world." Only the British could describe such a "situation" so subtly.

Of course it was not always thus.

Nearly a century has passed since Thomas Edison produced the first phonograph (in 1878), and for most of this period the record industry was considered a dud. Until 1948, it was, in *Forbes'* words, a "nothing industry," dominated by three companies, Decca, RCA Victor and Columbia, with Capitol trailing. Record sales were estimated at forty-eight million dollars in 1921, and in twenty-seven years had crawled to only eighty-two million. This was the era of the 78-r.p.m. record,

Billboard's latest count is 2,609, and the American Federation of Musicians (AFM) has more than 3,000 on its list.

when a number of Benny Goodman's hits, for example, sold under one hundred thousand copies (compared to today's multimillion-copy hits), and record stores and disc jockeys were as rare as perfect pitch.

In 1948 came the revolution, when Peter Goldmark, president of CBS Labs, introduced the long-playing record. His motive for developing the LP was to make it simpler, and cheaper, to produce symphonies. Until then, if you wanted a full symphony, you had to buy four or five separate records, each 78 providing only five or so minutes of music per side. With the introduction of the LP, an entire symphony could be recorded on one disc, making it convenient for the consumer, profitable for the manufacturer.

Perhaps it was pride that prompted the reaction of General David Sarnoff, president of RCA. He refused to accept the LP and introduced the 45-r.p.m., insisting it was superior. Whatever his argument, the 45 presented problems, just as the LP offered its own peculiar quandary. Neither innovation was practical. There weren't any record players available that could accomodate the advancements made.

This resulted in what became known as "the Battle of the Speeds." CBS (Columbia) had designed a phonograph that would take the LP, but found manufacturers preferred to make television sets, another "new" invention then being marketed on a consumer level for the first time. While RCA manufactured its own small 45-r.p.m. phonograph and found it had to sell it at cost (and sometimes less) to provide a market for the recordings planned.

High-pressure salesmanship and a growing demand for records—prompted, ironically, by television's changing the sound of radio from variety to music—in time created a market for both the 45 and the LP. Columbia and RCA both won, and everybody jumped on the bandwagon, with 78's joining button hooks and buggy whips in the local Museum of Science and Industry.

Almost simultaneously with the invention of the LP had come a radical change in economics and demography. People were getting richer and had more money for "leisure products" such as records . . . and they were moving to the suburbs; thus the system for marketing records changed, so that every store with high traffic—drugstores, supermarkets, etc.—became a potential record outlet.

In 1954, manufacturers' sales in the United States totaled eighty-seven million dollars, showing almost no growth over five years earlier. But in 1955, sales jumped to one hundred twelve million, and a year later to nearly one hundred fifty-six million. The industry was on its feet at last and moving at a discernible pace, only to accelerate to an even faster speed with the introduction of the mail-order record club (from Columbia in 1955) and the rack jobber, who began servicing supermarkets, drug and other nonmusic stores in 1957.

The maturation of marketing technique came only when the market itself had grown up, for in the middle 1950's "war babies" were becoming consumers. From 1950 to 1960, elementary school enrollments rose fifty-one percent to over thirty-two million, while the number of high school students jumped fifty percent to over ten million.

Today the five leading companies in terms of sales are Columbia, RCA, Warner Brothers-Seven Arts, Capitol and MGM/Verve, controlling nearly fifty-five percent of the total market. Decca, one of the original leaders, is included in the ninety or so other companies that make up another thirty-five percent, with more than two thousand sharing the leftovers (only ten percent). This would indicate most record companies aren't doing so well, that the debit sheets in the record industry far outnumber the credit sheets. They do, and in the time it takes to read this, not only are dozens of new companies being formed, an equal number are declaring bankruptcy. Many companies last no longer than a month, or the time it takes for one record to flop.

Forbes quoted Henry Brief: ". . . the average 45 single has to sell 11,200 copies to break even; the average pop LP, 7,800 copies; the average classical LP, 9,700 copies. In a nation of 200 million people, that may not seem like much, but the dismal fact is this: Last year U.S. record manufacturers turned out about 7,000 45's and 4,000 LP's. At last count, 74 percent of the 45's, 61 percent of the pop LP's and 87 percent of the classical LP's failed to break even. And when a pop record fails to break even, it's usually a total loss. A 45 that won't sell 11,200 copies probably won't sell 50."

"Record company strength depends on production of records that sell well," says Mickie Most, a record producer with eighty million in sales (Herman's Hermits, Lulu, Animals, Jeff Beck, Donovan). "Consider the awful fact that of every hundred records produced, only six really catch on . . . leaving ninety-four nasty smells around the place."

When a record does hit, though, it turns into the gold they talk about. "Ninety-six Tears" is a song of questionable merit musically, but in the sales department, it was certified a million-seller. "Ninety-six Tears" was recorded for under three hundred dollars in the Midwestern city that was home for a group called Question Mark and the Mysterians. Based on a profit of two cents for each 45 sold, this brought a return of twenty thousand dollars, which isn't a bad profit margin. In albums there is even greater profit—fifty cents per disc.

"The record industry is more like Las Vegas than it is like U.S. Steel," says William P. Gallagher, vice-president of *Leisure Time Marketing*.

One other point must be made before moving away from the record companies toward the allied businesses, and it merely provides one more indication of how much a part of the overall business community record production is. In all of industry today there is a trend toward forming conglomerates, massive commercial organizations absorbing businesses of variant interest. The record industry is now up to its annual stockholders' reports in this movement. Dot (Bonnie Guitar) and Volt (Otis Redding) Records, along with several smaller labels, are part of Gulf & Western, a conglomerate with sizeable interests in real estate, cigar manufacture, theater ownership and the production and distribution of auto parts. Liberty (Canned Heat) and World Pacific (Ravi Shankar) are among eight record companies owned by the Transamerica Corporation, which also owns insurance and financial firms. The management and production company of Charles Koppelman and Don Rubin (John Sebastian, Tim Hardin, Lovin' Spoonful) is owned by the Commonwealth United Corporation, whose other interests include theaters, oil and gas holdings and a jukebox manufacturer. While Mike Curb's Sidewalk Productions (soundtracks for films) and James William Guercio's Poseidon Productions (management, music publishing, records) are both owned by Transcontinental Investing, a corporation controlling the Arthur discothèques, *Hullabaloo* magazine, Love's barbecue restaurant chain and the Minisink Rubber Company.

Says Herm Schoenfeld in *Variety:* "Big business, which previously didn't know the difference between a copyright and an upright, has begun swinging into the publishing and disc fields and wrapping up every firm in sight. The takeovers during the last couple of years have gone well over the one hundred million mark."

It is for good reason that the record industry trade publications are now including Dow Jones figures each week.

It is nearly impossible to consider, let alone explore in depth, all the hundreds of other merchants committed in whatever style or field to pop music in so little as one chapter in a book. But a few of the specific areas should be mentioned, however superficially.

One of the more obvious is what is called the special products or novelty industry. Usually, this is that area of merchandising which is designed to capitalize on the idol current at the moment. A classic example, although not the most recent, is what in 1956 was called "The Great Elvis Presley Industry." This campaign of product saturation of all markets set the commercial style that was to follow when the Beatles and the Monkees, along with other groups to a lesser degree, captured the record-buying hearts of America.

Elvis became a star in January, 1956, with the release of "Heartbreak Hotel," and by midyear there were predictions being made that at least twenty million dollars' worth of gadgets and wearables would be sold with Presley's name on them in a year's time.

The forecasts proved conservative. Within a few months' time, the following were on the market: tee-shirts, knit pajamas, pencils, purses, wallets, gold-plated adjustable rings, bobby sox, necklaces, pins, guitars, shoes and sneakers, handkerchiefs, charm bracelets, buttons, scarves, skirts, jackets, hats, stuffed hound dogs, wristwatches, mirrors, decorative pillows, mittens, scrapbooks, diaries, plaster of paris busts, bookends, fan magazines, luminous posters and photographs, Bermuda shorts and toreador pants, lipstick (in Hound Dog Orange and Heartbreak Hotel Pink), games, jeans, shirts, colognes, photograph albums and trading cards.

"Perhaps," *Look* magazine said at the time, "it is to lighten our burdens that the Lord sends us from time to time gay and imaginative men like Colonel Parker (Presley's manager), who realize that life is a great big hilarious fruitcake loaded with potential profits."

What is significant here is the fact that what Presley did to the economy—creating new business for manufacturers of everything from lipstick to plaster of paris, boosting sales of everything else from postage stamps and stationery for fan letters to tickets to performances and jumping the payroll just about everywhere—has been tripled and quadrupled by others since. It was the soundest economic reasoning that caused the Beatles to be honored by British royalty; they were awarded the M.B.E. (a poor man's knighthood) for bringing not Rockefeller Center home with them, but nearly enough money to purchase it.

No matter how or where you turn in talking or thinking about rock 'n' roll, always the subject of money comes up, for, after all, no matter what else pop music may be—an art, a diversion, a plague—it remains a part of the economy. Everyone in rock faces this fact every day of life.

Consider the average five-man group starting out. Begin with the minimal five thousand dollars spent on instruments, amplifiers, costuming and gadgetry. Add a personal manager (who will lay claim to anywhere from fifteen to twenty-five percent of the group's earnings, off the top), a booking agent (who gets ten percent, also before expenses and taxes), a publicist (who may get five percent or merely one hundred to five hundred dollars a week plus expenses), and assorted salaried road managers, equipment handlers and hangers-on. In no time at all the "once-pure" musicians have spent the huge advance they got from a record company and now are counting gate receipts and worrying about whether their record has a bullet or not, meaning it took a significant jump on the best-selling record charts. They are also concerned about publishing, because if you form your own music publishing company . . . well, everyone knows that's the thing to do, because the songwriter gets two cents for every 45 sold, sometimes more (half that if he shares publishing with a record company or a manager, as is usually the case) . . . and if it's a hit, other artists will record the tune . . . and the royalties come rolling in.

Meanwhile, the songwriters are sharing royalty fees every time the song is played on the radio. (If a hit song is played at least ten, maybe twenty or thirty times a day, and there are more than a thousand rock 'n' roll stations . . . you go figure it out.) The concert price climbs toward the ten-thousand mark . . . there are posters to be merchandised . . . testimonials are asked . . . realtors and brokers stand in line . . . and Ed Sullivan is beckoning.

Says Saul Zaentz, president of San Francisco's Fantasy Records (Creedence Clearwater Revival): "It's all peace and love until it gets down to the nitty gritty of where's my money."

And it's no one's fault and it's everyone's fault.

Obviously there are a handful whose real interest in the music industry is much more music than it is industry. One of these is David Anderle, head of A&R for Elektra Records. He told the editor of *Cheetah* magazine, talking about the attitude he and his contemporaries (those under 30, generally) have toward the business: "If there is an importance to what we're doing, it's that we're making the business less uptight. All I want is for a whole bunch of nice albums to come out that I can listen to, and it really doesn't matter what label they're on. You know, the record business does have something to do with art, yet there never has been an artistic community in it, and that's what we're trying to establish.

"So we help each other out, and I'll tell a radio station guy that Van Dyke (Parks) has a great record, because it is a great record. Elektra will make money from the good records we put out, and I think that Warner Brothers (for whom Parks records) should make money from the great records *they* put out.

"It shouldn't be that the PR guy at Capitol should have to say to a distributor, 'Here's Bobbie Gentry, CAP-1506, would you like to have lunch with her?' and the distributor says, 'Hm, CAP-1506 sold five hundred thousand copies; sure I'd like to have lunch with it.'

"Perhaps, just perhaps, if all of us take over, if the young people take over, if we're the tastemakers, well, perhaps the taste we're making will be better, but the important thing is that the conditions will be better. We're not selling salami here. We're dealing in people's souls."

Anderle is not alone. There are others who feel as he does, most of them the creators of rock—the writers, singers, producers, A&R men, engineers.

"We're going to make record companies change their ideas," said Graham Nash, formerly of the Hollies, now one fourth of Crosby, Stills, Nash and Young. "We're not their private property. There's no reason why they should compete with each other, and no reason why people from different companies shouldn't play together if they're happier and making better music not staying in a rut."

Bob Dylan echoed Nash: "The most you can do is satisfy yourself. If you're doing it for them instead of you," he told *Sing Out!* magazine, "you're not in contact . . ."

Cream's lead guitarist Eric Clapton told *Rolling Stone:* "What we're doing now is simply concentration on LP's. And if by accident a single should come out of an LP session, then we'll put it on the market. Whereas before you'd have two sessions; you'd conscientiously go to an LP session and you'd conscientiously go to a single session. And single sessions are terrible. I can't make them at all. They're just like—you go in there and the whole big problem is whether it's commercial. That is the problem. No matter what the music is like, it's got to be commercial, it's got to have a hook line, you've got to have this and that and you just fall into a very dark hole. I can't take it at all. What we eventually would like to get into is using LP's in place of singles. Record an LP every two months, or every month, and record an extended LP which would be on 16-r.p.m. Do that twice a year. That would be like a complete concert."

And Phil Spector, the man who retired from the music industry a millionaire before reaching 25, said: "People don't think about what happened ten years ago. Nobody would have believed that a group could be worth a hundred thousand dollars to any record company. You could start twenty record companies with that hundred thousand. I don't care how good Janis Joplin is, there's no way in the world that she is worth a hundred thousand. Not if Ella Fitzgerald is not. I mean, there's got to be some comparison, you know; you've got to eventually come down to talent and then come down to commerciality. That is more important than talent. True, I agree, if you're making money, but still not a hundred thousand. Because if you make the very untalented, just because of commercial reasons, very expensive, you hurt a lot of talented people, but that is commercialism and that you are never going to get rid of in the record industry."

As this is written, Spector has returned to the studios. He likes to make hit records, he says, and you can't do that retired. He also likes to make good records and thinks talent and commercialism can be combined. He's right, of course.

"There's nothing fundamentally wrong with commerciality," Jefferson Airplane's Jorma Kaukonen said. "Most of the music and most of the shows kids go see are really insults to their intelligence. But, if they're given an opportunity to hear good things, I think the commercial standards will be raised. That's what's happening now."

In most respects, the pop music business seems to be no different from any other. There are good and bad used-car salesmen, and there are good and bad rock 'n' roll salesmen (includes the artist as well as the huckster-manufacturer). For the moment, most are honest only to a point, that mark being defined largely by convenience and circumstance . . . which are governed largely by ego and greed, the consuming desire to acquire more wealth, fame and/or power than any of the so-called competitors.

FROM AN ARTICLE ABOUT THE MONKEES IN THE *Saturday Evening Post:* "Teen-agers are already chewing Monkee gum, adorning themselves in Monkee wool caps, suede boots and stovepipe pants, and hopefully anticipating the grand opening of Monkee departments in over 1,600 stores from coast to coast."

FROM *Variety,* A HEADLINE: "Pub-Disc Industry Now Dominated by Wall St."

FROM A NEWS STORY IN *Billboard:* "First fiscal quarter sales for Warner Brothers-Seven Arts Records are running seventeen percent ahead of the comparable period last year. Second quarter figures are projected by the company to run from twenty to twenty-two percent over last year's like second quarter. Last year set a sales record for the ten-year-old company . . ."

FROM *Life,* A HEADLINE: "It's Money Music."

FROM A MEMO REGARDING THE FINANCES OF THE RASCALS: "Right from the start, the group incorporated. Their first year in business they grossed $250,000, getting an average of $2,000 a night. The second year they earned $800,000 making an average of $5,000 a night. This third year they will gross $1,500,000, average $12,500 for a night, will get $15,000 at the Hollywood Bowl and $17,500 at the Singer Bowl. In January, 1967, they began a profit-sharing plan. Currently the plan holds cash reserves of $150,000 and each member of the group also has considerable holdings in blue chip stocks. Each has a $100,000 straight life insurance policy. Each has bought a house for his parents except Felix, whose folks already owned their own home. The group just split a bonus of $45,000 tax-free for the second quarter of this year. Their fiscal year is September 1. The Rascals make 54 cents for every album they sell (30 cents for performing, 2 cents for each of the twelve tunes they write) and 12 cents per single (8 for performing plus 2 cents

133

for writing each side). Twenty-five percent of what they gross goes into profit-sharing and related areas."

FROM *Billboard,* A HEADLINE: "Retailing Aim: Youthful Dollars."

FROM AN INTERVIEW WITH DICK CLARK: "A myth has grown up over the years that I have something to do with what becomes popular. Generally, I reflect what's going on early enough to make a profit on it. I don't make culture. I sell it."

10

Radio: This Is Where
It's Happening

At precisely 9:03 P.M. Harvey Miller opens his microphone and mouth and says: "It's nine-oh-three in Boss Radio, gettin' into yo' head, gonna do it for the next three, Marvin Gaye 'n' Tammi say . . ."

The second record of his evening, Motown's "Good Lovin' Ain't Easy To Come By" comes crashing into the announcer's booth, goes screaming into the night—into an estimated half-million homes and cars.

"Ninety-three KHJ!"

The first record, "May I" by Bill Deal and the Rhondels, had been cued by the program's engineer as Harvey Miller, known to his listeners as Humble Harve, sent someone out for cigarettes. Then, BAM! right into the fast, jiving hello, introduce the next record, and get off!

After "May I" there is another recorded jingle, a chorus singing *"Humble Harve! Ninety-three KHJ!"* And then an "oldie" by Ray Charles, from 1963, which is followed by another recorded jingle—"MUCH MORE MEWWWW-SIC KHJ!"—and then Harvey Miller's deep, shorthand voice: *"Ray Charles did it! Nine-oh-eight at KHJ on the Humble Harve show! Look like it gonna rain, Baby, but don't worry about it. The Nichols Canyon Nightingale is here. You heard it*

first on Boss Radio—Mama Cass!" Then CRASH! right
into Cass Elliot's new single, the program's first "hitbound," a KHJ pick-to-hit.

9:08 P.M.

Only eight minutes into his three-hour show and
Harvey Miller has programmed four songs and four
jingles—mentioning the station's call letters at least six
times, his own name at least five. He has also, by
now, picked the next two songs to be played and is
leafing through the commercial book.

In Top Forty radio, the pace is fast.

KHJ is the major singles-oriented AM radio station
in the Los Angeles market, the station which since its
switch to rock 'n' roll in 1965 (from a middle-of-the-
road musical format) has almost always been in the
Number One position. It is the flagship station in a chain
owned by RKO General and one of the most important proving grounds used by Bill Drake, Top Forty's
master programming consultant. Surveys show it pulls
over two million *different* listeners each week, beam-
ing its high-pitched, up-tempo sound twenty-four hours
a day, seven days a week, from Tijuana, Mexico, to
Bakersfield, California, a distance of nearly two hundred miles, from the desert to the sea.

The "hipper" folk in Los Angeles say KHJ represents everything that is wrong with radio. "Top Forty
sludge," they call it (in milder moments). "Garbage
radio!"

Harvey Miller is 34, married, lives in a big, rambling
modern home balanced on the slope of a mountain in
Hollywood, with a 230-degree view that stretches from
Capitol Records to Catalina Island. In one corner of
one of the two living rooms is a jukebox stocked with
the latest hits. Miller says it was a gift from his good
friend Phil Spector, generally recognized as the best
record producer in the business. (Miller's wife, Gladys,
hangs out with Spector's wife, Veronica, who is the lead
singer of the Ronettes.) In the other living room—fires
going in both fireplaces—are two huge oil paintings, also
gifts from Spector. On still another wall are gold records
given Miller by the Beach Boys (for helping make

135

"Good Vibrations" a hit) and Jefferson Airplane (for "Somebody to Love"). The rest of the house looks about as it would if a successful used-car salesman lived there—nearly characterless. Miller parks his Cadillac and Jaguar XKE in the carport outside.

Rock 'n' roll has been good to Harvey Miller.

He came to the music business in 1953, when he was an 18-year-old record promotion man, pushing new discs for Mercury. Then he became a disc jockey for WHAT, a rhythm and blues station in Philadelphia, switching to WCAU (the CBS affiliate) and then to WIBG, where he established himself as Humble Harve, one of the city's leading jockeys.

"There was this guy in Baltimore, he was calling himself Long Lean Larry Dean. This was in 1959, and I heard it and it blew my mind, man. I figured I had to have something. I was fat as a bitch, man, so I figured I might as well be Heavy Harvey. I pronounced it Heh-vee Hah-vee. And it stuck. All the kids used to say 'Heavy!' when I came to the hops. And then I added Humble—Humble Heavy Harvey. Humble Heh-vee Hah-vee! After that all I had to say was 'It's Humble, baby!' or 'It's Heavy!' and the kids knew who was talkin' to them."

Miller came to Los Angeles in 1965, the same year KHJ switched to rock. But Miller did not join KHJ until a year later. His first Southern California job was at KBLA, a forerunner of what later would be called "underground" radio. On this show, Miller introduced the Astrological Gypsy, a character who has since then written daily horoscopes for Miller's listeners (this in a time years before astrology's recent "comeback"), and furthered his genuine appreciation of *good* popular music. He was the only disc jockey in town to play "Goin' Home," the eleven-minute-long opus by the Rolling Stones, for instance.

Harvey Miller is a strange bird—shallow and egoistic enough to select a word like "humble" as his own, yet deeply committed to and interested in the best popular music available. A paradox.

136

At 9:11 P.M., after Mama Cass has completed her Boss Hitbound and after a commercial that has two kids arguing over whether or not Tackle acne cream is to be used by a girl, Miller extracts a slip of paper from his atttaché case . . .

"And now . . . Prepared Exclusively For Humble Harve . . .

"Those of you born today, Monday, March tenth, fall under the sign of Pisces," Miller reads, serious. "Your character analysis: You appreciate kindness . . . you are secretive . . . you have a violent temper! The Stars' Destiny: The gypsy suggests you stand firm . . . stick to your own opinions . . . and tonight, follow your normal routine and things will straighten out . . . PISCES!"

From that right into the old familiar chorus stickily singing "Ninety-three KHJ!" Then BANG-O: "Day After Day" by Shango, that calypso song about an earthquake causing California to fall into the Pacific. And from that into another commercial, for Halo shampoo.

Miller explains how much freedom there is in the actual programming, how many decisions he is permitted to make: "Like, you can't put two R&B records together. There's no rule. It's just better programming in *their* judgment, sort of a balance to keep the thing on a Top Forty sound all the time. In other words, if you play two R&B records in a row, it's not that they don't want R&B, they do! It's just that it becomes too much R&B, y'dig, together. So we decide what song comes next, y'dig?

"There's also the decision to make . . . like, this is a down record, a ballad, strings. Now ya come outa that and you don't go into another ballad, because in that situation it would be like a KMPC thing, y'dig? In the KMPC bag. There has to be a flow, up and down, down and up."

He looks at the list the disc jockey who preceded him left—showing which of the Boss Thirty were not played during that show. "See those x's?" Miller asks. "That means Sam Riddle didn't get a chance to play those records, because of the structure of his show. So

I should try to work them in soon. They're hits and they haven't been heard for at least three hours.

"Each record gets treated individually, y'see; it goes where it fits.

"There's lots of decisions to make. Like, number one, right now, I gotta pick a record that's gonna fit into the time I have left between the (commercial) spots and I.D. (station identification), which should take me out for I.D. close to thirty—nine-thirty, nine-thirty and a half, something like that. So I pick a record that's gonna end on time.

"We got thirty records on the basic list, anywhere between ten and twelve hitbounds and four or five album cuts on top of the hitbounds, and that book of oldies there. It's a pretty good selection. It's repetitious but it's not that repetitious, or we wouldn't be Number One. People dig hits, man, or they wouldn't be hits. We play hits."

Miller is slipping into a defense of Top Forty programming—"garbage radio"—something he does often.

"KHJ has been accused of being plastic. Well, it's still the fastest thing on radio. It moves. It doesn't just sit there. Even people like Carpenter [John Carpenter, a writer for *The Los Angeles Free Press,* an underground newspaper], who are dead set against the whole concept, listen . . . because actually, man, you been raised on this sound. You really dig it, but you don't want to admit it."

At precisely 9:19 P.M. the red telephone rings. This is the station Hot Line, and when it "rings" (a light flashes), it's usually one of two people—Ron Jacobs, the station program director (Miller's boss), or programming consultant Bill Drake. Tonight it's Jacobs. He's calling from his mobile telephone (installed in his car) to see if Miller can pronounce the last name of a contest winner.

Miller glances at the hand-printed notice on the bulletin board in front of him. It says: *"Boss Radio congratulates Ronald Kuniyuki (Koo-Nee-Yoo-Kee) of Los Angeles . . . winner of a tape replay of the entire 48-hour history of rock and roll and a tape recorder to play it on!"* Miller says he can pronounce it—rattles it off. Hangs up.

138

If the call on the Hot Line had come from Bill Drake, it would have meant Drake had dialed a program line from wherever he was (anywhere in the world!), had listened to what Miller was saying and playing at that moment, had some comment to make and then had dialed the Hot Line number. In his home in Bel Air, Drake has several telephones, one tied into each of the half dozen or so stations he has as clients.

To the right of the Kuniyuki notice is a list of suggested one-liners for the disc jockeys, should their tongues ever fail them:

Boss Radio . . . getting it on with much more
 music—24 hours a day!
Boss Radio . . . where the hits always happen first!
Boss Radio . . . with much more music every hour
 of every day!
Boss Radio . . . radiating much more music, 24
 hours a day!
Boss Radio . . . handing you the heavy hits,
 'round the clock!
Boss Radio . . . where Robert W. awakens you
 electrically every Morgan from 6 to 9 A.M.!*
Boss Radio . . . where the magic is the music and
 the music is you!
Boss Radio . . . pluggin' you into the happening
 hits, 24 hours a day!
Boss Radio . . . where the top tunes turn, turn,
 turn, 24 hours a day!
Boss Radio . . . turnin' you on to a southland
 tune-in, 24 hours a day!

These slogans aren't used much now. They've been on the board for some time, reflecting a period when nearly everything in Los Angeles was Boss. It was even Boss Angeles! (This was during Beatlemania, when "boss," an English slang word for "great," entered American teen-age slang.) This sign, like much of the

---

*A reference to one of the station's deejays, Robert W. Morgan. The others on this Top Forty station are Sam Riddle (who precedes Miller from 6 to 9 P.M.), Johnny Williams (who follows Miller), Don Steele (called "The Real" Don Steele, "The Real" for short), Charlie Tuna, Scotty Brink.

room, tells not only what rock radio is like today but also what it was like in the past: much like it is today.

Between records, Miller talks about the past—about when he was spinning records in Philly, running two or three record hops each weekend in the suburbs. "It was groovy," he says. "We just played records and the kids danced. They even touched each other! They don't touch each other any more. Now they just get high and think about it. It's freaky, man. Why don't they stop smoking grass, man, and really do it? Really touch each other!"

None of this is heard on KHJ of course. It happens during records, and when the record ends, Miller is jumping in with another or cueing the engineer for another jingle, or saying something like *"Nine-thirty with Humble Harve in the City of the Angels and it's wet"* or *"I got nine-thirty-five at KHJ with Humble Harve!"* It is as if he is talking about someone else.

Miller talks some more about "the formula," what makes KHJ (and Top Forty nearly everywhere) what it is. He uses a fellow Boss Jock as a point of reference.

"Morgan, man, he really knows what he's doing. He can answer phones and be interesting. He can rap for maybe a whole minute and be interesting. But whatever he says is pretty valuable; nine out of ten times it's pretty groovy. Like, they wouldn't let him do that, man, if it wasn't groovy . . . and whatever comments I might have to make are thought out before I say them. Like if I say something really heavy, I'll write it down so I know what to say. I may be turned on by a story I heard, maybe, or the news. The astronauts . . . I might dedicate a record to them. Something that's current, man . . ."

He also talks about how the Boss Thirty playlist is compiled. It's really complicated, he says, but one of the main things is they all get on the telephone together every Tuesday—Bill Drake and program directors from all his stations on one great big conference call, swapping poop about which records are selling. "Say, the Box Tops are selling in Detroit," Miller says, "and maybe in a couple other cities, well, that maybe means it's time to start playing the Box Tops in L.A.

"Y'know, the real problem is not which songs to add

140

to the list but which ones to take off. Like, 'Indian Giver' is selling so you got to play it, right? But when does 'Indian Giver' stop selling? When do you stop playing it? At what point? Four weeks? Five? And if it's still selling at Wallach's Music City, what does that mean? How long should 'Hey Jude' have been played? Four *months?* How do you decide which ones go to make room for the new ones? That's the *real* problem, man."

A jingle comes in as he says this: *"And the hits just keep on comin'! KHJ in Los Angeles!"*

Toward the end of 1967, rock 'n' roll radio programming was revolutionized by a giant-sized, full-bearded disc jockey named Tom Donahue. By then, he had abandoned an approach to radio that started for him in 1948 in Charleston, West Virginia . . . going from there to disc jockey spots in Washington, D.C., and Philadelphia. He joined the staff of KYA in San Francisco in 1961, remained there until 1964, when he dropped out of radio into recording—forming his own label. He signed the Great Society (of which Grace Slick was then a member), and presented a number of rock concerts, including the Beatles' show at Candlestick Park. Then he dropped out of all of that, inventing, promoting and selling "underground radio."

He wrote his own mini-history of rock radio (and conducted quite an assault of Top Forty programming) in late 1967 in *Rolling Stone:*

"For the past six months KMPX in San Francisco has been conducting a highly successful experiment in a new kind of contemporary music programming. It is a format that embraces the best of today's rock 'n' roll, folk, traditional and city blues, raga, electronic music, and some jazz and classical selections. I believe that music should not be treated as a group of objects to be sorted out like eggs with each category kept rigidly apart from the others, and it is exciting to discover that there is a large audience that shares that premise.

"Alan Freed is generally acknowledged to have been the first rock 'n' roll disc jockey. He started in Cleveland, where he was known as Moondog, and later took his show to WINS in New York, where he gained national prominence, which was to end in the payola probe of 1960. In the mid-fifties a number of chain broadcasters initiated what we know today as Top Forty radio programming.

"As a rigidly formated presentation of popular music, it proved extremely successful for a chain of stations in the Midwest owned by Tod Storz, and those in the Midwest and South operated by the Plough Corporation, a Southern pharmaceutical house.

"The spectacularly successful concept of Top Forty radio spread quickly from city to city, and almost overnight rock 'n' roll music became an industry as record sales boomed. The stations were replete with jingles, sirens and explosions introducing the news and disc jockeys who worked at a frantic pace and never, never lost their jollity. Generally, the stations played about one hundred current records, but otherwise the format was almost identical to what is heard today in every city in the nation.

"Ten years later, the biggest deterrent to the progress, expansion, and success of contemporary music is that same so-called Top Forty radio.

"Once Top Forty stations dominated almost every radio market in the country. Now their audience and their ratings have been on a steady decline for the past three years, during a period of time when the music itself is gaining ever-increasing acceptance, as indicated by its sales popularity, the ballroom scenes all over the country, and the fact that rock entertainers are now an integral part of many variety entertainment programs on television.

"The music has matured, the audience has matured, but radio has apparently proven to be a retarded child. Where once Top Forty radio reflected the taste of its audience, today it attempts to dictate it, and in the process has alienated its once loyal army of listeners.

"There was a period when the so-called rock stations carefully scanned the sales figures from local record stores and made an attempt to play the records the public was buying. This theory in itself was partially invalid, since it was based on the idea that people only wanted to hear what they could buy. What they bought were popular 45's. Three or four months after a record was a hit, they could purchase an LP that contained one or two of the group's hits and ten other songs that had failed to gain public acceptance as singles or had been hastily recorded to fill up an LP.

"As time passed, the period between the release of a single and the release of an LP grew shorter, since companies found that if they waited three or four months their material might be 'covered' by other groups, such as the Ventures, who had a string of Top Ten LP's covering other people's hits.

"Then came the Beatles, whose explosive success changed the record scene, the radio scene, and, in many ways, changed the world. At KYA, where I was working at the time, we found ourselves playing six, eight, twelve Beatle cuts out of the fifty or so records we were playing on the air. There was a period of three or four months when the Beatles constituted about twenty-five percent of all the music being played on Top Forty radio stations. For the first time, Top Forty stations were playing cuts from LP's.

"By the spring of 1965, American groups like the Byrds, following the example of the Beatles, were putting out LP's that were carefully produced from start to finish. Twelve polished cuts—no rejects, no fillers, no junk. The sale of LP's began to rival the sale of singles. When faced with the fact that the Byrds' LP, or the new Bob Dylan album, was outselling the single records on their play lists, in most cases Top Forty programmers chose to ignore them rather than attempting to determine cuts to play.

"To select cuts from an LP for airing on a Top Forty station meant making independent decisions, reflecting taste and a good ear—attributes that are sadly lacking in most radio programmers and station managements. (Many of the current programmers have risen to their positions through their success in sales rather than their programming or musical background.)

"As a result, the bulk of the popular music radio programming in this country today is devoted to absurd jingles that in their content are almost totally divorced from the kind of music the stations are playing, babbling hysterical disc jockeys who are trying to cram into a ten- to fifteen-second period the inane slogans

143

that the program director has posted on the studio wall. The tempo is go! go! go!, the air is replete with such blather as 'here comes another twin spin sound sandwich' and 'here's a blast from the past, a moldy oldy that'll always last.'

"Somewhere in the dim misty days of yore, some radio statistician decided that regardless of chronological age, the average mental age of the audience was twelve and a half, and Top Forty radio aimed its message directly at the lowest common denominator. The disc jockeys have become robots performing their inanities at the direction of programmers who have succeeded in totally squeezing the human element out of their sound, reducing it to a series of blips and bleeps and happy, oh yes, always happy, sounding cretins who are poured from bottles every three hours. They have succeeded in making everyone on the staff sound alike —asinine. This is the much coveted 'station sound.'

"At the same time the station's top brass are telling the advertiser that they have the solid 18 to 45-year-old audience that represents the bulk of the buying public, they incessantly woo a subteen audience and seemingly do everything they can to offend the musical taste and common sense of everyone in their audience over twelve.

"Their selection of music is almost invariably determined by what is happening in some other market. They will seldom take a chance on a new record, even when performed by a local group. Their measure is never excellence, but rather acceptance in some other market. Most stations today are playing from a list of approximately thirty records with seven to ten so-called extras.

"Each week the stations call a selection of record stores and try to compute a top thirty. Most of them ignore the R&B stores. Few of them make any inquiry at all about LP's. If a record is selling that is more than seven inches in diameter, they don't care about it, don't want to hear it, and most assuredly are not going to play it.

"Top Forty radio, as we know it today and have known it for the last ten years, is dead, and its rotting corpse is stinking up the airways."

Tom Donahue had declared war! (Y'dig?)

Harvey Miller answers the charge by laying out his own definition of "underground" radio: ". . . two ballads together are death, because then you become, like, unrecognizable. That's the opposite view of the underground. The underground's view is that the more music you have, even a whole album, the music speaks for itself. It's an involvement. Here at KHJ it's not an involvement. It's a mood! This is a wake-up, exciting, dynamic thing. The only dynamic thing left on the radio.

"Underground radio is, like, for you to fill in the blanks. The unspoken things. It's the knowledge you have, like, if you're hip enough to know what they're doing, then you fill in the blanks. You're adult enough, mature enough to know where they're at . . . and then it's groovy music. Here you have to be more explicit . . ."*

Miller says his concept of what he wants the audience to be, and what it really is, aren't overwhelmingly similar. He says, "The person I like to think is listening to Top Forty radio is 17, man, is digging hit music and he is hip to everything. He reads the *Free Press* and is a liberal. That's the kid I want to be listening to me. I don't want to program to the kid that digs the Monkees. I'm programming to that 17-year-old kid. But what it really is is the truck driver in Northridge . . . the kid that's driving around with skirts on his car, a madonna on the front for good luck . . . the 9-year-olds buying *chazerei* like that bubble-gum hit, 'Indian Giver.' *Chazerei* is Jewish for 'the stuff you feed pigs.' "

Once during the show—for a period of nearly twenty minutes—Miller refused to program any *chazerei* and filled his show with some of the best music he had available: two oldies, "A Day in the Life" by the Beatles and "Fortune Teller" by the Rolling Stones; two hits from the current play-list, "You've

*Marshall McLuhan says radio is a "hot medium," which excludes the listener-participant, and that television is a "cool medium," which includes. Television, he says, demands intense participation because it demands the viewer "fill in" what is not shown. Radio is explicit. Using this yardstick, then, it is fair to say "underground" radio is "cooler" than Top Forty radio. (This is a very heavy footnote.)

Made Me So Very Happy" by Blood, Sweat and Tears"
(Number Twenty-four) and "Aquarius/Let the Sun
Shine In" by the Fifth Dimension (Number Eight);
and two Boss hitbounds, "Love Is a Four-Letter Word"
by Joan Baez and "Love Is All I Have to Give" by the
Checkmates Ltd. This last record is the first Phil Spector had produced in two years. It is also a record that
was three months in the making, employed about two
hundred and thirty people and cost eighteen thousand
dollars.

"Dig it, baby!" Miller said into the microphone.
"Turn that radio up!" Miller began playing along with
the fiddler in the record, moving his right hand as if
bowing a violin, grinning and pounding his foot.

Out of the song and into a jingle mentioning the call
letters again (in four-part harmony), then Miller
shouts: *"Live from Hollywood—the center of the
woild!"* And into the next record.

Like a circus juggler he works—crossing off songs on
the play-list as he plays them; reading part of a commercial; signalling the engineer what to cue next and
when; flipping through the Boss Thirty records he has
in a drawer to his right for some publishing information which he will share with the listeners; checking
times on one of two clocks; leafing through the Golden
Oldie book; joking with the station's telephone girl
(she takes requests); reading concert plugs; smoking
cigarettes; drinking Pepsi . . .

. . . while the engineer on the other side of the glass
meshes his energies with those of Miller.

Everything is coded—hits are numbered one through
thirty and hitbounds numbered thirty-one through however many there are. The jingles are numbered, too—
L-one, L-two, L-three, etc.; "L" for "Logo." So all
Miller has to do is say, "Twenty-two . . . with an
L-one," and the engineer makes two swift grabs and
has everything set to go. Often Miller will have his
engineer cue a record past an instrumental introduction,
because he doesn't feel that part of the music fits the
rest. Or he may talk over this instrumental part. The
weekly play-list of hits he has provides this information
—besides the overall length of the record, how many
seconds of instrumental there are before getting to the

vocal part, how many seconds in the closing instrumental part. A "map" of each record he plays.

"There's nothing left to chance," Miller says. "It's all covered. And if something goes wrong, it's the guy on the air's fault. Period.

"The play-list is constructed from sales and requests. Personal opinion is like one percent, because y'see, personal judgment leaves something to chance and that's what they don't take—chances."

"Opening Wednesday at theaters and drive-ins everywhere," says Miller, reading advertising copy, then going immediately into, *"Some clouds but mostly clear tonight sunny tomorrow overnight low . . ."*

Which is followed by a Mamas and Papas oldie.

A jingle.

Paul Anka's new hit.

Miller saying: *"That's Paul Anka, Lemme thank ya, Paul Ank-ya . . . Humble Harve! KHJ!"*

And into a commercial for Nutrament, which if consumed on a daily basis will add impressive inches to your chest and arms, not to mention make you feel very groovy.

Thanks to Tom Donahue and "underground radio," many Top Forty stations are now programming album cuts. Some are even checking the record stores in black neighborhoods before compiling play-lists. For the most part, however, most of what Donahue said about Top Forty three years ago in *Rolling Stone* continues as it was then.

Which is not to say Donahue is right and Miller is wrong.

They're both right and they're both wrong. And without Miller there couldn't be a Donahue.

Miller talks between records, rapping with his engineer about how nearly all recording artists have disappointed him over the years. ("Maybe we expect too much, though," he says.) He reminisces about his early days, talking about how "rock was a language and we were developing it." He praises the Beatles and Bob Dylan. He complains about how the Establishment took so much away from kids. ("The whole thing started

147

falling apart. Like Glad Wrap, man. Sears started selling Nehru jackets. Now that fuckin' cinched it! When Sears started selling Nehru jackets and beads, that did it, Jack!")

At 11:50 the next Boss Jock, Johnny Williams, enters the stained and cluttered studio, his own set of headphones in one hand, a coat and attaché case in the other.

Williams enters about the same time KHJ's first newscast in three hours is finishing, with the announcer saying, *"And that's what's happening today—March tenth 1969!"*

There is the sound of an explosion and Miller says: *"March tenth 1968!"* And the next thing you hear is the Box Tops singing their year-old hit, "Crying Like a Baby."

Which is followed by two commercials, one for a local drag-racing track, the other for Tackle medicated clear-gel.

At precisely 11:58 P.M. Harvey Miller opens his microphone and mouth and says: "Johnny Williams will be here at the midnight hour, just minutes from now. We'll see you tomorrow night and don't forget whatever you do—*spread lo-ovvvveeee, baby!"*

Into another song.

11

The Story of
the Electric Fan

On the evening of February 25, 1968, two girls who call themselves the Plaster Casters of Chicago—Cynthia, age 21, and Dianne, age 17—took a cab to the Chicago Opera House, where they waited outside for one of the top rock 'n' roll attractions to appear. He was at that moment completing his first show, and the Plaster Casters knew that he would be returning to his room in the Conrad Hilton Hotel between sets.

As the star they were seeking got into his limousine, Cynthia and Dianne followed in the cab. At the hotel, they approached him and introduced themselves. They were there, they said, to cast his genitals in plaster of paris. If he were agreeable, they'd all just go to his room . . . and this popular lead guitarist would become #00004 in the Plaster Caster's diary.

The rock 'n' roll star was agreeable.

This story (which will be continued later in this chapter) provides an interesting footnote to the chronicle of rock. In 1945, the noted film critic James Agee wrote in *Time* magazine: "The March of Time's issue about teen-age girls is worth seeing in the sense that one might examine with interest a slide of cancer tissue. These girls may be no worse than the teen-age girls of any other country, class or generation, but I would be sorry really to believe that. And am sorrier still to imagine their children."

The children Agee wrote about nearly a quarter-century ago had been conceived, raised and sent forth on this globe with the first real proliferation of rock that accompanied Beatlemania. For this is when the rock 'n' roll fan emerged from the screaming faces in the crowds and acquired a definite character.

This is the story of rock 'n' roll "fandom," that amorphous mass of humanity that has, in the immortal words of Sonny and Cher, "made it all possible." It includes the editors and writers of the sometimes erudite *Crawdaddy* magazine, and it includes the 23-year-old mother of two who just bought the latest Beach Boys album somewhere between the frozen foods and the supermarket checkout stand. (Six years ago she was a surfing bunny on the beach at Malibu.) It includes the 14-year-old who is squirming in a stiff new dress at the New York premiere of the Beatles' *Yellow Submarine,* and it includes the teen-ager in Dallas who is dialing her Top Forty radio station as you read this, hoping she's the fourth caller, because if she is, she wins a pair of tickets to a Grassroots concert. It includes the young English girl who was president of the Gerry Marsden (of Gerry and the Pacemakers) Fan Club and then married him, and it includes the thousands of other fan club presidents who must be content to fantasize fulfillment such as this. It includes the ten thousand who troop to the Fillmore West in San Francisco each weekend, and it includes the 1,250,000 who buy *16* magazine each month. Mostly it includes girls. Millions and millions of girls.

Ginger is a high school girl who lives on rural route 32 outside Terre Haute, Indiana, and she was not looking forward to returning to school when she wrote Terry Kirkman of the Association:

> School starts in about 2 weeks and I'm just sick to think about it. I guess I really shouldn't take that attitude, but school just seems to smother me. I think school is fabulous for those who have their life's work planned, but not for people like me who have no definite goals other than a search for their identity. If I could find a school that taught meditation or such, I would feel I was beginning to go somewhere. The truth is, I feel like I'm an old lady and I'm only 16.

What do you, as a wealthy singing star, say to such a plea? And what do you say to this, from Jeannete in Bismarck, North Dakota:

> Do you have very many friends. If you do your very lucky. Because I can't make very many friends. I was like my sister & mother.

Fifty percent of the 750 to 1,000 letters addressed to the Association each week are like these, reflecting in some way the communication gap that stretches between the letter-writer and his or her (usually her) parents. Quite simply, the letters are cries for help.

> What do you think of LSD and those other drugs? I think the young people of today are just taking their lives away. They say they want to get excitement. I'm sure that there are other ways in this world to get excitement than going on a trip. Do you feel this way?

> I've got a problem: this afternoon I saw *2001:*

A Space Odyssey. I don't understand it, especially the last part. Was Kubrick giving us . . .

I would greatly appreciate and respect any and all suggestions you could give me on how to help myself until I finish school. Your opinions mean a great deal.

Will you please do a favor for me? Please pray for Davy Casselman. He's my girlfriend's cousin. He was hit by a car last August and he's still unconscious. [Note: This letter was written nearly eleven months after the accident.] Maybe if everyone prays, God will make him well.

The letters come pounding in, and it becomes obvious that parents have become keepers, not confidantes. Youngsters are looking elsewhere for help.

Art Seidenbaum wrote in *The Los Angeles Times:* "Somewhere, over that manic guitar, your child has been receiving real messages—while you were digging the nineteenth hole," he said in an open letter to parents. "You may have waggled your finger; it probably proved you weren't listening. Or couldn't understand. Because out of the broken eardrums of pop, human affections are being glued. By default, celebrities have become father, mother and brother. And parents are those remote creatures who may be worshiped but never quite embraced."

Rock 'n' roll lives! The modern family sucks.

Obviously not every fan has troubles to share, an urgent problem to be solved.

Just finished a letter to my Mom and Dad, so now it's your turn. Wrote one to you today, but you deserve two. Yes?

The only address' I've got to send this is the fan club, so here's hoping they see that you receive this. My *16* magazines are at my previous residence. When I go there to visit, I'll hunt for your address.

Doggone it! Wish we could meet. I'm all emotional inside because this is a longing I need fulfilled. Maybe, to see if I really could come to love you. I mean truly. Not just a crush.

This will be my second Sunday in Sacred Heart church, and this time my prayer will be for God's hand to guide me. If He wants us to meet, I pray it's soon. If not, there just has to be a reason you've entered my heart so suddenly. God is so good to me. Without Him, I'd be lost. God is, well, my way of life.

In one week my cousin will be seeing you and the Association in concert. Oh! Well, my turn is coming. Time to sign off.

With love, Millie———

Others send elaborate bits of art and gifts—original posters, necklaces and bracelets, portraits, clothing, even an occasional joint. Thank you thank you thank you, they say. Love ya muchly . . . Suzanne.

Other fans are committed in still another way, not from a safe distance cloaked in dreams and fantasy, but close in. The fantasies exist here, too, but they are a different sort. This is the world of what has come to be called "the groupie."

"There are two kinds of groupies," guitarist Jimmy Page (of the Led Zeppelin) told *Rolling Stone*. "Those who are like friends, like San Francisco girls; and those Los Angeles and New York girls who are making a religion of how many pop stars they can fuck."

"Sure, some chicks are just star-fuckers," said Joe McDonald (of Country Joe and the Fish). "But it doesn't matter what their motivation is, you know. There's these times when they come around after somethin' and you're after somethin' too, so you get it together and everybody's happy. Groupies are beautiful. They come to hear you play, they throw flowers and underpants, they give you kisses and love, they come to bed with you. They're beautiful."

"Instead of saying, 'We're part of the love scene,' they're actually doing it," said Jimi Hendrix. "They take you around, they wash your socks and try to make you feel nice while you're in town because they know they can't have you forever. Used to be the soldiers who were the gallant ones, riding into town,

152

drinking the wine and taking the girls. Now it's the musician."

These girls also find themselves being written about in song. The Beach Boys, for example, sold more than a million records on which they praised the way Northern girls kissed and Southern girls talked, but said they wished they all could be "California Girls." Steppenwolf's leader John Kay wrote a song about groupies on his group's first album and called it "Everybody's Next One." The Sir Douglas Quintet had a hit in 1969 that began with the four words, "Teenybopper . . . my teenage lover. . . ." In another song, Mick Jagger sang (in "Stray Cat Blues") about a 15-year-old who knew how to scratch his back. And perhaps the bitterest of all came from Frank Zappa and the Mothers of Invention.

> A fine little girl
> She waits for me
> She's as plastic as she can be
> She paints her face
> With plastic goo
> And wrecks her hair
> With shampoo
> Plastic people
> Oh baby now—
> You're such a drag.*

When personal managers Chris Stamp and Kit Lambert first began to promote the Who in England, they organized the Hundred Faces, fans of the group who were permitted free entry wherever the Who performed. It is significant that they were called "Faces," for this is what most fans are; there are first names, sometimes, but surnames are seldom if ever used. "After you've come back home from a road tour and you've had all these chicks come at you in every city you hit, how can you remember names? And why bother?" one musician asks. "I mean, I might remember one of the girls had a mole on her ass, but that's all."

How do the girls themselves feel? Why do they pick

---

*"Plastic People" by Frank Zappa, Copyright 1967, Frank Zappa Music, a subsidiary of Third Story Music.

professional musicians instead of professional athletes? A San Francisco groupie named Anna told *Rolling Stone:* "I'm sure that it's the fact that they're on stage, lights are on, and they're involved so deeply. They're like gods. It's like the same feeling that girls got about movie stars. Look who they are. Look at how much money they've accumulated, how young they are. All the places they've seen . . . Every era has its gods—the ones that are worshiped by the female masses, and envied by the male masses, and rock stars, in this particular decade, have been on top of everything. They can have anything they want. Now they're introduced to royalty; they're given fantastic awards and achievements. It's quite an honor. They're put on the best TV shows, given prime time. People are constantly taking pictures of them. Why shouldn't they? They should be spoiled beyond belief. Look where they are. Why should they have to tolerate anything? That's the way it is and the sooner you accept that the better off you are . . . You're there three or four days, waited on hand and foot, and there's just all the dope and food you can eat, and all the people paying attention to you and your lover, it's very beautiful. I mean, you can go months in between, and live off just those few things."

Sex obviously plays a significant role in the relationships between stars and groupies. But other fans are committed on another level. They have, besides the emotional involvement, an economic interest in rock. These fans usually have jobs as barbers, photographers, publicists, personal secretaries, fan magazine writers, and clothiers. One such, a designer and clothier, is Jeannie Franklin, known in Los Angeles, for her two shops (one is inside the Whisky à Go Go), as Genie the Tailor. Genie came to California from New York, became a waitress at the Whisky à Go Go and started to build a business as a custom tailor to the musicians who appeared in the club. Zal Yanovsky and Steve Boone of the Lovin' Spoonful were her first customers. In a year's time, she had opened her first store near another Los Angeles club, the Troubadour, and had on her carefully typed list of customers more than fifty of the top rock 'n' roll stars.

Groupies are not necessarily always girls. Several

young men qualify—one of them being Rodney Bingenheimer, the unofficial "Mayor of the Sunset Strip." Rodney crashes parties so benignly and is so gracious once he gets close to a star, stars often find themselves adopting him. He was a stand-in for Davy Jones of the Monkees for a while, for example, and when one of the Beatles, George Harrison, came to Los Angeles, Rodney served as his native guide, helping him with his shopping and showing him around town. He is also reported to be getting a small allowance from Sonny Bono (of Sonny and Cher) for favors done in the past.

A second prominent male groupie-type is Augustus Owsley Stanley III, better known as "the LSD millionaire," for it was Owsley who manufactured and sold more than one million dollars' worth of the drug in California during the month or so before laws making it illegal went into effect. Drugs were much a part of the San Francisco scene when the bands and ballrooms were in their infancy and tribal gatherings (dances) were being called Acid Tests. Owsley adopted the Grateful Dead in this period, supplying them with perhaps a ton of fine electronic equipment (later designing and building some as well), a weight some say nearly equaled that of the drugs he provided. He's also befriended Jefferson Airplane and several other San Francisco bands.

Like the regular dancers on *American Bandstand* who became recognizable personalities, some of the groupie types actually became "stars" too. Genie the Tailor is on most of the "hip" party lists in Los Angeles and writes a column for one of the fan magazines. The Plaster Casters and Owsley Stanley are constantly being written up in national magazines. Rodney Bingenheimer was given a recording contract. And Linda Eastman was but another pretty New York photographer of rock groups until she was, quite suddenly, Beatle Paul McCartney's wife.

It may seem a pitiful parade of fans who are organized here. Dispel these thoughts immediately. The girls and their electric gypsy boyfriends regard this as rather prosaic and it must be remembered that morality, or the lack of it, is irrelevant.

155

"Groupies treat sex the same way an accountant treats his new Buick—as a status symbol," said Los Angeles psychologist Gerald Rochman.

"Besides," says one of the girls, "what's a groupie? Can't musicians have girlfriends, just like everybody else? I mean, I used to go with this guitar-player, right? And when I was going with him, most of the guys I saw were his friends—other musicians. So then when we broke up, well, the only guys I knew were, uh, like him. So I went from one musician to another. And probably my next boyfriend will be a musician, too, because the only people I see are in music. Does that make me a groupie?"

Guitarist Steve Miller told *Rolling Stone,* "We're all groupies sometimes. When Eric Clapton was in town, I went to see him, but I was so awed I was just like a groupie. I just stood around and couldn't say anything. He seemed so, uh, *important.*"

Everyone reading this book is a fan of one kind or another. Few of us buy a record or attend a nightclub or concert merely because we are curious; curiosity is a thing of our past now, and usually we expend our time and money because we like the group, or the individual performer.

We may not all be groupies—and if we are, on one level or another, so what? It's just a matter of who your heroes are. For nearly every one of us, there is someone in whose presence we'd go dumb.

16 magazine is the monolith of the once extremely lucrative but now sliding "teeny-bopper" fan magazine field, and its monthly paid circulation (not counting quarterly specials) is, as noted earlier, about one and one-quarter million, while its actual readership is esti- mated at about seven million.* The editor of *16* is Gloria Stavers, a former New York fashion model who once told a *Saturday Evening Post* writer: "I have this button in my head. I push it and I become thirteen again, and I remember all the things I longed for. I

---

*The competition is scattered and includes at this writing *Teen Screen,* *'Teen, Fave, AUM* (formerly *TeenSet*), *Flip, Tiger Beat, Disco Scene, Hullabaloo, Hit Parader, Outasite, In* and *Datebook* in the United States, and *Rave, Jackie, Mirabelle, Fabulous 208* and *Petticoat* in England.

don't want to sound conceited, but the other magazines can't reach these children the way I can." Gloria is in her middle 30's.

Among other things, *16* is known as the publication that made the peculiar phrases "Fab Fax" (for Fabulous Facts) and "Kissable Klose-Ups" (for you-know-what) part of sub-teen terminology. The former usually includes birthdate, favorite foods, number of brothers and sisters, and what the guy likes most in a girl, but little of more substance than that. The latter category—photographs—is emphasized; in any sixty-four-page issue of *16* there may be as many as two hundred. And between the Klose-Ups and Fax are the stories: "Spend a Perfect Night With Sajid Khan," "We're Not Too Young to Love" by John and Barry Cowsill, "Sure-Fire Ways to Please Boys" by Lucie Arnaz, "Bobby Sherman Answers Fifty Intimate Questions." Plus: a few contests ("Win a Trip to Dreamsville") and mail order ads ("Please send me *16's Popularity and Beauty Book.* I enclose one dollar").

Obviously *16* is edited for the younger (female) fan, and perhaps its editor—who takes many of the pictures, writes nearly all the copy and seems to appear in both —is the biggest fan of all.

In Los Angeles is a second fan mag called *AUM* (a phonetic spelling of *Om,* meaning all aspects of God . . . also representing America's Underground Magazine), which until recently was called *TeenSet.* The name change came with a broadening of format and an appeal to an older audience. Circulation is over two hundred thousand, and the magazine is, generally, quite intelligent in its approach to rock. This could be because its editor is a former teacher, but probably it is because there is some sort of "need" for a fan-type magazine for the 14 to 20 age group.

Much, but not nearly all, of this magazine is written by its close-to-thirtyish editor, Judy Sims. Her approach to writing about Jefferson Airplane's Paul Kantner epitomizes the magazine's attitude. For several days Judy and Kantner kept missing each other in an attempt to meet for an interview. In her story, Judy recounted all the episodes and closed the article this way: "He never came out. I sighed. I left. What the hell. It's only rock 'n' roll." In its reincarnation, *AUM* is more irreverent than that—with articles such as "Morality Is Not Good For You" and "Black and White" (a story about black militants in Watts); it also contains reviews of films such as *Candy* and *The Killing of Sister George*.

Fan magazines have filled a peculiar role in rock. Not so much now as once they did, but they have been responsible for helping "make" a number of stars. When the Byrds were introduced, for example, former Beatle press officer Derek Taylor spent weeks at the typewriter, grinding out copy about his five fledgling rock idols for the fan mags—and when it was all over, the Byrds had developed a strong fan magazine following (young record buyers, every one of 'em), and Taylor had by his own reckoning written the equivalent of half a dozen long novels. Of course the Byrds had more than fan magazine verbiage to offer, and it was the music, not the publicity, that won them stardom. Still, the fan magazines helped, just as they also helped the Beatles, the Monkees, Dino, Desi and Billy, Paul Revere and the Raiders (with emphasis on the pretty-boy in the group, Mark Lindsey), the Cowsills.

Many readers of these magazines also join fan clubs (such as the Steppenwolf Solidarity and the Association Admiration Aggregation). Membership usually costs a dollar or two, for which the member gets a selection of photographs, perhaps an autographed poster, a year's subscription to an irregularly issued Official So-and-So Fan Club Newsletter, and a psychedelic membership card. Plus: If you are the chapter president, you hold a slight edge on others in your locality in getting past guards into dressing rooms backstage and into the local Holiday Inn. Members of fan clubs write their heroes each week, write each other more often than that. Fan club pen pals are so close they make conventional togetherness seem anarchistic.

Wherever you find them—backstage at the Fillmore, in the letter columns of the fan magazines, padding along the corridors of the Holiday Inns of America, in fan clubs, wriggling together near an outdoor bandstand, anywhere—you learn: Fans are thick. Like rice.

Definition of terms: In the Plaster Caster's diary, a penis is called a "rig"; fellatio is called "plating" and a fellator is called a "plater." All the terms are part of British slang, taught the two girls by members of a popular British group.

From the diary of the Plaster Casters, pages seven and eight, concerning the popular lead guitarist mentioned at the beginning of this chapter:

Dianne: Plater

Cynthia: Mold and Plaster Caster

Marilyn: Cynthia's assistant

We needed a ratio of 28:28 and found this barely sufficient. ———has got just about the biggest rig I've ever seen! We needed to plunge him through the entire depth of the vase. In view of all these dodgy precedents, we got a BEAUTIFUL mold. He even kept his hard for the entire minute. He got stuck, however, for about fifteen minutes (his hair did), but he was an excellent sport —didn't panic . . . he actually enjoyed it and balled the impression after it had set. In fact, I believe the reason we couldn't get his rig out was that it wouldn't GET SOFT! We rubbed a little warm water around the top of his balls and eventually it slipped out. A beautiful (to say the least) mold with part of a ball and some random embedded hairs. Dig this—the plaster cast was a flop. Cynthia got uptight and didn't mix enough, and then after she'd gotten it set into the mold, she got anxious to get the finished product out before it was finished, and so it all crumbled. But it was kept intact in its crumbled heap for a couple days and it subsequently dried together and was only broken in 3 divisions—head, rig, and ball. A little Elmer's glue and we had our plaster cast—a little on the Venus De Milo side, but it's a real beauty.

Cynthia and Dianne call themselves groupies and are not ashamed of the term. "A groupie is a person who

159

regularly chases groups," Cynthia says. "It doesn't matter the approach or purpose—to get autographs, to go to bed with them, to get to know them. Most of my friends are groupies. Some people condemn you for seeking friendship with someone famous and they call you a groupie. I don't chase people just because they're famous—people like actors, vice-presidents, or war heroes—but only if they play good music. Music really moves me; it's a huge part of me."

Why this peculiar approach?

"I've been chasing groups for five years," Cynthia says. "We wanted to stand out from the other groupies and get to meet the groups first."

Cynthia left home when she was 19, after her mother discovered one of the diaries she had been keeping. (This was in the days before she began to make casts.) "She threatened me with a priest and a psychiatrist," Cynthia says. "So I moved in with Dianne. Dianne lives with her grandmother."

Diane says: "It all started when the Beatles came out . . . then Gerry and the Pacemakers, the Kinks, and Billy J. Kramer. I read *Rave, Fabulous* and *Big Beat*. I used to go downtown [Chicago] to buy the magazines all the time. Then when the Stones were here in May, 1965, I went down to their hotel. I ditched school for it."

Cynthia says: "The Stones were the first group I ever met. Since then . . . well, just everybody, I guess."

They live in a modest home in Elmwood Park, two blocks from the Chicago city limits. The casts are kept in a shoebox in Dianne's closet. Dianne is a student at Elmwood Park High School. Cynthia is an IBM key puncher. Both are native Chicagoans. When they go out on a "job," they carry the casts in a paper sack, to show musicians the quality of their craft. The casting equipment is in an attaché case; a huge sign on one side says PLASTER CASTERS OF CHICAGO. They even have tee-shirts that say the same thing—and business cards. "We look very official," Cynthia says.

Cynthia and Dianne say their idea has worked wonders in meeting new groups. It cuts through all the "groupie groveling," they say, and because people have heard of them, they usually are taken to hotel rooms straightaway.

There's been one problem, though. There are now some other young ladies in Chicago, and elsewhere, calling themselves the Plaster Casters. "I feel horrible about it," Cynthia says. "They're cashing in on our fame. They can get to groups real easy this way ... and we're the ones that pay for it when these others don't deliver. It hurts our reputation."

Frank Zappa of the Mothers of Invention is serving as an unofficial guardian of the Plaster Casters of Chicago, planning to publish their diaries and perhaps stage an exhibit of their work. About these impostors, he says: "Well, that's show biz."

12

My God,
the Rock Star

i-dol n. (Lat. *idolum*, Gk. *eidolon*, image; *eidos*, form) 1. an image of a divinity or a god used as an object or medium of worship; 2. a person or thing too greatly loved or adored; 3. a form having no substance; an apparition, as an image in a mirror; a phantom

All these definitions apply to the rock 'n' roll idol and none of them do, for who is to say whether or not Mick Jagger, say, is the image of a divinity or actually some kind of god, within the boundaries of what it is he does? Similarly, who is to make the value judgment that Elvis Presley was too greatly loved or adored? And there are those who will take both sides of the argument that rock stars are forms without substance.

Wherever any argument leads, however, there is no doubt we are talking about images here, and that love, adoration and a sense of worship are arguably involved. For good or evil, the rock idol exists (just as idols

161

exist in film, baseball and cooking), serving as a pivotal figure about which much of the entire medium revolves. They are the leaders, setting trends that may be musical, chemical or sartorial; they influence a developing life-style; they are the spokesmen, representing untallied millions of constituents, by choice or by default.

It is difficult, of course, to say exactly when idolatry is confirmed. Is it when you appear on the cover of *Life* (as Jefferson Airplane and the Beatles did), or when you get arrested for an obscene performance in New Haven, Connecticut (as the Doors were)? Is it when a multi-million-dollar industry is created to supply clothing, toys and assorted gimcracks carrying your name (as was the case with Elvis Presley, the Beatles and the Monkees), or when you've been asked to cut a Coca-Cola commercial (as hundreds have)? Is it when *Rolling Stone* gives you a six-page interview (Pete Townshend of the Who, Eric Clapton of Cream and Beatle John Lennon are included here), or when you command a minimum of ten thousand dollars for a single night's work (ten acts qualify the week this is written—the Doors, Jefferson Airplane, Supremes, Steppenwolf, Donovan, Jimi Hendrix Experience, Beach Boys, Janis Joplin, Monkees, Rascals, and the Association, forgetting the Beatles, the Rolling Stones and Bob Dylan, who aren't currently performing)? Is it when you've been forgotten by the record buyer but are acclaimed by today's Top Ten as an "influence" (Chuck Berry, Everly Brothers, Bo Diddley), or when the Whisky à Go Go in Los Angeles names a sandwich after you ("Jimi Hendrix Treat: super sausage on a wah-wah bun")?

When? No one truly knows, of course, for there are all kinds and levels of idolatry. In history, civilizations have worshiped trees, the Sun, the Moon, and the winds; our civilization often worships frail, two-legged gods, many with a song and an electric guitar.

Three "idols" will be considered here—Mick Jagger of the Rolling Stones, rock 'n' roll's fertility god; Davy Jones of the Monkees, pop's cuddly bear; and Frank Zappa of the Mothers of Invention, anti-idol.

FIRST VERSE

For more than four years—time enough in this rapidly accelerating age for one "generation" to replace another—Mick Jagger has been in the pop pantheon, appearing as part of the so-called English invasion of 1964, shooting straightaway to the pinnacle and remaining there since, nearly unassailable. He has been arrested and convicted for possession of "dangerous drugs" (pep pills). He has been blamed for inciting youngsters to riot. He has written and recorded songs so explicit in terminology and strong in position that they've been banned from the airwaves. (And when his songs were played—as they *usually* were—*Newsweek* called the result "air pollution.") He even knocked up his girlfriend, vocalist Marianne Faithfull, and not only announced the feat but also said he had no intention of marrying the girl. (They were in love, he said, and that was all that mattered.) Imagine what any one of these incidents would have done to the career of a more conventional star—a Jack Jones, say, or a Glen Campbell. Jagger just got more popular.

The former creative director of the Stones, 25-year-old Andrew Loog Oldham, explained this popularity by saying they were a natural outgrowth of the Beatles' popularity. "Pop music runs in three- to five-year cycles, semi-decades, let's say. And at the start, it's first come, first served. The first in the cycle make it big. Then out of all the contenders, the adults pick one. They like the sound, or they think the performers are the way kids ought to be, or they think it will help them get close to their kids. Adults took up the Beatles on that basis. And that left the market open again, because a certain large percentage of kids don't want to share with their parents. We filled that gap which the Beatles left."

A simple explanation and a misleading one, because the Stones were not at all like the Beatles, and whether they were first, second or last to come along, Mick Jagger and his boys would have had a fair crack at the brass ring. The major difference between the Stones and the Beatles was not that the Stones were (like Avis)

163

second, but that in 1964 the Beatles' image was asexual and the Stones' image was quite the opposite. According to the daily English press, the Stones were even obscene.

Michael Phillip Jagger came to rock from Dartford, England, and in 1962 had just been another rockertype hanging about in small London clubs with a desire to put rhythm and blues on the map. With him then was Keith Richards, now the Stones' lead guitarist and the Stone who shares writing credit with Jagger on most of their songs; they both were fans of a group led by Brian Jones, later the Stones' rhythm guitarist and sitarist. Soon the three boys were rooming together in Chelsea in a rather unglamorous single room with no cooking or heating facilities, and playing together at night but earning so little they were forced to sell their furniture to eat. In 1963, Charlie Watts, drummer, and Bill Wyman, bassist, joined them, and as public interest in the blues began to grow, the Rolling Stones began to build a following.

Heavily influenced by early American blues musicians such as Sonny Boy Williamson and Muddy Waters, and later Chuck Berry and Bo Diddley, they developed a heady style of their own around songs at first written by *their* idols and then written by themselves. Always the focus was wrapped about Jagger's brilliant, natural vocals.

"At the start, none of us knew what we were doing," Oldham recalls. "When we started, harmony was an unheard of thing for us. It was just the guys playing and Mick singing, joining in on harp."

Viscerally, about all Jagger had in common with any of the Beatles was the fact he didn't like barbershops. The Beatles were, by contrast, the epitome of sartorial magnificence. John, Paul, George and Ringo wore suits, for god's sake! While the Stones merely slouched out there in whatever they happened to find thrown over the foot of the bed when they got up that morning. (Only for early album photographs, did they put on clean shirts and coats.) When performing, Jagger would lean into the microphone, drop his fleshy eyelids to a sensual squint, touch his thick lips with the tip of his tongue, and begin to grunt and pant.

164

"Buzzin' 'round your hive/Together we can make money/Let me come inside," he sang ("King Bee").

"WOULD YOU LET YOUR DAUGHTER MARRY A ROLL-ING STONE?" was a headline that stretched across the front page of one of London's newspapers. (The parental response to this burning question, one assumed, was "Hell, no!" and it may also be safely assumed that nearly everyone's daughter at least *dreamed* of marrying a Stone once the headline appeared.) In the band's early days, the bad guy stories were practically unlimited, undoubtedly exaggerated and seldom if ever refuted. The Rolling Stones were dirty, rude, vulgar, indifferent (at their best), selfish, boorish, contemptuous . . . a Boy Scout's oath in reverse.

When they visited San Francisco a year later, in 1965, on their first American tour, the Diggers of that city issued a proclamation calling the Stones the embodiment of what they, the Diggers, represented: the sledge-hammer destruction of old values.

ROLLING STONES RULE! the graffiti read.

Contemptuous is the best word, and usually they were contemptuous of the fairer sex. In "Ride On, Baby," a girl on drugs was slammed: "You may look pretty/But I can't say the same for your mind." Another song, "Mother's Little Helper," was a musical predecessor to *The Valley of the Dolls,* about the pills suburbanites drop to get them through the day. "Yesterday's Papers" was a description of yesterday's girls. (Who needs them?) Even "Let's Spend the Night Together" was a strong put-down: "Don't hang me up/Don't let me down/We could have fun/Just groovin' around/Let's spend the night together . . ."

The ladies lapped it up.

When the Rolling Stones appeared on one of Ed Sullivan's shows, Jagger sang "Let's spend *some time* together . . ." but everyone knew he'd just substituted "some time" for "the night." Sort of like a joke on Sullivan. (Even if it *had* been Sullivan's idea.) Which, indeed, was Jagger's, and the Stones', attitude. It *was* a joke on Sullivan; take the man's money and run, and do something interesting, amusing. Like the time the Stones bought some authentic Nazi uniforms and wore them on Sullivan's show in answer to his request that the Stones appear in matching outfits instead of their usual casual attire. Fuck Ed Sullivan! That's what the Stones were saying.

And that's why Mick Jagger was (and is) an idol without (as they say) peer. Other lead singers who are recognized as symbols of sex or protest, notably Jim Morrison of the Doors, even Jimi Hendrix, studied Jagger's style. Which is not to say Morrison and Hendrix aren't valid; merely that Jagger is an original. During one of the Rowan and Martin *Laugh-In* shows of 1968, there came this joke: "Fifty-three percent of the population of the United States is under 35; the other forty-seven percent is under attack." There was no question which side Mick Jagger was (is) on, and this, coupled with his impressive talent, is why he is a rock olympian.

SECOND VERSE

A totally different sort of idol is Davy Jones of the Monkees. That he is English, has long hair and is in rock is all he has in common with Jagger or any of the Rolling Stones. The Monkees are much hipper and more talented than is generally acknowledged, but as idols they are little more than a teeny-bopper's delight, and currently fading fast. (As this is written, one of the four boys, Peter Tork, has dropped out, leaving the Monkees a trio.) Mick Jagger is a fan's erotic fantasy; Davy Jones is her first date.

Davy became an idol for one reason: Paul McCartney was an idol already. Before the Monkees were organized, y'see, the Beatles were the Kings of Pop, and they'd had this absolutely smashing film called *A Hard Day's Night* . . . soooooo, it seemed logical that this was the time for a teevee show that looked like the Beatles and their film. Lo and behold: the Monkees, a group in which Davy Jones was the match to the Beatles' Paul McCartney; they were, in their respective groups, the "cute" ones. (While Mike Nesmith was the Monkees' answer to John Lennon—they were the bright ones . . . and Micky Dolenz was Ringo's twin, both

166

being slightly funny-looking . . . and Peter Tork and George Harrison had something in common—the fact that they left no solid impression.)

The Monkees story began when four hundred and thirty-seven young men answered an ad in one of the Hollywood trade papers announcing tryouts for a new television series. Nearly everyone advised the men who created the Monkees, Bob Rafelson and Bert Schneider, to drop the project, telling them they would never find "stars" by advertising for them. Despite this generally uninspired start, four idols were born and within two years' time the Monkees could boast twenty-four million records sold, a television show near the top of the Nielsen rating chart, a fifty-thousand-dollar-a-night personal appearance fee, and very close to total domination of all the Fab Fax and Kissable Klose-Up pages in all the fan magazines in the world.

The four young men who survived those auditions were assiduously rehearsed (Dolenz had never played drums, for example), given ten thousand dollars worth of equipment, and placed in the hands of Donald Kirshner, known as "the Man with the Golden Ear" for producing over the previous seven years records selling one hundred fifty million copies (Herman's Hermits, the Animals, etc.). He in turn hired studio musicians for all the group's early recording sessions and the boys merely sang along. What the Monkees were, was: FAKES and PHONIES . . . SUPER-PLASTIC HOLLYWOOD B.S.!

That's the way the "hip" establishment felt. But there were millions who disagreed, apparently, for the Monkees were a commercial bonanza. And they were getting five thousand fan letters a day from SOMEBODY!

Mike Nesmith, now 27, explains the Monkee audience: "We wind up with the 11-year-olds who don't get along with Mommy and Daddy. At first we rejected them, but then you come to see how they identify with the band. They're not articulate. We speak for them in a way beyond semantics. I mean, I love Jimi Hendrix's music. It's a very powerful statement of what Jimi is. Chicks hear Jimi and they've got to ball him. They hear us and what they hear in us is themselves. We're a reflection. There's no need to ball us when they can

167

take the record home and it's like balling themselves every twenty minutes."*

Whatever the explanation, the Monkees hit in two media—radio and television—simultaneously, claiming the largest teen-age audience of the year for NBC and two Number One recordings, "Last Train to Clarksville" and "I'm a Believer."

"The teens have bought the Monkees," a spokesman for the Monkees' production company said. "They're the American Beatles!"

And they were. Just as John, Paul, George and Ringo had distinct images and personalities and no one was left out completely, Davy, Micky, Mike and Peter shared the spotlight and the fans. All were idols. With Davy Jones (like Paul McCartney in the beginning) claiming a noticeable edge.

From a letter to a fan magazine: "Please run more Monkee stories and pictures, especially pictures of Davy Jones. My girlfriend and I went to see the Monkees in concert and Davy looked so little, holding onto the microphone and sometimes a tambourine. I could just love him to death . . ."

The young fans wanted to mother Davy Jones. He *was* small—he'd been an apprentice jockey at Newmarket, England, when he was 15—and he was "cute." Girls wanted to take him home with them. Like Paul McCartney.

As it happened, he had some impressive credits as a performer before becoming a Monkee, first appearing as the Artful Dodger in *Oliver* on the London stage, them coming to Broadway in the same role. After that he was in a second Broadway production, *Pickwick,* and then he cut a single or two on his own and tried a few television roles. Still, it was not until he answered that advertisement that real notice came to him. Because he looked little older than the fans, it was extremely simple for them to identify.

In time, of course, the boys developed—like the Beatles developed. Not *just* like them, but like them. They played and sang at their own sessions, even wrote some of their own songs. They handled their weekly

---

*Pretty heavy for a Monkee, right?

television assignment with talent and dispatch. Even individually they progressed. Mike Nesmith, for example, wrote a hit song for another group (the Stone Poneys' "Different Drum") and joined jazzman Shorty Rogers to produce a pleasing album called *The Wichita Train Whistle Sings*. While Peter Tork became more involved with "causes," such as helping support the Free Clinics in the Haight-Ashbury and in Los Angeles . . . and Davy Jones opened a boutique in New York.

During this time, it was interesting what was happening to these four youthful idols. "Sure I object to the plastic Monkee image," Nesmith said. "But that's what I did, wasn't it? I mean, that's what that was. We made it stop after a while. I mean, the movie's not plastic (*Head*); our music is now very valid and very honest, but it's too late now, see, because we're off the air. *Headquarters* came out the same time as *Sgt. Pepper*, and so that didn't have a ghost of a chance. *Pisces, Aquarius* was a good album, but it was a fourth album, or fifth, and by that time nobody wanted to know any more. It was a very honest and hard thing we did, to break away, but the fact of the matter is that when it started off it was a manufactured, four-put-together, make-the-money-like-the-Beatles-made-it thing. And that's the way it was—Madison Avenue/Wall Street."

The Monkees had hit what is called an "identity crisis." They were no longer content to be what they had been, and probably it was largely because they had been made something they weren't. Nonetheless, they were idols. Like Herman's Hermits, Paul Revere and the Raiders, Tommy James and the Shondells, Dino, Desi and Billy and perhaps a dozen other acts, they appealed to the youngest rock fans, those who may have enjoyed the music of the Rolling Stones but who seldom were quite mature enough to *comprehend* the Stones.

Davy Jones' image was clean, and purposely so. Events and attitudes that enhanced Mick Jagger's position as a pop idol would have killed Davy Jones' popularity long before boredom did.

Mick Jagger's music was (and is) blues-based, revolutionary and contemptuous. Davy Jones' music was commercial, happy and innocuous. The difference in the music also spelled the difference in the types of idols they were.

THE BRIDGE

Throughout the history of rock, the concept of the idol has changed, just as the music has changed, and the audience that moved rock 'n' roll from the dance floor to the concert stage now seems to be seeking idols less physical and more mental. Thus, someone like Van Dyke Parks—whose glasses, scholarly vocabulary and fragile intensity made the old-style stardom he sought impossible—perhaps may find mass acceptance after all, now that the times are changing. Parks remains concerned with acceptance and rejection, but no longer is he in a time when, as he once said, "I wanted to be a rock and roll star like David Crosby and Jim McGuinn of the Byrds."

Parks shares the intellectual plateau of rock with several other exceptional composer-musicians (recognized first for their talent and second for any personality they might have)—Randy Newman, Harry Nilsson, Mike Bloomfield, Steve Stills, Eric Clapton, Al Kooper, Brian Wilson, Stevie Winwood and John Mayall among them. That any of these men have acquired a place in pop idolatry—and they all have, even if mass acceptance hasn't in each case been theirs—is a testimonial to the maturation of the rock audience. As never before, good music is qualification enough to earn a performer reverence, and the size of an audience or following, large or small, has absolutely nothing to do with whether or not idolatry exists. "The kids are getting brighter, faster," John Kay of Steppenwolf says. "You can't shuck them any more. If a musician wants respect—call it worship, call it anything you want—well, he better be prepared to deliver something besides tight leather pants or a cute hair style."

THIRD VERSE

Somewhere in the midst of all this public appreciation is a peculiar image named Frank Zappa, founder-leader and primary composer of the Mothers of Invention.

Beatles press officer Derek Taylor once advised a friend to "create and preserve the image of your choice." He did not say it to Zappa, but Zappa followed the advice—superbly—and the image he created was Freak. "He looks like a dying tree with suspenders," said one writer . . . and, presumably, the Mothers of Invention form the rest of the Black Forest.

Describing his group's appearances at the Garrick Theater in New York, Zappa said: "We had a system rigged with a wire running from the light booth at the back of the theater to the stage, and the lighting guy would send stuff down the wire. First, maybe a spread-eagled baby doll . . . followed by a salami, that would ram the baby doll in the ass. It was all carefully planned, and we played the right music for this sort of thing. Our big attraction was the soft giraffe. We had this big stuffed giraffe on stage, with a hose running up to a spot between the rear legs. Ray Collins would go up to the giraffe and massage it with a frog hand puppet . . . and then the giraffe's tail would stiffen and the first three rows of the audience would get sprayed with whipped cream shooting out of the hose. All with musical accompaniment, of course. It was the most popular feature of our show. People would request it all the time. We had a hawker standing outside the theater pulling people in from the street into that stinky room for a thrill, and we gave them a thrill."

If this sounds like nonsense, Zappa explains further, and thereby begins to take form as one of the real spokesmen of youth: "Music always is a commentary on society, and certainly the atrocities on stage are quite mild compared to those conducted in our behalf by our government. You can't write a chord ugly enough to say what you want to say, so you have to rely on a giraffe filled up with whipped cream."

Zappa is perhaps the most articulate of the idols, in interview and in concert, providing verbal jibes as well as some of the more brilliantly satiric musical thrusts. (The freak packaging is, in part, his means of attracting public attention to what he has to say.) But it is his talent as an arranger and composer that earns him such noticeable respect. As little as he may look like the straight world's concept of "musician of the year"—so designated by *Jazz & Pop* magazine in 1967—and as freaky an image as he and the Mothers of Invention have, he has done much to influence and guide pop music throughout the world.

Besides introducing a sense of musical anarchy long before it was popular (and now being copied by so many others), Zappa was also among the first to produce a rock album as if it were a single piece of music. (His second album, *Absolutely Free,* was released slightly earlier than the Beatles' tenth LP, *Revolver,* the latter being the one usually given credit for being the first "concept" album.) Utilizing what he calls "visual aids" (such as the soft giraffe) and creating a vast complex of musical style and technique based on nearly everyone from the Penguins to Edgar Varèse, Zappa perhaps more than anyone else represents the avant-garde of pop.

And . . . he's funny. Not funny like Don Adams or Jackie Gleason. More like Lenny Bruce. The titles of his songs alone tell you the man's view of life: "Hungry Freaks, Daddy" and "Who Are the Brain Police?" from the first LP, *Freak Out!;* "Plastic People," "Brown Shoes Don't Make It" and "America Drinks and Goes Home" from the second, *Absolutely Free;* "Flower Punk" and "What's the Ugliest Part of Your Body?" from *We're Only In It for the Money.*

> What's the ugliest
> Part of your body?
> What's the ugliest
> Part of your body?
> Some say your nose
> Some say your toes
> But I think it's your MIND . . .
> I think it's your mind
> (Fade out babbling inanities)*

This last song came from an album whose cover art was a biting parody of the artwork gracing the Beatles'

*"What's the Ugliest Part of Your Body?" by Frank Zappa, Copyright 1967, Frank Zappa Music, a subsidiary of Third Story Music.

Sgt. Pepper. And it was, according to the liner notes, all a product of the Nifty, Tough and Bitchen Advertising Agency, youth marketing consultants for Bizarre Productions. Zappa owned both companies.

"Very rare that chicks hit on me," Zappa told *Rolling Stone.* "I think they're afraid of me." At this thought, he flashed a small smile. "I would just like to take this opportunity to announce to the groupies of this country that I am a very pleasant fellow, so don't be afraid." After playing a set at the Fillmore West, fifteen to twenty girls approached Zappa backstage, not to hit on him but to ask him for an autograph.

And the Beatles, among others, get some of their ideas from him. It's that sort of idol Frank Zappa is.

He is an extremely serious young man:

> Unbind your mind
> There is no time
> To lick your stamps
> And paste them in
> Discorporate and we'll begin
> Freedom! Freedom!
> Kindly loving!
> You'll Be absolutely free
> Only if you want to be *

He is also a serious musician and he wants you to know it; the following is included on the liner of *We're Only In It for the Money:* "All the music heard on this album was composed, arranged and scientifically mutilated by Frank Zappa (with the exception of a little bit of surf music). None of the sounds are generated electronically . . . .they are all the produce of electronically altering the sounds of NORMAL instruments. The orchestral segments were conducted by Sid Sharpe under the supervision of the composer." Zappa wrote this.

Zappa's ego is enormous, however inoffensive it seems. It is not unusual for a rock star, an "idol," to have a sizable ego, of course. In other areas, however, Zappa seems less an idol, more an anti-hero of sorts.

*"Absolutely Free" by Frank Zappa, Copyright 1967, Frank Zappa Music, a subsidiary of Third Story Music.

Item: In 1966-68, drugs were *in* and an anti-drug position was *out*. So evident was this that when such divergent groups as Canned Heat and the Strawberry Alarm Clock were busted for possession of marijuana, they held *press conferences* to announce the fact. And when Neil Diamond tried to get popular musicians and singers to participate with him in an anti-drug concert in Carnegie Hall, everyone he asked refused because they felt it would hurt their "hip image." During this period, dope was hip and getting busted for possession seemed to guarantee at least a jump of ten points on the record charts, yet Zappa steadfastly urged young people to "put down" (not smoke).

Item: An editorial cartoon in *The Dallas Times-Herald* in 1969 had a teen-aged boy talking to his father: "Sure, I know you had heroes like Babe Ruth, but . . . aw, c'mon, Dad—you're too old to cry." On the wall in the boy's room was a poster of Tiny Tim, a man who was "ugly" before Zappa was but who succeeded only after Zappa had made ugliness—and "freaks"—acceptable.

Item: You usually note idolatry coming to an individual by watching the best-selling record charts; when that artist's name begins to appear there regularly, you know he (or she) probably is about to become an idol, to one degree or another. Zappa's music hasn't *ever* appeared on the singles charts, seldom on the album charts. And only on the "underground" stations is it even *played*.

Zappa is articulate and intelligent (besides writing music, he has written a thoughtful article for *Life* and assembled a book about groupies) . . . a composer deeply committed to noncommercial forms . . . anti-dope . . . and many other things that don't conform to the standard idol's image. He wasn't sexy. He wasn't even good-looking, let alone handsome. He wasn't *anything* conventional.

Despite all this, in *Eye* magazine's first annual rock poll (rating artists and pop music for 1968), the critics voted the Mothers of Invention the Top American Group of the Year and Frank Zappa the Beautiful Person of the Year, while readers (in a separate survey) named Zappa 1968's Private Delight.

Zappa was once suggested as a client for Billy James when James, a personal manager (Peanut Butter Conspiracy, Gordon Alexander, Penny Nichols) was considering a return to rock publicity. "I couldn't represent Frank," he said. "I'd feel like the White House press secretary."

It's *that* sort of idol Frank Zappa is. Sort of a presidential father-figure. Full freak.

13

Goin' Home/
On the Road Again

The Crazy World of Arthur Brown had arrived from England the night before, and even if it was nearly December, the hot morning sun was baking the roof of the Landmark Motor Hotel in Hollywood, where the band was staying. At ten-thirty Brown stood with his publicist under a steel umbrella on the patio adjacent to the motel's heated pool.

The publicist explained the day's promotional activities to hypo the box office for Brown's Los Angeles concert, then two days off. Brown grumbled a bit and went into conference with Tony Garland, a representative of Track Records, on which Brown had just had a hit single called "Fire."

Garland approached the publicist. "Y'have to realize how important we know these things are," he said, "but the real reason we came here two days early was to give the boys a rest. They've just come off an English tour and they spent fourteen hours on the plane last night and they're still eight hours ahead or behind because of the time difference. Let's do what we can. The boys need breakfast. I told them to have a good nosh and we'll get cracking, y' know?"

The day's first meeting, with NBC News, was cancelled when it was learned the instruments and special effects equipment hadn't arrived from London. "Can't do the interview without Arthur's flamin' helmet," Garland said.

At one o'clock the entire band was lounging under the same poolside umbrella with an unidentified blonde and Chris Stamp (brother of actor Terence Stamp and one of Brown's personal managers). Some of the boys threatened to throw the blonde into the pool, so she obligingly stripped to panties and blouse. Moments later she was underwater, and when she walked slowly out of the pool, she unbuttoned her blouse. The boys in the band matter-of-factly discussed the size and shape of her breasts.

Shortly after two o'clock the pop music writer for the afternoon newspaper arrived with a photographer, settling down with Brown in one of the motel rooms overlooking the pool. The interview began and the blonde entered, in dry clothing now but rubbing her damp hair with a towel. She curled up next to Brown.

"Luv . . . " said Chris Stamp.

The blonde looked at him.

"Look, luv . . . we're trying to conduct some business now. Can you split?"

She left and Stamp said to the publicist: "I don't mind these girls comin' 'round, but that one's boring. The least they should be is amusing. She's boring."

ON THE ROAD AGAIN #1

John Carpenter is a rock critic for *The Los Angeles Free Press*. He remembered a tour he went on this way:

"The Holiday Inn is at first a novel experience (room service, vibrating beds and swimming pools). After a week of hotel rooms differing only in what scenery surrounds them, the depressing plastic swankness of the place causes you to forget what city you're in. You're enacting the same drama night after night, telling some sweet young dumby from nowhere she's out of sight, you love her, but 'please hurry and get your clothes off 'cause the bus is leaving early in the morning.' The next night, unless she had an interesting birthmark or mole, you won't remember her name or be able to place her face with a particular city.

"To prove you are a buddy, he (the star of this

traveling show) reads you a letter from a 16-year-old from Tupelo, Mississippi, who proclaims her love for him despite the dose of the clap he gave her. He takes the proclamation as a fan letter, prompting his lead guitarist to open his bag, becoming a Gallagher to his Mr. Sheen by taking out a letter from a girl in Roxbury, Massachusetts, announcing she is with child. In case he doesn't remember her, she states, she is a 'brunette with a scar on her poo-poo.' She'll be no trouble to him, she goes on, and will see him in Nashville at the Holiday Inn where her parents have taken her to celebrate her sixteenth birthday. The star raps on and on about the difficulties of life at the top, of his responsibility to America's youth, of girls with scars on their poo-poos.

"And the tour progresses, spreading VD across the land while it puts on a stage what America's teens hold sacred . . ."

Of course it's not all sex on the road with a rock 'n' roll band; sex is merely a diversion, something to fill time, and the girls are there anyway, and this is what they want . . . isn't it?

No, the thing that characteriezs the mood of a road tour is not sex; it is, rather, a peculiar kind of monotony. (Thus, the need for diversion.) Groups may travel around the world several times, but always there are impenetrable walls—the walls in hotel and motel rooms, the walls of glass in buses and limousines, the walls of police holding back fans, the walls of chartered Lear jets. It is ironic that those who provide so much vitality and excitement for others should themselves be kept so remote from it.

"There were good nights and bad nights on the tours," Ringo Starr told Hunter Davies in the authorized Beatles biography.* "But they were really all the same."

"When we were away from it for a while," John Lennon said in the same book, "it was like the school holidays. You hadn't done any work for a bit and you'd

*The Beatles, the book that tells more about rock 'n' roll than any other (including this one), telling it dispassionately and without pretension or bull.

just remember the laughs. You'd quite look forwards to it again. Until you got back and were fed up."

"You're expected to go out there and do a Harry Belafonte job on the audience, something which you really haven't prepared for in front," said Jefferson Airplane's Grace Slick. "You've been standing around an airport, had some accomodation problem because someone's hair's too long, or you've been on some vehicle for hours without sleep and have only three hours till you go on stage. It's hard to do your thing then. You're really not there, and it's hard to get there with all the stuff coming up. People in the group start getting uptight, and music's an emotional thing, too, you know, so everybody's backstage yelling and screaming. Then we're supposed to walk out on stage and say, 'Hi, everybody, we're the new love group from San Francisco. Backstage everybody's killing each other, but here we are!' Audience reaction to the group at such a time is embarrassing, because they know—they can tell. The kids begin to wonder, and I don't blame them. They pay seven dollars or something, but even if they come in free you're supposed to do a thing, and we come out with long faces. People get really strange getting on and off buses and talking to a lot of different people all the time."

Usually the tours are of a type—incredible mind-bending grinds which, like basic training in the Army, became amusing or memorable only with the passage of time.

There were moments, however. There always are. Moments when even if people are killing each other backstage, it doesn't matter. One of these moments was described by David Crosby, a member of the Byrds when he made this appraisal of what performing is like in the *Oracle of Southern California:* Do you know what it's like, man, to have a cat playing drums, pounding you in the back, driving you, and then a bass like a big Pacific swell pushing you; you're riding on it, man, and that drum is kicking the whole time! Over the top of it, man, you're laying out the grooves, and accents, right? And over the top of that there's somebody riding and really cooling on top like froth, you dig? And he's playing lead, man, just cooking over it, and you're singing three bright chord colors at 'em and it's goin' out and you're digging it and the whole thing is like one big person that's sayin' the thing about how to move and feel good, dig? It goes and it runs and it gets OFF the ground and you get way . . . way . . . way . . . out."

GOIN' HOME #1

The telephone rang and it was Durrie Parks, Van Dyke's wife, to say that a friend who is a leather craftsman, well, he was making one of his rare visits to Los Angeles (from his home in Santa Barbara) and to ask friends if they'd like to come up. They said yes and took a checkbook along, thinking Chuck might have some of his purses and sandals laid out for display; this was how he picked up rent money sometimes, and Van Dyke and Durrie Parks liked to help him by collecting a few friends when he stopped by.

The Parks lived (then) in a green and brown two-story frame house pitched on a Hollywood mountaintop, set apart from the surrounding homes, in the middle of a spectacular wrap-around view, a shallow pool in the back, a garden in the front. The house came furnished, and only a few items—such as Van Dyke's piano and tape recorder, Durrie's looms, scattered paintings and mementoes—told you a gentle and talented man lived here.

Van Dyke Parks was 25, had been in entertainment for about ten years, appearing in nearly one hundred network television shows (*Studio One, Alcoa Theater,* etc.) before studying classical piano and composition at Carnegie Technical Institute. He had been a featured soloist with a folk ensemble, the Greenwood County Singers, had written and produced records for Harper's Bizarre, Skip Battyn and the Mojo Men. He appeared cloaked in the phrase "studio musician" on albums for the Gentle Soul, the Byrds, Judy Collins. His presence was noticeable as an arranger for Phil Ochs' LP, *Letter from California*. His lyric talent had been a part of two of the Beach Boys' best songs,

"Heroes and Villains" and "Vegetables." Now he was recording alone; his first album, *Song Cycle,* had been acclaimed as the complex musical statement from a genius it seemed to be. It had sold miserably.

The Parks' huge Airedale, Winston, greeted Harry and Bobbi at the open door of the modest home. Durrie was on the telephone in the living room and Van Dyke was in the adacjent kitchen, cutting meat for a stew. Harry and Van Dyke traded gossip about the music business. Harry told Van Dyke about the Plaster Casters, the teen-aged girls in Chicago who were making plaster casts of the genitals of touring rock stars, and Van Dyke offered a subtly off-color reaction. Then Van Dyke told Harry about how he might be working with the Beach Boys again, said he had been meeting with Brian Wilson nearly every day, and Harry said he was pleased. This burst of news out of the way, Harry met Chuck and began to look at his leather goods.

Soon several others entered the house, some carrying guitars, one of them Ruthann Friedman, who wrote "Windy" for the Association. Cigarettes were smoked and everyone settled into thoughts, textures and talk. Filling the room were the sounds of the Jim Kweskin Jug Band and the scents of cooking food and a peculiar but refreshing oil from India. Logs were burning in the fireplace.

Chuck sat in a rocking chair, telling how he met Van Dyke, seven years ago in Hermosa Beach. Since then, Chuck had worked on railroads in California and Utah, and had spent three years traveling around the world on his wits, letting his hair and beard fill, deciding to stain his hands each day working with the hides of animals. Van Dyke sat nearby, listening intently, nodding, occasionally interjecting a quietly funny anecdote. Durrie and the girls were in the kitchen, watching the stew and conducting one of those funny, conspiratorial domestic conversations men feel good knowing women conduct. Others in the house were strumming guitars.

Later, Van Dyke and Harry were standing by the large loom that was pushed into a corner with two windows, so Durrie could watch several hundred square miles of Los Angeles below as she made pillow covers for a cabin they had just rented in Big Sur. Van Dyke held a piece of her weaving.

"Durrie says the pillows will look like this," he said, "except she says there won't be any mistakes."

Van Dyke adjusted his dark-rimmed glasses and smiled as if to say: The mistakes are very small ones and I don't see them, do you? He turned toward one of the windows, peered into the Saturday dusk, mentioned the Beach Boys again, then talked of his album.

Often at Van Dyke Parks' house there is talk about *Song Cycle*. Not only because it is good, but also because it didn't sell. In the year since its release, Warner Brothers-Seven Arts had recouped only an eighth of the forty thousand dollars it cost to produce. "I think the album can sell millions," he had said on another afternoon. "I listened to it today. I don't listen to it often. Of course when the scenery changes, it enhances something. The scenery was changing and it really sounded great. I really loved it. I think the reason I'm committed to it is not only because I continue to be touched by it—and I know no more clumsily self-effacing person than myself—I think that it's just fucking great. And I think that the people who don't buy it just haven't come to their senses yet."

The conversation slid into other fields, and college and conservation were talked about. They deplored the rape of public land. They laughed about fraternity stunts.

Van Dyke had a wheelchair in the room, and they took turns pushing each other around the room. Van Dyke said he was going to use the chair to help him get those smooth moving shots in the film he hoped to make.

A couple of hours passed. People moved from one room to another, changing verbal alliances. Chuck sold nearly a hundred dollars' worth of purses and had taken an order for a pair of sandals and a man's shoulder bag. A few people left and stew was served to those remaining. Van Dyke dodged a couple of calls from Brian Wilson, having Durrie say he wasn't home.

Outside it was Saturday night in Los Angeles.

181

Only a little way from Van Dyke's house of that time is Laurel Canyon, a paisley gash that runs from Schwab's Drugstore on Sunset Boulevard through the Santa Monica Mountains to the suburban sprawl to the north. Van Dyke Parks calls Laurel Canyon "the seat of the beat" in his album *Song Cycle,* for it is here that many of Los Angeles' music-makers create and rehearse, using the canyon walls as a natural baffle—the neighbors don't seem to mind too much. Laurel Canyon is a shabby, ocean-less Big Sur, a Woodstock with hot and cold running commuter traffic, honored in recent song (as well as sometime residence) by dozens of musicians, from John Mayall to Jackie DeShannon.

Stand on the wood porch outside the Canyon Country Store halfway up the hill and watch the neighborhood file in for supplies. In a few days' time you will have seen Richie Furay (formerly of the Buffalo Springfield, now the leader of Poco), Danny Hutton of Three Dog Night, Lee Michaels, the Monkees' Micky Dolenz, Joni Mitchell, Ted Bluechel of the Association, A&M's Michael Vosse, Elektra's engineer John Haeny, Phil Austin and Phil Proctor of the Firesign Theater, Carol King (of the songwriting team Goffin and King), Eric Burdon of the Animals, Frank Zappa of the Mothers of Invention, Harry Nilsson, and half their managers, fans and hangers-on.

The attraction of the small store, with a dry cleaners and small restaurant nearby, is social as much as domestic. It is here where chicks are picked up, new homes are found (on a bulletin board or through friends), where grass might be scored, and where you usually get some sort of vague answer to the question: "What's happening?"

"If there were more mobility in this town, the Canyon Store would look like MacDougal Street on Saturday night," says Billy James, a personal manager and music publisher who lives just up the hill from the store.

James lives on Ridpath Drive, a steep twisting road that puffs to a dead end after dividing seventy-five to one hundred small frame houses slammed up against the mountainside. An afternoon stroll along this block reveals the essence of canyon existence. (And the essence of rock home life—in Los Angeles, New York and nearly anywhere else.)

At 8504 Ridpath, where Billy lives with his wife Judy and son Mark, there is a mailbox with a typewritten list of the legitimate addresses for 8504; there are at least twenty companies, groups and individuals on the list. Inside the house this day, the dutiful wife is preparing a one P.M. breakfast of hamburgers for Billy and for Jackson Browne, a singer-songwriter Billy represents. Between phone calls, in a small dark "office" cluttered with albums, photographs, collages, tapes and acetates, Billy talks about the canyon.

"I lived in Beverly Hills my first two years here," the former Columbia and Elektra records publicist said, "and then I moved into the clear air of the hills. It was either the hills or the ocean; both are here and it seemed silly not to live comfortably.

"I wasn't the first to move into Laurel, but there weren't too many here then—Arthur Lee (of Love) lived nearby—and that was about it. It's all happened in the last year or so. I don't know why, really. If creative artists need to live apart from their community at large, they also have a desire to live among their own kind, and so an artistic community develops."

As Billy talks, you hear someone in the near distance rehearsing. Billy explains that it is the drummer for the International Submarine Band. The drumming becomes louder as you pass the house and walk another few yards to 8524, Barry Friedman's home. There you find him listening to tapes he has just produced for Elektra Records. Outside and on a different level from the house itself someone is cleaning the swimming pool, and in another room of the sparsely furnished but rambling home, a young Canadian songwriter named Rolf Kempf is picking and singing quietly.

Barry turns up the tapes for a visitor and begins to hype the group, the Holy Model Rounders. You can see his lips move and barely hear him as an earthslide of sound fills the room from two huge studio speakers mounted near the ceiling.

When the volume is cut, Rolf returns to his picking.

In November, 1968, Frank Zappa called a rehearsal of his Mothers at the Lindy Opera House in Los Angeles, to plan an order of "events" for an upcoming concert at the Shrine Exposition Hall. Much of Zappa's program is visual, and it was as much for visual as musical reasons he'd called the gang together. The music came first, certainly, but the music —changes of key, instrumental breaks, segues from one song to another, etc.—was hooked to visuals. Zappa was asking his band to connect a song from one of his albums, "Who Needs the Peace Corps," with another, newer and grosser song they'd been playing in concert, called something like "Do You Wanna Get (Something Really Obscene)?" That night's rehearsal was devoted in part to making both songs one.

"Hold it," Zappa said, not saying it, but moving a hand rapidly across his throat, a symbol to "cut," causing the musicians to halt. "On G, Ian comes in . . . and then after eight bars we all stop and we go like this." He bent his arm and ran his other hand along that arm. "When our hands reach the elbow, maybe it would be a good idea if we all made a sucking noise . . ."

The Mothers tried it again and again, finally getting it down. Zappa grinned almost imperceptibly, lighted a cigarette and stuck it in the fret of his guitar, jumped into the air, and when he landed, hit two notes. The band started playing the next song.

"The only part of the show that's planned is the building blocks," he had once explained. "Certain items, the noises, the songs, the cues for the songs and noises. The elements are assembled in different ways. The sequence is the most important part of the show and it will tell you how to listen to the music. It's all controlled by signals. When I jump up and hit the ground, for instance, the first two notes I play on the guitar tell the guys what song is next. Sometimes I use hand signals to cue a vomiting sound, or snorking. That sort of thing."

Rehearsals for nearly all good rock bands follow the

same pattern, although visual signals usually aren't so important and never are the songs quite what the Mothers play.

The members of the band gather in a studio, rehearsal hall or in someone's living room and spend hours going over songs, changing rhythms and times, ad-libbing and then polishing drum and guitar solos, dropping verses and adding new ones, introducing harmony and taking it away again, changing key, saying "fuck it!" or "that's it!" and moving on.

Between songs they smoke cigarettes, gossip, eat cold hamburgers, drink, and smoke dope. Some rehearsals are machine-like, Taking Care of Business. Others are sloppy. Either way, time is filled and the music advances, falls back, or marks time.

GOIN' HOME #2

The homes are as different as the voices are.

Joni Mitchell lives in Laurel Canyon, in a small wooden cottage you have to walk up a lot of steps to get to, into which she's tugged and hauled a dozen pieces of tastefully massive antiques and panels of stained glass. Around the house is the green of bush and grass and tree.

Members of the Jefferson Airplane live in the sixty-five-year-old Tiffany mansion facing Golden Gate Park in San Francisco. A pool table is in the dining room. A recording studio baffled with paisley drapes and Persian rugs is in the cellar, adjacent to the creaky old furnace, built in 1909. A ten-foot-long boa constrictor has the run (or slither) of the morning room. The Tiffany windows, the painted ceilings, the lace curtains and pink velvet drapes . . . it's all still there. New tenants, that's all.

John Sebastian took some of his Lovin' Spoonful money and bought a farm in Sag Harbor, Long Island, where he is raising organic vegetables.

John and Michelle Phillips live in the old Jeanette MacDonald place in Bel Air, one of those truly grand spreads: swimming pool, stable, four other outbuildings, three floors through, all of that.

Penny Nichols is sleeping in her manager's basement guest room in Laurel Canyon.

Dino Valente is sleeping on a houseboat in Sausalito.

Paul McCartney is hanging about in his spacious three-story home in St. John's Wood, not far from London's cricket ground and the EMI studios where he's spent so much time making records with his mates, John, Ringo (both of whom have their homes up for sale) and George (still happy with his pad to the city's north).

And Jim Morrison is living in a small hotel in a commercial neighborhood of Los Angeles not far from some topless joints, the Doors' office and the Elektra studios.

ON THE ROAD AGAIN #3

If much of a rock group's time is spent either on the road or onstage and in rehearsal, sometimes even more is spent in the studio grinding out next month's hit or flop records. In another time, recording was a simple thing, only calling for everyone's getting together and singing and playing in a semblance of harmony, somebody else pushed a button, and that was it, repeating the process until a "take" was considered acceptable. Today it's different. Ever since the Beatles spent all that time and money in the studio recording *Sgt. Peppers Lonely Hearts Club Band*, recording techniques have changed. Today the complex recording machinery available is a fourth, or fifth or sixth "member" of the group, and four months in a studio for one album is no longer the record in elapsed time.

"While we're in the studio with tapes and things, why ignore them?" Paul McCartney asks. "You can make them a part of it. They're the instruments now." Grace Slick says: "Electricity is just something available to us. Hundreds of years ago they invented a new kind of oil paint and the artists went nutty learning how to use it, adapting it to their style and art. Now we all have electricity. We're playing with it. We're using it to translate what we have in our heads onto tape."

186

It is the six-, eight- and ten-track recording facility that makes this possible, a technique that is like a layer cake: a rhythm track (drums, bass guitar and rhythm guitar, for example) can be made, then a vocal track can be laid down, followed by a lead guitar or harmonica track, followed by some sound effects on still another track. Ad infinitum, or at least until the tracks are exhausted. (Twenty-four track machines are now being built.) "It allows the artist all sorts of time and opportunity for introspection," one recording engineer says. " 'How do I like this here? Does it fit in?' 'Maybe it would be better if we overdubbed a female chorus at this other point.' You see, the options are increased. By the time they're done, it's like a collage. The beauty of it is that not everybody has to be present at once. Mistakes are only one-track mistakes. You just go back and re-record all or part of that track."

Musicians have become electricians; guitarists have become electronics experts. Several even have studios built into their homes—John Phillips of the Mamas and the Papas, Brian Wilson of the Beach Boys, Steve Miller, Jefferson Airplane, Alex Hasilov of the Lime-liters, Micky Dolenz among them.

There is much to be done each day: auditioning a new bass player or auditioning yourselves for a gig at a new club; meeting with a publicist or a personal manager or an accountant; buying clothes or recording what may be the follow-up hit; trying to write a new song or correct a weakness in an old one; rehearsing long hours to get the "sound" right or spending all day in a forest for a photographer; recording radio promotional spots for an upcoming concert in Denver or signing autographs at a Teen-age Fair; going into Golden Time (after midnight) in a studio or finding yourself in a strange city with a concert beginning in an hour and the airline has lost your guitar.

It's sometimes no wonder a lot of booze is consumed, a lot of dope is smoked.

GOIN' HOME #3

What do the stars say they do at home?

Cass Elliot says: "I get up early in the day with the baby and my day is her day. At seven-thirty I watch the Huntley-Brinkley report, watch a little television, and go to sleep. On weekends, man, it's somethin' else. I guess it's because I know all the people. We've all been friends for many, many years, and we've maintained our relationships. So if you come over to my house and you see Eric Clapton and David Crosby and Steve Stills playing guitar together and Buddy Miles walks in, it's not because I got out my Local 47 book and called up and said let's get a bunch of musicians together. My house is a very free house. It's not a crash pad and people don't come without calling. But on weekends, I always get a lot of delicatessen food in, because I know David is going to come over for a swim and things are going to happen. Music happens in my house, and that pleases me."

Stevie Winwood says: "I go sit in the fields and talk to the rats. Just walk around in the country."

ON THE ROAD AGAIN #3
(Being a return to Arthur Brown & Los Angeles)

Brown's interview with the newspaperman ended short of schedule when his manager said Brown had a doctor's appointment. The publicist drove Brown to a doctor's office, where the singer got a vitamin shot ("in me bum, of all places," he said later) and a prescription for some pills.

All the band was to assemble at the motel for inspection at three-thirty, prior to leaving at four for an appearance on a local television show. Brown and his manager, who were to conduct the inspection, didn't arrive until nearly four-fifteen. Two of the three sidemen were there and all piled into cars for the cross-town drive.

Brown was interviewed after waiting for more than an hour, and once again it was back to the Landmark, to pick up all the costumes and musical paraphernalia —which finally had arrived from London—for the day's final appointment, the NBC News interview, which had been rescheduled.

Almost an hour passed with the Crazy World of

Arthur Brown setting up, NBC rigging cameras and lights, and everyone almost understanding what was wanted. The band was to go through the motions of rehearsing for Friday night's concert, moving their lips and playing in time to a record of their Number One hit, "Fire." When NBC had filmed the number twice, Brown was soaked with sweat. His costuming, including a mask and heavy, flaming headpiece, was tiring.

Driving back to the motel, plans for the evening were discussed. Brown said he thought it might be interesting to see an Andy Warhol film, never having seen one before. Two others in the group talked about a party and finding a band in town to jam with. All talked about food.

The following day—Thanksgiving—the Crazy World of Arthur Brown relaxed, with girls and parties and meals and conversation they'd found. Friday, early, they went into rehearsal for the evening's concert. They talked hesitantly about the minimal number of advance tickets sold (under fifteen hundred of eighteen thousand available) and wondered if the ten thousand dollars' worth of advertising was properly spent.

The concert that night was a bomb (under two thousand attended and everything that could have gone wrong, did) and the Crazy World of Arthur Brown left Los Angeles for the next date on the tour.

14

The Rise & Fall
of a Group

The lifespan of a popular musical group today is often measured in terms of records, not years, and listing the groups that have either disappeared in the past half year, or been through so many personnel changes as not to be recognized, is to compile a *Who's Who* of rock—including the Lovin' Spoonful, Cream, Traffic, Electric Flag, the Mamas and Papas,

Country Joe and the Fish, Animals, Buffalo Springfield, Stone Poneys, Righteous Brothers, Big Brother and the Holding Company, Yardbirds, Byrds and Them. (To name a few.)

The groups have shifted and crumbled like the earth above the San Andreas Fault, and the reasons for the slippage are numerous.

"Any time you're dealing with emotions and business, which it always turns into because that's the structure we're using, you're going to have hassles," Jefferson Airplane's Spencer Dryden says.

Ed Densen, manager of Country Joe and the Fish, explains it this way: "When a band gets together it is in the situation of an underdeveloped country. It needs everything and has no money to get anything. This necessitates a period of hard work and desperate scuffling during the period when amplifiers are bought and insurance is paid for, road managers found, and early publicity done. At the same time the band is having a hard time finding work, and everyone's worries are very real and short-term. Will we get a gig next week at the Avalon? Will I be able to pay my rent this month? Can we get a set together in time for the gig? Once some measure of success is achieved, these problems ease up and other problems which had been hidden before emerge. Who is the band leader? Who makes decisions? What decisions does he make? You mean he decides when I get a lead? Who are we? Do we do commercials? For who? You mean I am responsible for the success of the band? And those creeps are just hanging on? Everyone is around with advice, and nobody knows what's going on. So people begin intrigues in the band . . . "

Roger McGuinn says of the early Byrds: "I think about all the old show-business people who keep talking about vaudeville and how it was a great place to get their thing together. There isn't anything like that any more. So you are thrust right out into the big time right away and either you make it or you don't. I think we were lucky we stayed around as long as we did, considering how we were when we started."

Eric Clapton says of the Cream: "We formed on a very sort of superficial basis to begin with, really. It

190

was like an all-star group. And that's all wrong. It's like a kind of fantasy idea. A group should be a natural thing that just happens, you know, after you break from school—you just go on doing the same things with four guys or whatever it is. The way the Beatles did it. You can't just, like, pick people out of a magazine and say, 'Well, that would be a great group, put them together.' Because the point of reference will be different for each guy."

Dick Davis, who was Buffalo Springfield's partner, manager, flunkie and friend, tells the whole story, and the story of that group is the one that seems most typical. It begins in 1966 when Steve Stills, a young blond folksinger who played rhythm guitar, left Greenwich Village for Los Angeles.

"Steve stayed with me when he first got to L.A.," Davis said. "Then a few weeks later he moved next door. We kept talking about forming a group. It would be with Van Dyke Parks. But that didn't happen, so Steve sent for Richie, he called Richie on the phone. I paid for the call, by the way, not knowing it was to New York . . . "

Richie Furay was another folk artist, another rhythm guitarist, from Ohio. "Richie stepped off the plane in a Brooks Brothers suit and a crewcut," Davis recalled. "Steve and I didn't look like that at all. I thought right then nothing was going to happen . . . "

A few weeks later Steve was in the living room of Barry Friedman, a former circus fire-eater and free-lance publicist then organizing and producing bands for Randy Sparks. (Dick Davis had earlier been a road manager for the Back Porch Majority, one of Randy Sparks' groups.) They were busy on the telephone, tracking a bass player from city to city in Canada, using Randy Sparks' telephone credit card. (Friedman was planning to quit.) They found him—his name was Ken Koblun—and arranged to fly him to Los Angeles, where he began rehearsing with the group, couldn't hack the pressures, and soon went back to Canada.

Shortly thereafter Richie and Steve were caught in a Los Angeles traffic jam and noticed a hearse with Ontario plates ahead of them. Richie remembered a Canadian who'd taught him a song called "Nowadays

Clancy Can't Even Sing" and said to Steve, "I'll bet that's Neil Young."

Neil provided the lead guitar the group needed, and Bruce Palmer, who was in the hearse with Neil, played bass. Barry Friedman told them about a drummer in the Dillards, a bluegrass group. His name was Dewey Martin. That made the group.

The name—Buffalo Springfield—came from a steamroller. There had been one parked in front of Friedman's house on Fountain Avenue in Hollywood.

"In the beginning," Davis recalled, "Barry was a big help. He gave them money every day for hamburgers. They had a place to stay. He hustled them around. He managed to talk Eddie Ticknor (the Byrds' manager) into putting the Buffalo on a five-date tour with the Byrds. I was running lights for the Byrds then and I went along. The Buffalo were interesting, although you couldn't say they were good, even if David Crosby of the Byrds said so."

After that Friedman (who is now Frazier Mohawk, a record producer for Elektra) asked Davis to become "involved" in management. "Barry had signed Steve and Richie for management, and now they were trying to sign them to Epic records. I happened to see the recording contracts. I guess it was a standard contract, but being young and idealistic, I couldn't accept it. It was atrocious. The royalties were only two and a half percent. There were clauses in the contract giving the name to the company. It came to me that I couldn't work with that contract and I really wanted to work with the group. I finally said don't sign them; they'll take your name away from you if you oversleep.

"I got the group," Davis said, "and I lost Barry's friendship."

Davis asked Chris Hillman of the Byrds if he would speak to Elmer Valentine, one of the owners of the Whisky à Go Go, about getting the Buffalo booked into the club. Davis was running lights for Johnny Rivers there then, but Valentine wasn't listening, and Davis thought he might listen to Hillman. The Buffalo went into the Whisky as the "second group" for six weeks. Meanwhile, Davis "bopped around town between Dunhill Records and Warner Brothers and a couple of others."

Warners was offering a ten-thousand-dollar advance, and he'd accepted (verbally) Dunhill's five. He didn't know what to do, so he called two friends, Charlie Greene and Brian Stone, who had been the managers of Sonny and Cher and then had the Daily Flash, a group from the Pacific Northwest, and Bob Lind, who'd had a hit with "Elusive Butterfly." They said nothing was firm until contracts were signed. Davis told Warners they had a deal, but he'd first have to tell Dunhill no.

That night Greene and Stone called, saying they wanted a crack at it. "I took the group to meet them and Brian and Charlie charmed them. They did their act, and the group said, 'This is our kind of people; they should produce us and manage us and publish us . . . ' I thought so too.

"We ended up contracted to Atlantic Records. The money was in the bank—twelve thousand! Plus: Green-Stone had given us all our instruments."

The Buffalo, meanwhile, were tearing them apart at the Whisky. Everybody in town was coming to hear them. In three weeks, Richie had turned into a fireball. "He'd bounce from one end of the stage to the other on his tiptoes backward, and he'd be playing and screaming, and it meant something," Davis says. "It was his stage presence that would develop the Buffalo technique of splitting from the microphone the minute the verses were over and hitting the mike just as the words were to start again, the rest of the time being nowhere near the microphones. It was characteristic of them on stage."

Bruce was the real star, though—playing the most incredible bass ever heard: warped neck, bad pickups, only one knob that worked and four bottom E guitar strings, all tuned low, everything on the amp turned to bass. Despite this, Bruce was incredible.

The Buffalo was an eclectic group. Neil was a sensitive and poetic songwriter, bringing country-western and rock influences with him, while Steve's influences were folk, rock and Latin. Others added some bluegrass. It all merged as one, and as Davis said, "At the

Whisky it seemed they'd been together three years, not three weeks."

"We had money in the bank, which Greene-Stone kept for us and gave to us," Davis says. "They'd rented cars for all of us. We had our rent paid. Whenever we needed money, we'd just ask for it. And we got credit anywhere we wanted it."

The Buffalo were working six nights a week. They also were going into a studio to record. Things couldn't have looked better. On the surface. Beneath the surface, the earth was beginning to slip.

Neither Neil nor Bruce were in the country legally, and there were problems changing this status. Bruce seldom turned up for rehearsals. Egos were developing.

"In front of an audience, egos were more important than music," Davis says, "and although it drove the group for quite a while, it was also a fatal flaw.

"Steve and Neil were always involved. Even then you could see it. Steve always wanted to become a lead guitar player and felt a loss of prestige or love or whatever it was from the audience because of Neil's lead guitar playing. Steve wasn't singing anything but 'Burned' and background harmonies at the time, and he pushed more and more for lead positions in vocals and justified this by saying, 'I wrote the song and nobody else can sing it,' although the whole idea originally had been for Richie to be the lead vocalist.

"So Richie was going through a hard ego blow. He began to feel out of place in the group. He didn't play that good a guitar then. He felt he was required to do something besides sing, because if he wasn't going to be the lead singer, what was his value in the group to be? His feelings were hurt as much as anything else. But it was another blow the group never recovered from."

A week before leaving the Whisky, the group went into Gold Star Studios. Sonny and Cher, most of Phil Spector's groups, the Beach Boys and Herb Alpert were recording hits in this small complex of studios in Hollywood, but the Buffalo thought Gold Star was terrible.

"We had decided Gold Star was not good for a vocal sound," Davis says. "So we took our four-track (recording) over to Columbia and played it back on their eight-track, and as a consequence we lost a generation on nearly everything on the first album . . . sometimes two generations. We did some vocals there, then we did a final mix-down at Gold Star. And then we went to Columbia again, re-recording as many vocals as we could. By now, Atlantic was screaming: 'You have to have a November release or we can't get it out for Christmas!' They gave us two weeks. The pressure was on."

In the midst of this, the group's first single was released—the song Neil had taught Richie so long ago, "Nowadays Clancy Can't Even Sing." Its release as the A-side of the first single infuriated the Buffalo.

" 'Clancy' was supposed to be the B-side," Davis recalls, "and the A-side was to be 'Go and Say Goodbye.' It was pressed that way and sent to the distributors. Then the next day we got a call that due to heavy distributor demand, the A-side was being switched to 'Clancy.' We said fine; we were convinced it was going to be a hit, because we figured distributors wouldn't have bothered to demand anything if they didn't think it was going to be a hit, right? Well, we were lied to a lot in those days."

"Clancy" wasn't a hit (it barely made the Top Twenty-five in Los Angeles), and Davis thinks it was because it was a song impossible to promote. "It was twenty-five seconds too long for a single and it had the word 'damn' in it," Davis said. "So naturally it didn't get much radio play."

In the meantime, the group was nurturing a growing dissatisfaction with its managers. Steve even went to Barry Friedman asking him to take over as producer or help find someone else. Somehow, Greene and Stone stayed on and the LP was finished. Not on time, but finished. By December, which Davis thinks now was amazing.

"We got a two-sided master dub of the album and charged to Steve Sanders' house, where there was the best sound equipment we knew about," Davis said. "Sanders was working for the Mamas and Papas then, and John Phillips was there when we arrived. We put the dub on the record player and I could have hidden for shame. Levels were so far off from one track to the next, it sounded like they were from two different albums. There were places where harmony parts were practically unapparent. It was terrible."

They screamed. They wanted to go back into a studio. They wanted to do it again. The album was released anyway. (The label wasn't at fault after all.) And it made just about as much impact as "Clancy" had.

There were other problems, too. Prior to the release of "Clancy," Neil had been arrested on the Sunset Strip while a friend of his was driving Neil's new gold Corvette. They were taken to the West Hollywood sheriff's station and questioned. Neil thought the whole thing was a laugh; he hadn't done anything, and so what if he didn't have any identification. Then someone said, "Put those animals in the cage." Neil turned to the guy, who was wearing a green suit, and said, "Who you calling an animal, grasshopper?"

"The guy left," Davis said, "and returned with two huge cops. One of them beat the living hell out of Neil. Then Brian arrived to bail him out, and they asked *him* for identification. Brian got uptight. He said what did they need identification for? He had the money and that was all they needed. So they put Brian in jail, on an old traffic ticket. So Charlie had to come down and as they were trying to get him into jail, I showed up."

It was a tragicomedy, but more tragic than fun as things turned out. The beating, Davis says, sent Neil to the UCLA neurospychiatric hospital for some time for tests, and perhaps was the cause of attacks Neil would have for some time.

As the album was released, the money ran out. Davis says he was down to three or four meals a *week*, paying his phone bill rather than buying food because he felt it was his duty to have a phone. (All the others in the band had lost theirs by now.) Neil and Richie were even sleeping on Davis' couch. The only job he remembers was one where they were second-billed to the Turtles in Redondo Beach.

"We were interesting, you have to give us that," Davis says. "We had appeared with the Rolling Stones at the Hollywood Bowl—for very little money, I might add; it was a prestige sort of gig—and now we couldn't get work."

Sometime after that Steve found a small club in Sausalito that would let them play. There wasn't much money involved, but they were at least guaranteed regular meals. So for several weeks they jammed at the Ark, alternating sets with a new group from San Francisco called Moby Grape. (A band that sounds in some of its songs very much like Buffalo Springfield—in "Omaha" for example.) During the day they stayed close to home, an apartment in the Haight-Ashbury immediately next door to that of Marty Balin and Jack Casady of Jefferson Airplane.

"We played the Fillmore the same time," Davis says. (Third-billed to Bola Sete and Country Joe and the Fish.) "Charlie and Brian drove up in their chauffeured limousine. They brought two of the agents who'd had something to do with our early career . . . "

The agents were Skip Taylor (now Canned Heat's manager) and John Hartmann, who had conducted what Davis calls "an amazing interagency campaign for the group, where they had on their own initiative been sending memos to everybody at the William Morris Agency with pictures of buffalo drawn on them and little typewritten messages about the group." Davis adds that the campaign was a failure.

Reception at the Fillmore had been polite . . . at the Avalon Ballroom, where they did a guest set (no pay), considerably better. Still: "We came back to Los Angeles completely discouraged, broken up."

Once they had returned, Steve retired to a friend's ranch in the rustic Topanga Canyon section to write. Recently there had been what the newspapers called "riots" on the Sunset Strip. The kids had been protesting a ten o'clock curfew. The cops had said it was a riot. Steve came away from his friend's ranch with a song called "For What It's Worth":*

> What a field day for the heat
> A thousand people in the street
> Singin' songs and a-carryin' signs

Mostly say: Hooray for our side.
I think it's time we
STOP
Children, what's that sound?
Everybody look what's goin' down.

Steve played this song for Richie, and Richie said he thought it was a neat song. Then Richie learned the song. And Steve said he wanted to record it.

"We went into a studio," Davis says. "By now, Greene-Stone had agreed to get someone to help us with production, so Stan Ross came in and helped work out a sound on snare, bass and footpedal which actually characterized the Buffalo's recording sound from that point on. Other than that, Steve produced the record. He sang most of the parts. I thought the song was so obvious it was ridiculous. I couldn't accept it."

"For What It's Worth" became the group's first, and only, real national hit, going to the Number Seven position on the record charts following a slow fourteen-week climb.

Before the record hit, however, the group borrowed money from Atlantic Records (being broke, still) and flew to New York for ten days at Ondine's. There they stayed in a three-room suite in the Wellington Hotel, two Buffalo (counting Davis, there were six) to a room.

Unfortunately, one night there were too many camp-followers picked up between Ondine's and the Wellington, and the Buffalo were forced to rent another room in the hotel. It was in that room, late one Saturday night, that Bruce was arrested for possession of marijuana. The hotel detective was checking to see if Bruce had snuck a friend into the extra room, and he had, and apparently the friend had brought pot with him.

Bruce had to remain in New York for court when the rest of the group returned to Hollywood to tape the *Hollywood Palace*. (Davis appeared on the show as Bruce, back to the camera—in keeping with Bruce's onstage stance and to hide the fact there had been a replacement.) Bruce was found guilty, the federal authorities found him and locked him up for three weeks, then returned him to Canada on a "voluntary departure" (not a deportation). The Buffalo, meanwhile, went another two to three thousand deeper in debt because of lawyer's bills.

Following the *Palace* taping, the group went into Gazzarri's on La Cienega Boulevard, with Ken Forssi, the bass player from Love, filling in until Kenny Koblun arrived from Canada. (Kenny being the bass player who'd freaked and left the group before Bruce joined it.) Koblun finished the gig at Gazzarri's.

"And while all this was happening," Davis says, "the record company had decided to take one of the cuts off the album and put 'For What It's Worth' in its place, rather than cut a second album, putting a sticker on the outside saying it contained the hit single. I think it boosted sales a hundred and fifty thousand albums."

Following the Gazzarri's job, they were booked into the Hullabaloo in Hollywood for two nights at a thousand dollars a night. Then they played a concert at Rolling Hills High School, where "the group went on stage and the place came apart; the kids never stopped screaming." Davis says, "Everything they'd dreamed about was happening."

They also appeared at a benefit to raise money to support the continuing demonstrations on Sunset and to provide money for legal fees for those arrested. The Buffalo Springfield were second-billed to Peter, Paul and Mary and billed *over* the Byrds and a number of other groups which not so long before had been billed ahead of them.

Then came a tour that had been arranged—for three thousand a week—while they were in New York. This was a road show package assembled by Tony Ferra, who owned a Hollywood discothèque, the Red Velvet Supper Club. Co-billed with the Buffalo on the tour were the Seeds, one of the more uninspired Los Angeles rock groups.

Davis describes the tour and the other acts also with them: "The first part of the show featured one of Tony Ferra's acts—his 12-year-old daughter Tina who sang songs like 'You're a Dum Dum,' dressed up in cute little mod boots. He also had someone named Jimmy

Velvet who'd had a cover hit on 'Teen Angel,' which was about the girl who got killed on the railroad tracks rushing back for her boyfriend's ring, remember that great one? Rudy Dee and the Skyliners; they played 1956 rock 'n' roll songs. And three girls called the Carousels. Rudy and the Skyliners backed everybody, and the Carousels vocally backed everybody. The second half was the Seeds and the Buffalo, whoever turned up first going on first."

The tour was a fiasco. The first show they played to about twenty percent capacity. A second show, back in Hollywood at the Palladium, they played across the street from Love (at the Hullabaloo) and drew an audience of between seventy-five and one hundred. The third show was at the Cinnamon Cinder, a teen-age night club in Long Beach owned by a Los Angeles disc jockey.

"Three dates into the tour and we still hadn't left town," Davis groaned, remembering what it was like. "Then, in Albuquerque, we played to about fifty percent of a large house. And the next show, there was nobody there. A week of this and we decided to hell with it. We could be in town working for seven-fifty to a thousand a night and doing television—we'd lost *The Smothers Brothers Show* because of this tour—and starting to record again. So we jumped ship in Texas. They were twelve hours late in paying us, and I said we're not going on."

The second album was begun without a producer and Ahmet Ertegun flying in from New York to supervise sessions. The group recorded at nearly every studio in town. Steve appeared for those sessions involving songs he'd written and Neil would do the same, neither making an appearance for the other's songs. Only one of about a dozen songs recorded then—"Pretty Girl Why"—ever appeared on an album. (And that one appeared not on the second but the third.)

"Steve was trying to take over the group," Davis remembers. "The happiness (about getting out of the tour) dissolved as soon as we got back to town."

The Buffalo also picked up still another bass player after the Seeds tour. Kenny Koblun had freaked again. ("He wasn't able to play the kind of bass we knew

200

he could," Davis says. "He couldn't find his fingers. He was having problems enjoying life in the city again.") When he returned again to Canada, he was replaced by Jim Fielder—coming from the Mothers of Invention where he'd been unhappy playing twelve-string guitar.

Davis says the group hit another new low then. Yet, Davis adds, "Nobody ever really thought we'd break up. We thought we'd stay together until we made the million dollars we thought we were entitled to—apiece. We thought the people who wanted to become stars would become stars and those who wanted to be rich would be rich, and the songs would be known and everybody would be famous and happy."

Midway through completion of what they thought would be their second LP, the Buffalo went on tour again, back to the Midwest—second-billed to the Turtles in Moline and Decatur; earning twelve-fifty a night in Algonquin and Aurora, in Illinois. But they were working only on weekends, left to sit idly in Chicago hotel rooms five days each week. Boredom and impatience quickly gained control of the group.

"After the first week everybody was flying to Los Angeles to record and flying back to Chicago to play," Davis said. "Meaning we made zero money. No money at all for this period."

Davis also recalls the relationship between Steve and Neil was getting worse. They didn't speak to each other, he says, and "they'd walk off the stage ready to kill each other."

Within a few months of when Jim Fielder had joined the group, there was also some complaining about him. "Steve was very unhappy that Bruce wasn't there," Davis says. "He was furious at Greene-Stone and blamed them for Bruce's being away. He felt that anybody with the right connections and the right bread and the right juice and who knew the right people could get anything done no matter who it was that had done whatever, you know? He just felt that whoever was managing him was at fault for whatever was wrong. He even threw rocks at Charlie and Brian's windows once. He insisted Jimmy Fielder could not play bass."

(Leaving the Buffalo, Fielder joined Blood, Sweat, and Tears and became recognized as one of the best bass players in rock.)

While flying back and forth from Chicago to Los Angeles to record, Neil began working with Jack Nitzsche, a young arranger-composer-producer who had worked successfully with Phil Spector and the Rolling Stones, among others. They were, in Davis' words, "producing pieces of Neil's songs for the Buffalo." Slowly, Neil was retreating from the group.

"Neil felt Nitzsche and he could produce and make a lot more money and be happier than he was with the Buffalo," Davis says.

"Neil called a meeting. Now, we never called meetings. Sometimes maybe we'd run into each other. But Neil called a meeting. So we walked into Greene-Stone's office and Neil said, 'I'm leaving the group.' Most were surprised. Steve was angry. I thought it was a drag. We were making a thousand a night and we were looking forward to some good bookings—the Monterey Pop Festival, the Newport Folk Festival (at which the Buffalo were to be the only rock group). We tried to talk him out of it. We had another single out, 'Bluebird,' and in that we'd not been able to promote our earlier singles because of Neil's illness and Bruce's bust, I thought it unfair to hang the group up now. I told Neil I thought his attitude was temporary. He finally said he'd play through the pop festival. Then Steve said that was a lousy idea, because why should Neil get all that recognition from the festival because of the group if he was going to leave anyway. We were about to go on the road again, to Boston, and I thought that was good because the group always got tighter on the road together, and so I thought he'd get over it. I made the mistake of saying that to Greene-Stone, who told Neil that's what I felt. So Neil disappeared and we had to leave without him."

It was at this point that Jim Fielder was canned—three hours before the Buffalo were to leave Los Angeles. He was called and told he wouldn't be needed; Bruce was back. Bruce had sneaked back into the country illegally and moved into Steve's beach house. (He had two—the beach house in Malibu, costing him

202

six-fifty a month, another closer into town and renting for slightly less. Steve was the only one living in a semblance of luxury at the time, largely because of the royalties he'd received as writer of "For What It's Worth.")

"So we took off with no lead guitar player and a bass player who hadn't played with us in nearly six months," Davis recalls. "And it was a disaster. It was so embarrassing I agreed to take reduced money for the Boston gig. Neil wasn't there and the kids knew it; they were waiting for that fringed jacket. The next place we were supposed to play was the Where It's At Club, and we were so bad, we cancelled after one night."

Back to Los Angeles.

Where they recruited Doug Hastings from the Daily Flash as their new lead guitarist . . . and found an old friend, David Crosby of the Byrds, volunteering his services. He was leaving the Byrds, he said, and he said he'd rehearse with the Buffalo and play with them in Monterey.

Crosby played with both the Byrds and the Buffalo at the pop festival (although few truly noticed it) and Davis said the new alliance "really cooked—musically. Vocally, they weren't together and something was lacking—the friendship, something. We got a nice review from an important reviewer. We got a lot of applause. But we weren't as good as we should have been or could have been, and the people knew it."

They returned home again, Crosby deciding to remain with the Byrds (only to leave a few months later), Richie going into the hospital to have his troublesome tonsils removed. This last caused the group to miss the Newport Folk Festival and what Davis called "four weeks of the best bookings ever . . ."

When Richie had recovered, the Buffalo went on the road again, earning between a thousand and fifteen hundred a night. Another artistic fiasco, Davis says.

"Slowly, though, it began to come back. Doug began to fit in. Bruce's playing was coming back. We did gigs all over—in Wisconsin and Illinois for about a month."

What happened with the Monkees in Chicago illustrates as well as anything what it sometimes is like on the road; at all times, tense—but sometimes a lot of fun.

"We were supposed to leave for Hayward, Wisconsin, all the way at the top of the United States," Davis remembers. "The night before we were to leave, there was a party at the Monkees' hotel. Peter Tork called and said, 'Hey, there's a group of girls here called the Plaster Casters that you've got to meet.' So everybody went, and they didn't get back to the hotel until five the next morning and we were supposed to leave at six or seven to drive to Hayward.

"We'd pulled away from Greene-Stone again by this time, and I was hoping we'd come home with some money. We were twenty thousand in debt. So we were taking cars around. Well, everybody but Richie and I refused to leave that morning. They said the Monkees would fly them up in their private plane. That was fine, but there was no way back. You couldn't rent a car in Hayward; I'd called to find out. Then the Monkees said they'd take us to our next gig, to Waupaca. But there was no way of getting from Waupaca. So Richie and I drove for ten hours that day, stopped at Oclare at the hotel because it was the closest hotel to Hayward, then drove for another hour to Hayward.

"Hayward was an Indian reservation. There was this big pavilion with a tent, and a light show, the first light show we'd seen outside California. And right next to the stage was a train on a siding, with old 1940's-type club cars, dining cars and Pullman cars. That was where we were to eat, and our dressing rooms were in the Pullmans. Well, the plane didn't show up, and we couldn't find it. We called every airport within a hundred miles. Nothing.

"Then we heard something about a plane having trouble and landing in Duluth, that they were on the way by bus. They finally arrived, three hours late. The promoter didn't care, because the Monkees were with them. But it was so late when we finished the gig, we couldn't drive back to the hotel in Oclare. And where do you stay on an Indian reservation? There was nowhere to stay. So I rented the train."

Richie and Davis got up at four the next morning

to drive on to Waupaca, stopping at Oclare to pick up the stuff they'd left at the hotel and pay for the rooms they hadn't used. They arrived in Waupaca about the same time the rest of the group arrived in the Monkees' bus.

Back in Los Angeles again, Neil began hanging around Davis' apartment and slowly began to be a part of the group again—working in the studio, using some of the knowledge he had gained from Nitzsche to help mix the group's third album. Then, the night before they were to open at the Teen and Twenty Club in Huntington Beach, a beach city an hour's drive from Hollywood, Doug Hastings was canned. Neil was back. Officially.

They'd also been wooed by Greene and Stone once again, being promised five-thousand-a-night gigs within a month's time.

"By the end of September [1967] we were making less money than if I'd taken the offers *I'd* been made," Davis says.

What happened next should have saved the group, Davis says. Ahmet Ertegun suggested the name of an attorney, and the attorney recommended an accountant. Both were hired to straighten the Buffalo's tumbled books, finances and contracts. Davis says the attorney told him the contract with Greene-Stone could be broken, but they'd need money. Davis went to Ertegun for this money.

"Atlantic Records didn't want to help," Davis says, "so I told the lawyer, okay, fine, if you say we can break the Greene-Stone contract, if you say we have a good case, well, then Atlantic's contract falls, too, because they have a contract with us through Greene-Stone. You might tell Ahmet Ertegun . . . you know . . . [Davis chuckles] . . . he's gonna have to pick sides. The next week Ahmet came in with a great plan as to how we were gonna get rid of Greene-Stone and he was going to give us a certain amount of money to do it."

Greene-Stone were out of the Buffalo picture in October, and about the same time Davis visited an agent at William Morris, who asked him if he wanted a tour with the Beach Boys.

"I had been asking for a major tour for two years, and although the money offered wasn't much, I said, 'We'll take it, we'll take it, we'll take it!' We took it. We went on tour in November."

It was a peculiarly successful tour. The current single, "Rock and Roll Woman" (a song written by Steve) was a stiff, but the second album was getting decent promotion through press parties held in each city. But Bruce was hit with pneumonia in Richmond, Virginia, and missed concerts in Washington and Connecticut. "Steve had to play bass," Davis says, "and he was furious. He was getting into playing lead guitar and he didn't want to play bass. He played great bass, but he didn't want to. So he went on stage and he was so furious, when it came to 'Bluebird,' which was where he really wailed on guitar in the long instrumental break, he started finger-picking the bass rapidly, as if it were his guitar. I don't know what he thought he was doing, but the audience came right up out of their chairs and started screaming, and these were college students, not teeny-boppers.

"He was still mad when he came off stage. He didn't even see it happen. And the Beach Boys were fascinated: Who but the Buffalo could go out under the worst possible subcreative conditions and come off-stage with cheers? There wasn't a thing they didn't cause for themselves, but still they pulled it off."

Back, again, to Los Angeles, where they had not one or two, but three records on the local charts—"Mr. Soul" (which had been the flip side of "Bluebird"), "Rock and Roll Woman," and the album, *Buffalo Springfield Again*. Plus: In their absence, a local "underground" disc jockey, B. Mitch Reed, had stayed at Steve's house and had found a ten-minute version of "Bluebird" and even that was getting additional air-play locally. Reed had taken the tape and because of subsequent demand, had started bicycling copies around the country to other "underground" rock stations.

Things were looking up again. Davis thought he could get fifty thousand a month for the group, for a period of at least two months, and was taking orders for ten thousand on weekends through late winter and early spring.

Then in January (1968) Davis got a frantic call from Bruce: "Hey, man, I'm in jail."

"I said, 'What happened?' and he said, 'Well, it seems I was driving real fast and I was drunk and they found this joint under the seat.' So I said, 'Okay, hang on.' I got our lawyer out of bed, he got a criminal lawyer out of bed, and we got Bruce out of jail. This time we knew what to do. The immigration authorities didn't even know."

The next day Bruce moved into a hotel and immediately was busted again. Davis quotes Bruce as explaining, "There was this guy upstairs from me making noise and I called the police; I didn't know there was any grass in my room, and they came to my room first."

In the legal confusion that followed—including Bruce's failing to show up at one hearing—federal authorities found him and sent him to a detention camp near San Diego prior to deportation. Jim Messina, who had been working with the group as an engineer on the second and third albums, took Bruce's place on bass.

Also during this time the Buffalo had been looking for another manager, settling on Elliot Roberts (who now manages Joni Mitchell, among others), who promised to put the Buffalo in the Rome Pop Festival. The Rome Pop Festival never happened and Roberts lasted two weeks, at which point the Buffalo began to talk with Nick Grillo, the Beach Boys' manager. They made a deal with him, giving him three percent of their income for serving as business manager . . . then they began to talk about Grillo taking control of everything.

And suddenly, after a blowup during a gig in Fresno, California, Dick Davis was out. "I acted stupid and petty and got embarrassed and quit," he remembers. "I didn't actually say 'I quit,' I just stayed home and they never called."

For two years, Davis had been an equal partner in the Buffalo. Now he was to get a letter from the band's attorney, Irwin Spiegel, saying the group was suspending any payment of moneys earned as "some sort of road manager."

"They stayed together about a month and a half after that," Davis says. "Maybe it was two months, I don't remember."

There was to be another marijuana arrest first—in March, when Los Angeles County sheriff's deputies raided a party in Topanga and busted Neil, Richie and Jim Messina, along with Eric Clapton of the Cream, following a noisy party complaint. Neil also said he was leaving the group again, to try making it as a solo artist.

In May, there were several "farewell concerts" held in the Los Angeles area, the last held in Long Beach. A couple of months later a third album, *Last Time Around,* was released, and since then Atlantic has issued a "best of" LP.

The Buffalo were gone—dropped by the bullets of pride, ego and greed, but also doomed from the start, because unlike the Beatles and the Beach Boys (two of the best examples), there had been no close ties before the group was formed. Forming a rock group is like forming a marriage; you usually have to spend a hell of a lot of time together before you make it "official." Else you're heading for the divorce court before you take the vows.

The Buffalo Springfield was one of many marriages that didn't take.

POSTSCRIPT: As this is written, Richie Furay and Jim Messina are in a group called Poco, a fine country-rock group signed to Epic and being managed by Dick Davis. (Richie is the leader of the group and writes nearly all its material.)

Steve Stills and Neil Young have joined forces with David Crosby and Graham Nash (formerly of the Hollies) in an alliance called Crosby, Stills, Nash and Young, recording for Atlantic.

Neil Young also has two albums on the Reprise label, as a solo artist. (One was produced and arranged in part by Jack Nitzsche.)

While Dewey Martin has signed with Uni Records.

Coda

What's it all mean? What *is* rock 'n' roll, when everything has been (paraphrasing Bob Dylan) analyzed and categorized, finalized and advertised . . . selected and dissected, inspected and rejected?

(There is an impulse to answer this question with another line from Dylan: "The answer, my friend, is blowin' in the wind . . .")

The Reverend David A. Noebel, an associate of the Reverend Billy James Hargis of the Christian Crusade, says it's all a Communist plot. In his books, *Communism, Hypnotism and the Beatles* and *Rhythm, Riots and Revolution,* he explains that the "music of the Beatles, like other more innocuous-sounding rhythms heard daily by American children, is in actuality a part of a systematic plan geared to making a generation of American youth mentally ill and emotionally unstable." Rock 'n' roll is aimed at high school students, he says, while folk music is intended to subvert college students. The goal: "to hypotize American youth to prepare them for future submission to subversive control."*

Those who create the music make a different sound about rock, offer a different explanation.

Cass Elliot says rock is the voice of change, an international communicative force: "How can you negate the fact that it has mass appeal? It gets into millions of homes and lives. Like this song Spanky and Our Gang recorded. It turns me on so much when they sing, 'And if I can make you give a damn about your fellow man . . .' Let's take the people who have

*From David A. Noebel, *Communism, Hypnotism and the Beatles* (1965) and *Rhythm, Riots and Revolution* (1966). Published by The Christian Crusade, Box 977, Tulsa, Oklahoma 74102

latent thoughts about maybe the United States isn't always right. They hear a song like 'Give a Damn' and maybe it'll awaken them."

Jimi Hendrix says: "You can't mess with people's heads, that's for sure. But that's what music's all about, messing with people's heads."

"Dear Fellow Musicians," Joan Baez wrote in *Jazz & Pop*. "You can make the sounds that remind us that we are part of without beginning to without end, that we all are sacred, and that we all need each other."

Says Arlo Guthrie: "It's not a question of how the new world gets started but how the old one goes out —beautifully, gently, or with fear, hatred and bloodshed."

"I'm very aware of the value and power of speaking through a song," says Brian Wilson of the Beach Boys. "Not messages—just what you can say through music itself."

According to Marty Balin, founder and lead vocalist of Jefferson Airplane, "It's *real,* that's what this new music is—and that's what makes it different from anything which has ever happened in pop music before."

"The blues is the truth," says Lightnin' Hopkins.

Judy Collins says: "In the future we will have pop song cycles like classical *lieder,* but we will create our own words, music and orchestrations, because we are a generation of whole people."

And the articulate Frank Zappa says: "If you want to come up with a singular, most important trend in this new music, I think it has to be something like: it is original, composed by the people who perform it, created by them—even if they have to fight the record companies to do it—so that it is really a creative action and not a commercial pile of shit thrown together by business people who think they know what John Doe and Mr. Jones really want. I think that as far as music in America today is concerned, rock is probably the most vital, most alive sort. Gradually, rock has made everything possible because it is capable of and willing to assimilate everything, because a fantastic number of kids are willing to listen."

Richie Havens: "Music is the major form of communication. It's the commonest vibration, the people's broadcast, especially for kids."

Joan Baez: "It is such perfect wallowing music."

Rock 'n' roll (in all its variant manifestations) is, as *The New Republic* said, "verbal, tuneful, visual, rhythmic and communicative—a combination which is putting everybody else out of business." When *The New Republic* said this, was it referring only to non-rock record sales? Or did the editors know more than they were telling?

It has to do with what Dylan meant when he said "something is happening, and you don't know what it is, do you Mr. Jones?"

Rock is a sound and motion collage.

It's nearly fifty thousand young people gathering in Golden Gate Park in San Francisco to celebrate life, for a gathering of the tribes, a baptism . . . and it's another fifty thousand buying a single record *(The Beatles)* in a single city (Los Angeles) on a single day (the first day it was available).

It's a band called that—the band—and really answering to no name at all, holed up in a pink house in Woodstock, New York, to rehearse for a year before recording or appearing anywhere . . . and it's John Lennon facing you nude from an album sleeve.

The draft is white people sending black people to make war on yellow people to defend the land they stole from red people. Tomorrow morning on the front steps of City Hall there will be a huge suck-in for peace. Bring your blankets and something to suck.*

It's Aretha Franklin's record producer, Jerry Wexler, who lives in New York, flying his hit singer from Detroit, where she lives, to Muscle Shoals, Alabama, to record, and bringing in musicians from Memphis to join her backup band . . . and it's a poet named Leonard Cohen becoming a recording artist while a recording artist named Jim Morrison becomes a poet.

It's Jim Guercio dropping out of school "when John Kennedy died and the Beatles were born" and a few

*From *Hair*, "The American Tribal Love-Rock Musical."

years later being declared a millionaire record producer by *Time* at the ripe old age of 22 . . . and it's the music played by the inmate band to help quash a riot at South Carolina's main penitentiary in Columbia.

It's Phil Ochs in 1968 telling New York Police Captain Daniel O'Connell, "Tomorrow we are going to declare the war over and celebrate its end in Washington Square Park—whether or not we receive a permit for a revolution from the Parks Department" . . . and it's the Armed Forces the same year banning sale of Joan Baez records in PX's around the world because Miss Baez was refusing to pay sixty percent of her income tax, a figure that matched the government's allotment for defense. (If she won't support an army, then the army won't—by damn—support her.)

> To sing is to love and to affirm, to fly and to soar, to coast into the hearts of the people who listen, to tell them that life is to live, that love is there, that nothing is a promise, but that beauty exists, and must be hunted for and found.
> —Joan Baez, writing in *Daybreak*

It's the young Steve Miller sitting cross-legged in a Texas field, listening to T-Bone Walker play guitar in a roadhouse nearby . . . and it's an older Steve Miller spending days in a recording studio creating with electronic gadgetry the sounds he hears in his head.

> . . . everything in the universe is composed basically of vibration—light is a vibration, sound is a vibration, atoms are composed of vibrations— and all these vibrations just might be harmonics of some incomprehensible fundamental cosmic tone.
> —Frank Zappa, writing in *Life*

It's *Life* magazine bidding for the serial rights to the official Beatles biography . . . and it's a writer in *Esquire* describing at inordinate length the significance of Janis Joplin's left nipple.

It's a young San Francisco band calling itself Dancing, Food and Entertainment because that name looks good on the marquee . . . and it's Jim Morrison giving his group (the Doors) a name because he believes "there are things that are known and things that are unknown and in between are doors."

It's musicians passing joints in a recording studio while overdubbing harmonica and vocal parts . . . and it's included this week on *The Ed Sullivan Show* between a precision drill team and Alan King.

> I think it's time we STOP,
> Children,
> What's that sound?
> Everybody look what's going down.*

It's the Bank of California saying pop music could become San Francisco's fourth largest industry (after construction, manufacturing and finance) a year from now, grossing upwards of forty million dollars in 1970 . . . and it's George Harrison's mother personally answering two hundred fan letters each week.

> We're more popular than Jesus now. I don't know which will fade first—rock 'n' roll or Christianity.
> —John Lennon

It's Elektra Records leasing a lodge on California's Feather River as "a recording retreat, a quiet place in the country where musicians can get their heads, bodies and music together . . . to free artists from the urban pressures that have caused them to use their instruments and music as an escape . . . to permit emancipated music to pass through them and back into the city" (quoting Frazier Mohawk, a producer whose idea it was) . . . and it's the Beatles opening a London boutique, then closing it and giving all the clothing away—free!

It's Jefferson Airplane being featured in Jean-Luc Godard's first American film, *An American Movie,* and Art Garfunkel of Simon and Garfunkel appearing in *Catch-22* . . . and it's someone holding up an applause sign at the end of Country Joe McDonald's wedding to a very pregnant Robin, and everybody applauding.

*"For What It's Worth," by Stephen Stills, Copyright 1966, Ten East, Springalo and Cotillion Music.

It's cavernous dance halls splashed with patterned moving light; satiric political comment traveling in 4/4 (and, lately, 5/4, 7/4 and 11/4) time; thousands of young men growing hair and sideburns and playing in local groups and tens of thousands of radios, all turned on and tuned in to one sound; magazines called *Fave* and *Rave,* and *Flip* and *Hip;* tight pants and no underwear; Laura Nyro, Booker T and the MGs, Procol Harum, Johnny Winter, Jeff Beck, Carla Thomas, Clarence (Frog Man) Henry, Buck Owens, Jerry Butler, Jim Reeves, Murray the K, Gale Garnett, Richard Alpert, David Blue, Big Bill Broonzy, Andy Warhol, Janis Ian, Tom Jones, Vanilla Fudge, Bobby Goldsboro, Linda Ronstadt, Barry Mann and Cynthia Weil, Gene Vincent, David Ruffin, the 1910 Fruitgum Company, Eldridge Cleaver, John D. Loudermilk, the Bar-Kays, Pigmeat Markham, Nancy Sinatra, Peaches and Herb, Gary Lewis and the Playboys, Mary Hopkin (and hundreds more) whose names have not been mentioned in this book.

Plato put it this way: "Forms and rhythms in music are never changed without producing changes in the most important political forms and ways. The new style quietly insinuates itself into manners and customs and from there it assumes a greater force . . . goes on to attack laws and constitutions, displaying the utmost impudence until it ends by overthrowing everything, both in public and in private."

And Dylan said: "The times they are a-changin' . . ."

Discography

Chapter 1: WE'RE GONNA SHAKE, RATTLE & ROLL

The Best of the Legendary Jimmie Rodgers (incl. "Muleskinner Blues"; "T for Texas") RCA Victor LSP-3315.

All Time Greatest Hits (Roy Acuff) (incl. "Great Speckled Bird"; "Wabash Cannonball"; "Pins and Needles") Hickory 109.

Country Sounds of the Original Carter Family (incl. "Cannonball Blues") Harmony 7422.

Hank Williams/Greatest Hits (incl. "Hey Good Lookin' "; "Your Cheatin' Heart"; "Cold Cold Heart"; "I'm So Lonesome I Could Cry") MGM 3918.

Best of Muddy Waters (incl. "Hoochie Coochie Man"; "Rollin' Stone"; "I'm Ready") Chess 1427.

From the Beginning (B. B. King) (two discs incl. "Rock Me Baby"; "Sweet Sixteen"; "Treat Me Right") Kent KST-533.

Best of Little Walter (incl. "My Babe") Checker 3004.

History of Rhythm & Blues Vol. 1, The Roots 1947-1952 (incl. the Ravens; Orioles; Leadbelly; Clovers; Cardinals; Joe Turner; Ruth Brown) Atlantic SD 8161.

18 King Size Rhythm & Blues Hits (incl. Hank Ballard and the Midnighters; Little Willie John; Five Royales; Billy Ward and the Dominoes; Otis Williams and the Charms) Columbia CS 9467. (Note: Also available on the original label as *18 All Time King Hits*, King 1026.)

History of Rhythm & Blues Vol. 2, The Golden Years

1953-1955 (incl. the Diamonds; Drifters; Chords; Tommy Ridgeley; LaVern Baker; Ray Charles; Clovers; Ruth Brown) Atlantic SD 8162.

Chuck Berry's Golden Decade (two discs incl. "Maybelline"; "Johnny B. Goode"; "School Days"; "Rock and Roll Music"; "Back in the U.S.A.") Chess LPS-1514D.

Little Richard's Grooviest 17 Original Hits (incl. "Lucille"; "Tutti Frutti"; "Long Tall Sally"; "Good Golly Miss Molly") Specialty SPS 2113. There are a number of other albums with similar titles on the market. None are the original except this one by Specialty.

16 All Time Greatest Hits (Bo Diddley) (incl. "Bo Diddley"; "You Can't Tell a Book by Its Cover"; "I'm a Man") Checker 2989.

The Ray Charles Story Vol. 1 (15 hits from 1952 to 1956 incl. "I've Got a Woman"; "Hallelujah I Love Her So") Atlantic 8063.

Fats Domino Swings (incl. "Fat Man"; "Blue Monday"; "Blueberry Hill"; "I'm Walkin'"; "My Blue Heaven"; "Ain't That a Shame") Imperial 12091.

Encore of Golden Hits/The Platters (incl. "The Great Pretender"; "My Prayer"; "Only You") Mercury SR-60243.

History of Rhythm & Blues Vol. 3, Rock & Roll 1956-1957 (incl. Clyde McPhatter; the Robins; Clovers; Joe Turner; Ivory Joe Hunter; LaVern Baker; Coasters) Atlantic SD 8163.

Bill Haley's Greatest Hits (incl. "Rock Around the Clock"; "Shake, Rattle & Roll"; "See You Later, Alligator") Decca DL 5027.

Chapter 2: THE FIRST ROCK CORONATION

Elvis' Golden Records (incl. "Heartbreak Hotel"; "Hound Dog"; "Teddy Bear"; "Jailhouse Rock") RCA Victor LSP-1707.

Million Sellers (artists from the Sun label incl. Jerry Lee Lewis; Johnny Cash; Carl Perkins) Sun 1250.

The Golden Hits of Jerry Lee Lewis (incl. "Whole

Lotta Shakin' Goin' On"; "Great Balls of Fire") Smash
SRS-67040.

Johnny Cash's Greatest Hits, Vol. 1 (incl. "I Walk
the Line"; "Ring of Fire") Columbia CS 9478.

The Very Best of the Everly Brothers (incl. "Wake
Up Little Susie"; "Bird Dog"; "Bye Bye Love") Warner Bros.-7 Arts WS-1554. (Note: The early songs on
this LP, originally cut for the Cadence label, have been
re-recorded here for Warner Bros. because the original
tapes had been lost or destroyed. The sound is quite
close to the original, however, in that the same studio
and producer were used, and the Everlys actually
hadn't altered the arrangements much in the interim.)

The Buddy Holly Story (incl. "Peggy Sue"; "That'll Be
the Day"; "Oh Boy") Coral CRL 57279.

Coasters/Greatest Hits (incl. "Poison Ivy"; "Yakety
Yak"; "Charlie Brown"; "Along Came Jones") Atco
SD 33-111.

Chapter 3: THE OTHER PHILADELPHIA STORY

Best Sellers by Rick (Nelson) (incl. "Be-Bop Baby";
"Poor Little Fool"; "Stood Up") Imperial 12218.

15 Greatest Hits/Frankie Avalon (incl. "Venus";
"Gingerbread"; "De De Dinah") United Artists 6382.

Best of Little Anthony and the Imperials (incl. "Tears
On My Pillow"; "Shimmy Shimmy Ko Ko Bop")
Veep 16512.

Paul Anka's 21 Golden Hits (incl. "Diana"; "Puppy
Love"; "Put Your Head on My Shoulder"; "Lonely
Boy") RCA Victor LSP-2691.

*History of Rhythm & Blues, Vol. 4, The Big Beat
1958-1960* (incl. hits by the Coasters; Bobby Darin;
Drifters; Ray Charles; LaVern Baker; Ben E. King)
Atco 8164.

Golden Goodies, Vol. 4, For a Dance Party (incl. hit
versions of the Bristol Stomp; the Fly; the Mashed
Potato; the Loco-Motion; the Pony, etc.) Roulette R
25208.

The Midnight Special (Leadbelly) (16 songs incl. title song; "Rock Island Line"; "Easy Rider") RCA Victor LPV-505.

The Asch Recordings 1939-1945, Folk Singers Vol. 2, Record 1 (incl. Leadbelly; Burl Ives; Woody Guthrie; Pete Seeger; Josh White; Bess Lomax; Brownie McGhee) Asch AA 3.

Pete Seeger's Greatest Hits (although all were hits for others, it includes "Little Boxes"; "Wimoweh"; "Where Have All the Flowers Gone"; "Turn Turn Turn"; "Bells of Rhymney") Columbia CS 9416.

This Land Is Your Land (Woody Guthrie) (incl. title song; "Pastures of Plenty") Folkways FTS 31001.

Best of the Weavers (incl. "Goodnight Irene"; "Kisses Sweeter Than Wine"; "On Top of Old Smokey") Decca DXSB 7-173.

Calypso (Harry Belafonte) (incl. "Jamaica Farewell"; "Day-O") RCA Victor LSP-1248.

The Best of the Kingston Trio (incl. "Tom Dooley"; "M.T.A."; "Where Have All the Flowers Gone"; "Tijuana Jail") Capitol T-1705.

Peter, Paul and Mary in Concert (incl. "Blowin' in the Wind"; "If I Had A Hammer"; "Puff the Magic Dragon"; "The Times They Are A-Changin' "; "500 Miles") Warner Bros.-Seven Arts WB 1555.

Folk Festival at Newport 1959, Vol. 2 (incl. Joan Baez; Bob Gibson; Odetta; New Lost City Ramblers; Barbara Dane) Vanguard VSD-2054.

Joan Baez, Vol. 2 Vanguard VSD-2097.

The Freewheelin' Bob Dylan (incl. "Blowin' in the Wind"; "Don't Think Twice, It's All Right") Columbia CS 8786.

The Times They Are A-Changin' (Bob Dylan) (incl. title song; "One Too Many Mornings"; "With God On Our Side"; "Only a Pawn in Their Game") Columbia CS 8905.

Other SIGNET Books of Current Interest

☐ **THE ARMIES OF THE NIGHT—History as a Novel, the Novel as History by Norman Mailer.** The Pulitzer Prize-winning chronicle of the three days of anti-Vietnam demonstrations in Washington during October 1967 by the bestselling author of **The Naked and the Dead.** "Brilliant writing, brilliant reportage."—Chicago Sun-Times
(#Y3712—$1.25)

☐ **THE MARIHUANA PAPERS edited by David Solomon.** In this basic reference on marihuana, the author calls on works from Rabelais to Terry Southern, Baudelaire to Allen Ginsberg, as well as evidence from leading pharmacologists and sociologists to show exactly what effects the controversial drug has and to expose as illogical, the fears with which Americans have reacted to its use.
(#W3442—$1.50)

☐ **HOW TO GET OUT OF VIETNAM: A Workable Solution to the Worst Problem of Our Time by John Kenneth Galbraith.** The distinguished economist, political theorist, and bestselling author offers a practical plan for U.S. withdrawal from "a war we cannot win, should not wish to win, are not winning, and which our people do not support."
(#S3414—35¢)

☐ **I PROTEST! by David Douglas Duncan.** A powerful condemnation of the war in Vietnam in photographs and text by the world-famous photographer who was assigned by **Life** Magazine and ABC News to cover the action in Khe Sanh.
(#N3546—$1.00)

SIGNET Books of Current Interest

☐ **TELLING IT LIKE IT WAS: THE FREAK-OUT IN CHICAGO edited by Walter Schneir.** An anthology of articles on the Chicago Riots surrounding the Democratic Convention of 1968. (#T3856—75¢)

☐ **VIOLENCE: AMERICA IN THE SIXTIES by Arthur Schlesinger, Jr.** One of the most eminent historians of our time speaks out on the emerging pattern of violence in America and suggests ways in which we might uncover the roots of hatred and move towards self-control. (#D3747—50¢)

☐ **WRITERS AND ISSUES, edited by Theodore Solotaroff.** A provocative collection by outstanding writers on the political, social, and moral changes taking place in America. (#Y4046—$1.25)

☐ **AMERICA VS. AMERICA: The Revolution in Middle-Class Values by James A Michener.** Written out of concern for the rebellion of the younger generation against the values of their parents, this Broadside explores present middle-class guidelines and the contradictions between what many Americans say they believe and what they actually do. (#P3819—60¢)
